病原生物与感染性疾病
文献索引

田德桥 编

科学技术文献出版社
SCIENTIFIC AND TECHNICAL DOCUMENTATION PRESS
·北京·

图书在版编目（CIP）数据

病原生物与感染性疾病文献索引 / 田德桥编. —北京：科学技术文献出版社，2023.11
ISBN 978-7-5235-0977-7

Ⅰ.①病… Ⅱ.①田… Ⅲ.①病原微生物—关系—感染—疾病—文献—索引
Ⅳ.①Z89：R37 ②R4

中国国家版本馆CIP数据核字（2023）第223040号

病原生物与感染性疾病文献索引

| 策划编辑：郝迎聪 | 责任编辑：韩 晶 | 责任校对：张 微 | 责任出版：张志平 |

出 版 者　科学技术文献出版社
地　　址　北京市复兴路15号　邮编　100038
编 务 部　（010）58882938，58882087（传真）
发 行 部　（010）58882868，58882870（传真）
邮 购 部　（010）58882873
官 方 网 址　www.stdp.com.cn
发 行 者　科学技术文献出版社发行　全国各地新华书店经销
印 刷 者　北京厚诚则铭印刷科技有限公司
版　　次　2023年11月第1版　2023年11月第1次印刷
开　　本　787×1092　1/16
字　　数　559千
印　　张　28.25
书　　号　ISBN 978-7-5235-0977-7
定　　价　118.00元

版权所有　违法必究

购买本社图书，凡字迹不清、缺页、倒页、脱页者，本社发行部负责调换

编写说明

　　病原生物及感染性疾病自古以来对民众健康和人类社会构成巨大威胁。天花、鼠疫在历史上造成了大量人员死亡，仅欧洲14世纪的"黑死病"——鼠疫就导致2500万人死亡。1918年，甲型H1N1流感在全球流行，造成全世界近5000万人死亡。近30年来，严重急性呼吸综合征（SARS）、H5N1禽流感、2009 H1N1流感、中东呼吸综合征（MERS）、H7N9禽流感、埃博拉病毒病、寨卡病毒病、2019新型冠状病毒感染（COVID-19）等新发再发传染疾病层出不穷，对民众健康、社会稳定、经济发展和国家安全产生巨大影响。例如，2019年底暴发的COVID-19截至2023年2月已造成全球7.5亿人感染，680多万人死亡。

　　病原生物与感染性疾病相关文献数量庞大，包括大量图书与期刊文献，特别是新冠疫情后，相关的图书、期刊文献很多，梳理这些文献可为相关研究与管理人员提供参考。为此编者检索整理了与病原生物和感染性疾病相关的一些重要中英文图书、期刊文献，检索时间2023年3月。

　　文献检索关键词如下：

　　英文：Infectious OR Communicable OR Pathogen OR Pathogenic OR Pandemic OR Pandemics OR Bacteria OR Virus OR Viruses OR Parasite OR Mycoplasma OR Chlamydia OR Chlamydophila OR Rickettsia OR Vaccine OR Vaccines OR Influenza OR HIV OR AIDS OR COVID OR SARS OR Yersinia pestis OR Vibrio cholerae OR Anthrax OR Smallpox OR Ebola OR Hepatitis OR Tuberculosis

　　中文：感染 OR 传染 OR 病原 OR 细菌 OR 病毒 OR 寄生虫 OR 支原体 OR 衣原体 OR 立克次体 OR 疫苗 OR 流感 OR 艾滋 OR HIV OR 新冠 OR SARS OR COVID OR 鼠疫 OR 霍乱 OR 炭疽 OR 天花 OR 埃博拉 OR 肝炎 OR 结核

　　文献检索策略如下：

1. 图书检索

通过以下网站，根据检索关键词在标题中进行检索，选择出版时间在 2010 年以后的图书，筛选重要图书，整理相关信息。

美国科学院出版社（https://www.nap.edu/）；

德国施普林格出版社（https://link.springer.com/）；

荷兰爱思唯尔 SD 数据库（https://www.sciencedirect.com/browse/journals-and-books）；

约翰威立父子出版公司在线图书馆（https://onlinelibrary.wiley.com/）；

英国泰勒 - 弗朗西斯出版集团（https://www.taylorfrancis.com/）；

哈佛大学出版社（https://www.hup.harvard.edu/）；

麻省理工学院出版社（https://mitpress.mit.edu/）；

牛津大学学术资源库（https://global.oup.com/academic/online）；

剑桥大学出版社（https://www.cambridge.org/core）。

在京东商城网站（https://www.jd.com/）检索、筛选相关中文图书。在国家版本数据中心网站（https://pdc.capub.cn/）进行信息核准。

按年度由近及远顺序编排图书信息，年度相同的按标题字母或拼音编排。

2. 期刊文献检索

英文期刊文献通过 Web of Science 核心合集进行检索，选择综述、引用次数较高的文献。

中文期刊文献通过中国知网进行检索，选择综述、引用次数较高的文献。

出版时间选择 2000 年以后的文献，按年度由近及远顺序编排文献，年度相同的按标题字母或拼音编排。

书中文献信息基于原始来源，未做过多调整。书中不当之处，请读者批评指正。

编者

2023 年 5 月

目 录

一、图书

NAP ······1
Springer ······23
ScienceDirect ······206
Wiley ······251
Taylor Francis ······272
Harvard ······355
Mitpress ······356
Oxford ······358
Cambridge ······374
中文图书 ······375

二、期刊

SCI 期刊文献 ······411
中文期刊文献 ······433

一、图书

NAP

标题	Addressing the Long-Term Effects of the COVID-19 Pandemic on Children and Families
年度	2023
DOI	https://doi.org/10.17226/26809
序号	1
标题	Emerging Stronger from COVID-19: Priorities for Health System Transformation
年度	2023
DOI	https://doi.org/10.17226/26657
序号	2
标题	Partnerships for Equitable Pandemic Response and Recovery
年度	2023
DOI	https://doi.org/10.17226/26892
序号	3
标题	Addressing the Impact of COVID-19 on the Early Care and Education Sector
年度	2022
DOI	https://doi.org/10.17226/26463
序号	4
标题	Aviation After a Year of Pandemic: Economics, People, and Technology: Proceedings of a Workshop
年度	2022
DOI	https://doi.org/10.17226/26375
序号	5
标题	Caring for People with Serious Illness: Lessons Learned from the COVID-19 Pandemic: Proceedings of a Workshop
年度	2022
DOI	https://doi.org/10.17226/26596
序号	6

续表

标题	Countering the Pandemic Threat Through Global Coordination on Vaccines: The Influenza Imperative
年度	2022
DOI	https://doi.org/10.17226/26284
序号	7
标题	COVID-19 Vaccines: Studying Historical Successes (and Failures) for Equity-Centered Approaches to Vaccinating Indigenous Communities, Undocumented Immigrants, and Communities of Color: Proceedings of a Workshop-in Brief
年度	2022
DOI	https://doi.org/10.17226/26622
序号	8
标题	COVID-19, Health Equity, and the Asian American, Native Hawaiian, and Pacific Islander Communities: Proceedings of a Workshop-in Brief
年度	2022
DOI	https://doi.org/10.17226/26700
序号	9
标题	Evaluating COVID-19-Related Surveillance Measures for Decision-Making
年度	2022
DOI	https://doi.org/10.17226/26578
序号	10
标题	Evolving Crisis Standards of Care and Ongoing Lessons from COVID-19: Proceedings of a Workshop Series
年度	2022
DOI	https://doi.org/10.17226/26573
序号	11
标题	Flying in the COVID-19 Era: Science-Based Risk Assessments and Mitigation Strategies on the Ground and in the Air: Proceedings of a Workshop
年度	2022
DOI	https://doi.org/10.17226/26426
序号	12

续表

标题	Future Planning for the Public Health Emergency Preparedness Enterprise: Lessons Learned from the COVID-19 Pandemic: Proceedings of a Workshop
年度	2022
DOI	https://doi.org/10.17226/26805
序号	13
标题	Globally Resilient Supply Chains for Seasonal and Pandemic Influenza Vaccines
年度	2022
DOI	https://doi.org/10.17226/26285
序号	14
标题	Increasing Uptake of COVID-19 Vaccination Through Requirement and Incentive Programs
年度	2022
DOI	https://doi.org/10.17226/26545
序号	15
标题	Innovation in Cancer Care and Cancer Research in the Context of the COVID-19 Pandemic: Proceedings of a Workshop
年度	2022
DOI	https://doi.org/10.17226/26470
序号	16
标题	Innovations for Tackling Tuberculosis in the Time of COVID-19: Proceedings of a Workshop
年度	2022
DOI	https://doi.org/10.17226/26530
序号	17
标题	International Workshop on COVID-19 Lessons to Inform Pandemic Influenza Response: Proceedings of a Workshop
年度	2022
DOI	https://doi.org/10.17226/26352
序号	18
标题	Lessons Learned from the COVID-19 Pandemic to Improve Diagnosis: Proceedings of a Workshop-in Brief
年度	2022

续表

DOI	https://doi.org/10.17226/26567
序号	19
标题	Lessons Learned in Health Professions Education During the COVID-19 Pandemic, Part 2: Proceedings of a Workshop
年度	2022
DOI	https://doi.org/10.17226/26484
序号	20
标题	Long COVID: Examining Long-Term Health Effects of COVID-19 and Implications for the Social Security Administration: Proceedings of a Workshop
年度	2022
DOI	https://doi.org/10.17226/26619
序号	21
标题	Long-Term Impacts of COVID-19 on the Future Academic Careers of Women in STEM: Proceedings of a Workshop-in Brief
年度	2022
DOI	https://doi.org/10.17226/26687
序号	22
标题	Materials Science and Engineering in a Post-Pandemic World: A DoD Perspective: Proceedings of a Workshop
年度	2022
DOI	https://doi.org/10.17226/26226
序号	23
标题	Public Health Lessons for Non-Vaccine Influenza Interventions: Looking Past COVID-19
年度	2022
DOI	https://doi.org/10.17226/26283
序号	24
标题	Rapid Expert Consultation on Self-Tests for Infectious Diseases: Lessons Learned from COVID-19
年度	2022
DOI	https://doi.org/10.17226/26694
序号	25

续表

标题	Rental Eviction and the COVID-19 Pandemic: Averting a Looming Crisis
年度	2022
DOI	https://doi.org/10.17226/26106
序号	26
标题	Standing Committee on Emerging Infectious Diseases and 21st Century Health Threats: Annual Report 2020
年度	2022
DOI	https://doi.org/10.17226/26715
序号	27
标题	Standing Committee on Emerging Infectious Diseases and 21st Century Health Threats: Annual Report 2021
年度	2022
DOI	https://doi.org/10.17226/26716
序号	28
标题	Supporting Children with Disabilities: Lessons from the Pandemic: Proceedings of a Workshop
年度	2022
DOI	https://doi.org/10.17226/26702
序号	29
标题	Supporting Individual Risk Assessment During COVID-19
年度	2022
DOI	https://doi.org/10.17226/26629
序号	30
标题	Systematizing the One Health Approach in Preparedness and Response Efforts for Infectious Disease Outbreaks: Proceedings of a Workshop
年度	2022
DOI	https://doi.org/10.17226/26301
序号	31
标题	Toward a Post-Pandemic World: Lessons from COVID-19 for Now and the Future: Proceedings of a Workshop
年度	2022
DOI	https://doi.org/10.17226/26556
序号	32

续表

标题	Vaccine Research and Development to Advance Pandemic and Seasonal Influenza Preparedness and Response: Lessons from COVID-19
年度	2022
DOI	https://doi.org/10.17226/26282
序号	33
标题	Virtual Public Involvement: Lessons from the COVID-19 Pandemic
年度	2022
DOI	https://doi.org/10.17226/26827
序号	34
标题	A Pandemic Playbook for Transportation Agencies
年度	2021
DOI	https://doi.org/10.17226/26145
序号	35
标题	Addressing Disaster Vulnerability Among Homeless Populations During COVID-19
年度	2021
DOI	https://doi.org/10.17226/26220
序号	36
标题	Back in School: Addressing the Well-Being of Students in the Wake of COVID-19: Proceedings of a Workshop–in Brief
年度	2021
DOI	https://doi.org/10.17226/26296
序号	37
标题	Communication Strategies for Building Confidence in COVID-19 Vaccines: Addressing Variants and Childhood Vaccinations
年度	2021
DOI	https://doi.org/10.17226/26361
序号	38
标题	COVID-19 Addendum to Critical Issues in Transportation
年度	2021
DOI	https://doi.org/10.17226/26047
序号	39

续表

标题	COVID-19 and the K-12 Teacher Workforce: Seizing the Moment to Reimagine Education: Proceedings of a Workshop–in Brief
年度	2021
DOI	https://doi.org/10.17226/26356
序号	40
标题	COVID-19 and the Present and Future of Black Communities: The Role of Black Physicians, Engineers, and Scientists: Proceedings of a Workshop
年度	2021
DOI	https://doi.org/10.17226/26146
序号	41
标题	Critical Findings on COVID-19: Select Publications from the National Academies of Sciences, Engineering, and Medicine
年度	2021
DOI	https://doi.org/10.17226/26100
序号	42
标题	Emergency Evacuation and Sheltering During the COVID-19 Pandemic
年度	2021
DOI	https://doi.org/10.17226/26084
序号	43
标题	Innovations for Tackling Tuberculosis in the Time of COVID-19: Current Tools and Challenges: Proceedings of a Workshop-in Brief
年度	2021
DOI	https://doi.org/10.17226/26404
序号	44
标题	Learning from Rapid Response, Innovation, and Adaptation to the COVID-19 Crisis: Proceedings of a Workshop-in Brief
年度	2021
DOI	https://doi.org/10.17226/26131
序号	45
标题	Lessons Learned in Health Professions Education During the COVID-19 Pandemic, Part 1: Proceedings of a Workshop
年度	2021

续表

DOI	https://doi.org/10.17226/26210
序号	46
标题	Meeting Regional STEMM Workforce Needs in the Wake of COVID-19: Proceedings of a Virtual Workshop Series
年度	2021
DOI	https://doi.org/10.17226/26049
序号	47
标题	Mental Health and Substance Use Disorders in the Era of COVID-19: The Impact of the Pandemic on Communities of Color: Proceedings of a Workshop-in Brief
年度	2021
DOI	https://doi.org/10.17226/26102
序号	48
标题	Pivotal Interfaces of Environmental Health and Infectious Disease Research to Inform Responses to Outbreaks, Epidemics, and Pandemics: Proceedings of a Workshop-in Brief
年度	2021
DOI	https://doi.org/10.17226/26270
序号	49
标题	Rapid Expert Consultation on Allocating COVID-19 Monoclonal Antibody Therapies and Other Novel Therapeutics (January 29, 2021)
年度	2021
DOI	https://doi.org/10.17226/26063
序号	50
标题	Rapid Response by Laboratory Animal Research Institutions During the COVID-19 Pandemic: Lessons Learned: Proceedings of a Workshop-in Brief
年度	2021
DOI	https://doi.org/10.17226/26189
序号	51
标题	School-Based Strategies for Addressing the Mental Health and Well-Being of Youth in the Wake of COVID-19
年度	2021

一、图书

续表

DOI	https://doi.org/10.17226/26262
序号	52
标题	Short-Term Strategies for Addressing the Impacts of the COVID-19 Pandemic on Women's Workforce Participation
年度	2021
DOI	https://doi.org/10.17226/26303
序号	53
标题	Strategies for Building Confidence in the COVID-19 Vaccines
年度	2021
DOI	https://doi.org/10.17226/26068
序号	54
标题	The Critical Public Health Value of Vaccines: Tackling Issues of Access and Hesitancy: Proceedings of a Workshop
年度	2021
DOI	https://doi.org/10.17226/26134
序号	55
标题	The Impact of COVID-19 on the Careers of Women in Academic Sciences, Engineering, and Medicine
年度	2021
DOI	https://doi.org/10.17226/26061
序号	56
标题	The Utility, Feasibility, Security, and Ethics of Verifiable COVID-19 Credentials for International Travel: Proceedings of a Workshop-in Brief
年度	2021
DOI	https://doi.org/10.17226/26409
序号	57
标题	Undergraduate and Graduate STEM Students' Experiences During COVID-19: Proceedings of a Virtual Workshop Series
年度	2021
DOI	https://doi.org/10.17226/26024
序号	58

续表

标题	Understanding and Communicating about COVID-19 Vaccine Efficacy, Effectiveness, and Equity
年度	2021
DOI	https://doi.org/10.17226/26154
序号	59
标题	Using Syndemic Theory and the Societal Lens to Inform Resilient Recovery from COVID-19: Toward a Post-Pandemic World: Proceedings of a Workshop-in Brief
年度	2021
DOI	https://doi.org/10.17226/26259
序号	60
标题	A Pandemic Playbook for Transportation Agencies
年度	2020
DOI	https://doi.org/10.17226/25993
序号	61
标题	Airborne Transmission of SARS-CoV-2: Proceedings of a Workshop-in Brief
年度	2020
DOI	https://doi.org/10.17226/25958
序号	62
标题	COVID-19 Testing Strategies for Colleges and Universities
年度	2020
DOI	https://doi.org/10.17226/26005
序号	63
标题	Decarcerating Correctional Facilities during COVID-19: Advancing Health, Equity, and Safety
年度	2020
DOI	https://doi.org/10.17226/25945
序号	64
标题	Encouraging Adoption of Protective Behaviors to Mitigate the Spread of COVID-19: Strategies for Behavior Change
年度	2020

一、图书

续表

DOI	https://doi.org/10.17226/25881
序号	65
标题	Encouraging Protective COVID-19 Behaviors Among College Students
年度	2020
DOI	https://doi.org/10.17226/26004
序号	66
标题	Evaluating Data Types: A Guide for Decision Makers Using Data to Understand the Extent and Spread of COVID-19
年度	2020
DOI	https://doi.org/10.17226/25826
序号	67
标题	Framework for Equitable Allocation of COVID-19 Vaccine
年度	2020
DOI	https://doi.org/10.17226/25917
序号	68
标题	Genomic Epidemiology Data Infrastructure Needs for SARS-CoV-2: Modernizing Pandemic Response Strategies
年度	2020
DOI	https://doi.org/10.17226/25879
序号	69
标题	Opportunities to Improve Opioid Use Disorder and Infectious Disease Services: Integrating Responses to a Dual Epidemic
年度	2020
DOI	https://doi.org/10.17226/25626
序号	70
标题	Rapid Expert Consultation on Crisis Standards of Care for the COVID-19 Pandemic(March 28, 2020)
年度	2020
DOI	https://doi.org/10.17226/25765
序号	71
标题	Rapid Expert Consultation on Critical Issues in Diagnostic Testing for the COVID-19 Pandemic(November 9, 2020)
年度	2020

DOI	https://doi.org/10.17226/25984	
序号	72	
标题	Rapid Expert Consultation on Data Elements and Systems Design for Modeling and Decision Making for the COVID-19 Pandemic（March 21, 2020）	
年度	2020	
DOI	https://doi.org/10.17226/25755	
序号	73	
标题	Rapid Expert Consultation on SARS-CoV-2 Laboratory Testing for the COVID-19 Pandemic（April 8, 2020）	
年度	2020	
DOI	https://doi.org/10.17226/25775	
序号	74	
标题	Rapid Expert Consultation on SARS-CoV-2 Surface Stability and Incubation for the COVID-19 Pandemic（March 15, 2020）	
年度	2020	
DOI	https://doi.org/10.17226/25751	
序号	75	
标题	Rapid Expert Consultation on SARS-CoV-2 Survival in Relation to Temperature and Humidity and Potential for Seasonality for the COVID-19 Pandemic（April 7, 2020）	
年度	2020	
DOI	https://doi.org/10.17226/25771	
序号	76	
标题	Rapid Expert Consultation on SARS-CoV-2 Viral Shedding and Antibody Response for the COVID-19 Pandemic（April 8, 2020）	
年度	2020	
DOI	https://doi.org/10.17226/25774	
序号	77	
标题	Rapid Expert Consultation on Severe Illness in Young Adults for the COVID-19 Pandemic（March 14, 2020）	
年度	2020	
DOI	https://doi.org/10.17226/25752	
序号	78	

续表

标题	Rapid Expert Consultation on Social Distancing for the COVID-19 Pandemic（March 19, 2020）
年度	2020
DOI	https://doi.org/10.17226/25753
序号	79
标题	Rapid Expert Consultation on Staffing Considerations for Crisis Standards of Care for the COVID-19 Pandemic（July 28, 2020）
年度	2020
DOI	https://doi.org/10.17226/25890
序号	80
标题	Rapid Expert Consultation on the Effectiveness of Fabric Masks for the COVID-19 Pandemic（April 8, 2020）
年度	2020
DOI	https://doi.org/10.17226/25776
序号	81
标题	Rapid Expert Consultation on the Possibility of Bioaerosol Spread of SARS-CoV-2 for the COVID-19 Pandemic（April 1, 2020）
年度	2020
DOI	https://doi.org/10.17226/25769
序号	82
标题	Rapid Expert Consultation on Understanding Causes of Health Care Worker Deaths Due to the COVID-19 Pandemic（December 10, 2020）
年度	2020
DOI	https://doi.org/10.17226/26018
序号	83
标题	Rapid Expert Consultation Update on SARS-CoV-2 Surface Stability and Incubation for the COVID-19 Pandemic（March 27, 2020）
年度	2020
DOI	https://doi.org/10.17226/25763
序号	84
标题	Rapid Expert Consultations on the COVID-19 Pandemic: March 14, 2020—April 8, 2020
年度	2020

续表

DOI	https://doi.org/10.17226/25784
序号	85
标题	Reopening K-12 Schools During the COVID-19 Pandemic：Prioritizing Health，Equity，and Communities
年度	2020
DOI	https://doi.org/10.17226/25858
序号	86
标题	Resilience of the Research Enterprise During the COVID-19 Crisis：Proceedings of a Workshop Series-in Brief
年度	2020
DOI	https://doi.org/10.17226/26014
序号	87
标题	Vaccine Access and Hesitancy：Part One of a Workshop Series：Proceedings of a Workshop-in Brief
年度	2020
DOI	https://doi.org/10.17226/25895
序号	88
标题	Airport Roles in Reducing Transmission of Communicable Diseases
年度	2019
DOI	https://doi.org/10.17226/25367
序号	89
标题	The Convergence of Infectious Diseases and Noncommunicable Diseases：Proceedings of a Workshop
年度	2019
DOI	https://doi.org/10.17226/25535
序号	90
标题	Toward Understanding the Interplay of Environmental Stressors，Infectious Diseases，and Human Health：Proceedings of a Workshop-in Brief
年度	2019
DOI	https://doi.org/10.17226/25493
序号	91

续表

标题	Integrating Responses at the Intersection of Opioid Use Disorder and Infectious Disease Epidemics: Proceedings of a Workshop
年度	2018
DOI	https://doi.org/10.17226/25153
序号	92
标题	Urbanization and Slums: Infectious Diseases in the Built Environment: Proceedings of a Workshop
年度	2018
DOI	https://doi.org/10.17226/25070
序号	93
标题	A National Strategy for the Elimination of Hepatitis B and C: Phase Two Report
年度	2017
DOI	https://doi.org/10.17226/24731
序号	94
标题	Building Communication Capacity to Counter Infectious Disease Threats: Proceedings of a Workshop
年度	2017
DOI	https://doi.org/10.17226/24738
序号	95
标题	Integrating Clinical Research into Epidemic Response: The Ebola Experience
年度	2017
DOI	https://doi.org/10.17226/24739
序号	96
标题	Preparing Airports for Communicable Diseases on Arriving Flights
年度	2017
DOI	https://doi.org/10.17226/24880
序号	97
标题	Public Transit Emergency Preparedness Against Ebola and Other Infectious Diseases: Legal Issues
年度	2017
DOI	https://doi.org/10.17226/24795

续表

序号	98
标题	Big Data and Analytics for Infectious Disease Research, Operations, and Policy: Proceedings of a Workshop
年度	2016
DOI	https://doi.org/10.17226/23654
序号	99
标题	Eliminating the Public Health Problem of Hepatitis B and C in the United States: Phase One Report
年度	2016
DOI	https://doi.org/10.17226/23407
序号	100
标题	Global Health Risk Framework: Pandemic Financing: Workshop Summary
年度	2016
DOI	https://doi.org/10.17226/21855
序号	101
标题	Global Health Risk Framework: Resilient and Sustainable Health Systems to Respond to Global Infectious Disease Outbreaks: Workshop Summary
年度	2016
DOI	https://doi.org/10.17226/21856
序号	102
标题	Potential Research Priorities to Inform Public Health and Medical Practice for Domestic Zika Virus: Workshop in Brief
年度	2016
DOI	https://doi.org/10.17226/23404
序号	103
标题	Rapid Medical Countermeasure Response to Infectious Diseases: Enabling Sustainable Capabilities Through Ongoing Public- and Private-Sector Partnerships: Workshop Summary
年度	2016
DOI	https://doi.org/10.17226/21809
序号	104

续表

标题	The Ebola Epidemic in West Africa: Proceedings of a Workshop
年度	2016
DOI	https://doi.org/10.17226/23653
序号	105
标题	The Neglected Dimension of Global Security: A Framework to Counter Infectious Disease Crises
年度	2016
DOI	https://doi.org/10.17226/21891
序号	106
标题	International Infectious Disease Emergencies and Domestic Implications for the Public Health and Health Care Sectors—Workshop in Brief
年度	2015
DOI	https://doi.org/10.17226/21773
序号	107
标题	Ranking Vaccines: Applications of a Prioritization Software Tool: Phase III: Use Case Studies and Data Framework
年度	2015
DOI	https://doi.org/10.17226/18763
序号	108
标题	A Guide for Public Transportation Pandemic Planning and Response
年度	2014
DOI	https://doi.org/10.17226/22414
序号	109
标题	Research Priorities to Inform Public Health and Medical Practice for Ebola Virus Disease—Workshop in Brief
年度	2014
DOI	https://doi.org/10.17226/19004
序号	110
标题	The Global Crisis of Drug-Resistant Tuberculosis and Leadership of China and the BRICS: Challenges and Opportunities: Summary of a Joint Workshop by the Institute of Medicine and the Institute of Microbiology, Chinese Academy of Sciences
年度	2014

续表

DOI	https://doi.org/10.17226/18346
序号	111
标题	The Influence of Global Environmental Change on Infectious Disease Dynamics: Workshop Summary
年度	2014
DOI	https://doi.org/10.17226/18800
序号	112
标题	Developing and Strengthening the Global Supply Chain for Second-Line Drugs for Multidrug-Resistant Tuberculosis: Workshop Summary
年度	2013
DOI	https://doi.org/10.17226/13524
序号	113
标题	Infectious Disease Mitigation in Airports and on Aircraft
年度	2013
DOI	https://doi.org/10.17226/22512
序号	114
标题	Perspectives on Research with H5N1 Avian Influenza: Scientific Inquiry, Communication, Controversy: Summary of a Workshop
年度	2013
DOI	https://doi.org/10.17226/18255
序号	115
标题	Ranking Vaccines: A Prioritization Software Tool: Phase II: Prototype of a Decision-Support System
年度	2013
DOI	https://doi.org/10.17226/13531
序号	116
标题	Adverse Effects of Vaccines: Evidence and Causality
年度	2012
DOI	https://doi.org/10.17226/13164
序号	117

续表

标题	Facing the Reality of Drug-Resistant Tuberculosis in India: Challenges and Potential Solutions: Summary of a Joint Workshop by the Institute of Medicine, the Indian National Science Academy, and the Indian Council of Medical Research
年度	2012
DOI	https://doi.org/10.17226/13243
序号	118
标题	Monitoring HIV Care in the United States: A Strategy for Generating National Estimates of HIV Care and Coverage
年度	2012
DOI	https://doi.org/10.17226/13408
序号	119
标题	Monitoring HIV Care in the United States: Indicators and Data Systems
年度	2012
DOI	https://doi.org/10.17226/13225
序号	120
标题	Prepositioning Antibiotics for Anthrax
年度	2012
DOI	https://doi.org/10.17226/13218
序号	121
标题	Public Engagement on Facilitating Access to Antiviral Medications and Information in an Influenza Pandemic: Workshop Series Summary
年度	2012
DOI	https://doi.org/10.17226/13404
序号	122
标题	Ranking Vaccines: A Prioritization Framework: Phase I: Demonstration of Concept and a Software Blueprint
年度	2012
DOI	https://doi.org/10.17226/13382
序号	123
标题	HIV Screening and Access to Care: Exploring the Impact of Policies on Access to and Provision of HIV Care
年度	2011

续表

DOI	https://doi.org/10.17226/13057
序号	124
标题	HIV Screening and Access to Care: Health Care System Capacity for Increased HIV Testing and Provision of Care
年度	2011
DOI	https://doi.org/10.17226/13074
序号	125
标题	Preparing for the Future of HIV/AIDS in Africa: A Shared Responsibility
年度	2011
DOI	https://doi.org/10.17226/12991
序号	126
标题	Preventing Transmission of Pandemic Influenza and Other Viral Respiratory Diseases: Personal Protective Equipment for Healthcare Personnel: Update 2010
年度	2011
DOI	https://doi.org/10.17226/13027
序号	127
标题	Review of the Scientific Approaches Used During the FBI's Investigation of the 2001 Anthrax Letters
年度	2011
DOI	https://doi.org/10.17226/13098
序号	128
标题	The Emerging Threat of Drug-Resistant Tuberculosis in Southern Africa: Global and Local Challenges and Solutions: Summary of a Joint Workshop by the Institute of Medicine and the Academy of Science of South Africa
年度	2011
DOI	https://doi.org/10.17226/12993
序号	129
标题	The New Profile of Drug-Resistant Tuberculosis in Russia: A Global and Local Perspective: Summary of a Joint Workshop by the Institute of Medicine and the Russian Academy of Medical Science
年度	2011

续表

DOI	https://doi.org/10.17226/13033
序号	130
标题	What You Need to Know About Infectious Disease
年度	2011
DOI	https://doi.org/10.17226/13006
序号	131
标题	Considerations for Ensuring Safety and Efficacy of Vaccines and Therapeutic Proteins Manufactured by Using Platform Approaches: Summary of a Workshop
年度	2010
DOI	https://doi.org/10.17226/12899
序号	132
标题	Hepatitis and Liver Cancer: A National Strategy for Prevention and Control of Hepatitis B and C
年度	2010
DOI	https://doi.org/10.17226/12793
序号	133
标题	HIV and Disability: Updating the Social Security Listings
年度	2010
DOI	https://doi.org/10.17226/12941
序号	134
标题	HIV Screening and Access to Care: Exploring Barriers and Facilitators to Expanded HIV Testing
年度	2010
DOI	https://doi.org/10.17226/12932
序号	135
标题	Infectious Disease Movement in a Borderless World: Workshop Summary
年度	2010
DOI	https://doi.org/10.17226/12758
序号	136
标题	Priorities for the National Vaccine Plan
年度	2010

续表

DOI	https://doi.org/10.17226/12796
序号	137
标题	Strategic Approach to the Evaluation of Programs Implemented Under the Tom Lantos and Henry J. Hyde U.S. Global Leadership Against HIV/AIDS, Tuberculosis, and Malaria Reauthorization Act of 2008
年度	2010
DOI	https://doi.org/10.17226/12909
序号	138
标题	The 2009 H1N1 Influenza Vaccination Campaign: Summary of a Workshop Series
年度	2010
DOI	https://doi.org/10.17226/12992
序号	139
标题	The Domestic and International Impacts of the 2009-H1N1 Influenza a Pandemic: Global Challenges, Global Solutions: Workshop Summary
年度	2010
DOI	https://doi.org/10.17226/12799
序号	140

Springer

标题	**2000 Years of Pandemics**
副标题	Past, Present, and Future
作者	Claudia Ferreira, Marie-Françoise J. Doursout, Joselito S. Balingit
年度	2023
出版社	Springer Cham
DOI	https://doi.org/10.1007/978-3-031-10035-2
序号	1
标题	**Challenges and Opportunities of mRNA Vaccines Against SARS-CoV-2**
副标题	A Multidisciplinary Perspective
作者	Siguna Mueller
年度	2023
出版社	Springer Cham
DOI	https://doi.org/10.1007/978-3-031-18903-6
序号	2
标题	**Changing Law and Contractual Relations Under COVID-19**
副标题	Reallocation of Social Risks in Asian SME Sectors
系列标题	Kobe University Monograph Series in Social Science Research
作者	Yuka Kaneko
年度	2023
出版社	Springer Singapore
DOI	https://doi.org/10.1007/978-981-19-4238-9
序号	3
标题	**Coronavirus Pandemic & Online Education**
副标题	Impact on Developing Countries
作者	Imtiaz A. Hussain, Jessica Tartila Suma
年度	2023
出版社	Palgrave Macmillan Singapore
DOI	https://doi.org/10.1007/978-981-19-6853-2
序号	4

续表

标题	Covid-19 and Insurance
系列标题	AIDA Europe Research Series on Insurance Law and Regulation
作者	María Luisa Muñoz Paredes, Anna Tarasiuk
年度	2023
出版社	Springer Cham
DOI	https://doi.org/10.1007/978-3-031-13753-2
序号	5
标题	COVID-19 in Zimbabwe
副标题	Trends, Dynamics and Implications in the Agricultural, Environmental and Water Sectors
作者	Lazarus Chapungu, David Chikodzi, Kaitano Dube
年度	2023
出版社	Springer Cham
DOI	https://doi.org/10.1007/978-3-031-21472-1
序号	6
标题	COVID-19 Metabolomics and Diagnosis
副标题	Chemical Science for Prevention and Understanding Outbreaks of Infectious Diseases
作者	Frank N. Crespilho
年度	2023
出版社	Springer Cham
DOI	https://doi.org/10.1007/978-3-031-15889-6
序号	7
标题	COVID-19, Tourist Destinations and Prospects for Recovery
副标题	Volume One: A Global Perspective
作者	Kaitano Dube, Godwell Nhamo, MP Swart
年度	2023
出版社	Springer Cham
DOI	https://doi.org/10.1007/978-3-031-22257-3
序号	8

续表

标题	COVID-19, Tourist Destinations and Prospects for Recovery
副标题	Volume Two: An African Perspective
作者	Kaitano Dube, Ishmael Mensah, Lazarus Chapungu
年度	2023
出版社	Springer Cham
DOI	https://doi.org/10.1007/978-3-031-24655-5
序号	9
标题	COVID-19: Search for a Vaccine
系列标题	Essentials
作者	Patric U. B. Vogel
年度	2023
出版社	Springer Spektrum Wiesbaden
DOI	https://doi.org/10.1007/978-3-658-38931-4
序号	10
标题	Digital and Sustainable Transformations in a Post-COVID World
副标题	Economic, Social, and Environmental Challenges
作者	Salvador Estrada
年度	2023
出版社	Palgrave Macmillan Cham
DOI	https://doi.org/10.1007/978-3-031-16677-8
序号	11
标题	Digital Management in Covid-19 Pandemic and Post-Pandemic Times
副标题	Proceedings of the International Scientific-Practical Conference(ISPC 2021)
系列标题	Springer Proceedings in Business and Economics
作者	Richard C. Geibel, Shalva Machavariani
年度	2023
出版社	Springer Cham
DOI	https://doi.org/10.1007/978-3-031-20148-6
序号	12

续表

标题	Discovery of Small-Molecule Modulators of Protein–RNA Interactions for Treating Cancer and COVID-19
系列标题	Springer Theses
作者	Wan Gi Byun
年度	2023
出版社	Springer Singapore
DOI	https://doi.org/10.1007/978-981-19-7814-2
序号	13
标题	Domestic Violence and COVID-19
副标题	The 2020 Lockdown in the European Union
系列标题	SpringerBriefs in Criminology
作者	Joachim Kersten, Michele Burman, Jarmo Houtsonen, Paul Herbinger, Norbert Leonhardmair
年度	2023
出版社	Springer Cham
DOI	https://doi.org/10.1007/978-3-031-15335-8
序号	14
标题	Drug Repurposing for Emerging Infectious Diseases and Cancer
作者	Ranbir Chander Sobti, Sunil K. Lal, Ramesh K. Goyal
年度	2023
出版社	Springer Singapore
DOI	https://doi.org/10.1007/978-981-19-5399-6
序号	15
标题	Explore Business, Technology Opportunities and Challenges After the Covid-19 Pandemic
系列标题	Lecture Notes in Networks and Systems
作者	Bahaaeddin Alareeni, Allam Hamdan
年度	2023
出版社	Springer Cham
DOI	https://doi.org/10.1007/978-3-031-08954-1
序号	16

续表

标题	**Exploring What Drives Indian Stock Market During Covid-19**
副标题	Fads or Fundamentals
系列标题	SpringerBriefs in Economics
作者	Indrani Chakraborty
年度	2023
出版社	Springer Singapore
DOI	https://doi.org/10.1007/978-981-19-8001-5
序号	17
标题	**GCC Hydrocarbon Economies and COVID**
副标题	Old Trends, New Realities
作者	Nikolay Kozhanov, Karen Young, Jalal Qanas
年度	2023
出版社	Palgrave Macmillan Singapore
DOI	https://doi.org/10.1007/978-981-19-5462-7
序号	18
标题	**Global Health, Humanity and the COVID-19 Pandemic**
副标题	Philosophical and Sociological Challenges and Imperatives
作者	Francis Egbokhare, Adeshina Afolayan
年度	2023
出版社	Palgrave Macmillan Cham
DOI	https://doi.org/10.1007/978-3-031-17429-2
序号	19
标题	**Governments' Responses to the Covid-19 Pandemic in Europe**
副标题	Navigating the Perfect Storm
作者	Kennet Lynggaard, Mads Dagnis Jensen, Michael Kluth
年度	2023
出版社	Palgrave Macmillan Cham
DOI	https://doi.org/10.1007/978-3-031-14145-4
序号	20

续表

标题	Industrial Engineering in the Covid-19 Era
副标题	Selected Papers from the Hybrid Global Joint Conference on Industrial Engineering and Its Application Areas, GJCIE 2022, October 29-30, 2022
系列标题	Lecture Notes in Management and Industrial Engineering
作者	Fethi Calisir, Murat Durucu
年度	2023
出版社	Springer Cham
DOI	https://doi.org/10.1007/978-3-031-25847-3
序号	21
标题	Infectious Diseases (Second Edition)
系列标题	Encyclopedia of Sustainability Science and Technology Series
作者	Lester M Shulman
年度	2023
出版社	Springer New York
DOI	https://doi.org/10.1007/978-1-0716-2463-0
序号	22
标题	Innovation of Businesses, and Digitalization During Covid-19 Pandemic
副标题	Proceedings of the International Conference on Business and Technology (ICBT 2021)
系列标题	Lecture Notes in Networks and Systems
作者	Bahaaeddin Alareeni, Allam Hamdan
年度	2023
出版社	Springer Cham
DOI	https://doi.org/10.1007/978-3-031-08090-6
序号	23
标题	Intelligent and Transformative Production in Pandemic Times
副标题	Proceedings of the 26th International Conference on Production Research
系列标题	Lecture Notes in Production Engineering
作者	Chin-Yin Huang, Rob Dekkers, Shun Fung Chiu, Daniela Popescu, Luis Quezada
年度	2023

出版社	Springer Cham
DOI	https://doi.org/10.1007/978-3-031-18641-7
序号	24
标题	**Migrants and the COVID-19 Pandemic**
副标题	Communication, Inequality, and Transformation
作者	Satveer Kaur-Gill, Mohan J. Dutta
年度	2023
出版社	Palgrave Macmillan Singapore
DOI	https://doi.org/10.1007/978-981-19-7384-0
序号	25
标题	**Paediatric Infectious Diseases**
副标题	A Practical Guide and Cases
作者	Yhu-Chering Huang, Ping-Ing Lee, Po-Yen Chen
年度	2023
出版社	Springer Singapore
DOI	https://doi.org/10.1007/978-981-19-7276-8
序号	26
标题	**Pandemic and the City**
系列标题	Footprints of Regional Science
作者	Mehmet Güney Celbiş, Karima Kourtit, Peter Nijkamp
年度	2023
出版社	Springer Cham
DOI	https://doi.org/10.1007/978-3-031-21983-2
序号	27
标题	**Pandemic in the Metropolis**
副标题	Transportation Impacts and Recovery
系列标题	Springer Tracts on Transportation and Traffic
作者	Anastasia Loukaitou-Sideris, Alexandre M. Bayen, Giovanni Circella, R. Jayakrishnan
年度	2023

续表

出版社	Springer Cham
DOI	https://doi.org/10.1007/978-3-031-00148-2
序号	28
标题	**Plural Policing, Security and the COVID Crisis**
副标题	Comparative European Perspectives
系列标题	Palgrave's Critical Policing Studies
作者	Monica Den Boer, Eric Bervoets, Linda Hak
年度	2023
出版社	Palgrave Macmillan Cham
DOI	https://doi.org/10.1007/978-3-031-19177-0
序号	29
标题	**Pseudotyped Viruses**
系列标题	Advances in Experimental Medicine and Biology
作者	Youchun Wang
年度	2023
出版社	Springer Singapore
DOI	https://doi.org/10.1007/978-981-99-0113-5
序号	30
标题	**Social Vulnerability to COVID-19**
副标题	Impacts of Technology Adoption and Information Behavior
系列标题	Synthesis Lectures on Information Concepts, Retrieval, and Services
作者	Xiaojun Yuan, Dan Wu, DeeDee Bennett Gayle
年度	2023
出版社	Springer Cham
DOI	https://doi.org/10.1007/978-3-031-06897-3
序号	31
标题	**Sustainable Business Management and Digital Transformation: Challenges and Opportunities in the Post-COVID Era**
系列标题	Lecture Notes in Networks and Systems
作者	Marko Mihić, Sandra Jednak, Gordana Savić

一、图书

续表

年度	2023
出版社	Springer Cham
DOI	https://doi.org/10.1007/978-3-031-18645-5
序号	32
标题	The Chemical and Biological Nonproliferation Regime After the Covid-19 Pandemic
副标题	Dealing with the Scientific Revolution in the Life Sciences
作者	Malcolm Dando
年度	2023
出版社	Palgrave Macmillan Cham
DOI	https://doi.org/10.1007/978-3-031-19108-4
序号	33
标题	The COVID-19—Health Systems Nexus
副标题	Emerging Trends, Issues and Dynamics in Zimbabwe
系列标题	Global Perspectives on Health Geography
作者	Lazarus Chapungu, David Chikodzi, Kaitano Dube
年度	2023
出版社	Springer Cham
DOI	https://doi.org/10.1007/978-3-031-21602-2
序号	34
标题	The Covid-19 Pandemic
副标题	A Public Choice View
系列标题	Studies in Public Choice
作者	Panagiotis Karadimas
年度	2023
出版社	Springer Cham
DOI	https://doi.org/10.1007/978-3-031-24967-9
序号	35
标题	The Effect of Covid-19 on Loan Loss Provisions and Earnings Management of European Banks
系列标题	BestMasters

续表

作者	Merjona Lamaj
年度	2023
出版社	Springer Gabler Wiesbaden
DOI	https://doi.org/10.1007/978-3-658-40060-6
序号	36
标题	The Political Economy of Global Responses to COVID-19
系列标题	International Political Economy Series
作者	Alan W. Cafruny, Leila Simona Talani
年度	2023
出版社	Palgrave Macmillan Cham
DOI	https://doi.org/10.1007/978-3-031-23914-4
序号	37
标题	The Post-Pandemic Landscape of Education and Beyond: Innovation and Transformation
副标题	Selected Papers from the HKAECT 2022 International Conference
系列标题	Educational Communications and Technology Yearbook
作者	Anna Wing Bo TSO, Steven Kwan Keung NG, Locky LAW, Tiffany Shurui BAI
年度	2023
出版社	Springer Singapore
DOI	https://doi.org/10.1007/978-981-19-9217-9
序号	38
标题	Tourism Analytics Before and After COVID-19
副标题	Case Studies from Asia and Europe
作者	Yok Yen Nguwi
年度	2023
出版社	Springer Singapore
DOI	https://doi.org/10.1007/978-981-19-9369-5
序号	39
标题	Transnational Employment Strain in a Global Health Pandemic
副标题	Migrant Farmworkers in Canada

续表

系列标题	Politics of Citizenship and Migration
作者	Leah F. Vosko, Tanya Basok, Cynthia Spring
年度	2023
出版社	Palgrave Macmillan Cham
DOI	https://doi.org/10.1007/978-3-031-17704-0
序号	40
标题	**Varicella-Zoster Virus**
副标题	Genetics, Pathogenesis and Immunity
系列标题	Current Topics in Microbiology and Immunology
作者	Ann M. Arvin, Jennifer F. Moffat, Allison Abendroth, Stefan L Oliver
年度	2023
出版社	Springer Cham
DOI	https://doi.org/10.1007/978-3-031-15305-1
序号	41
标题	**Virus-Host Interactions**
副标题	Methods and Protocols
系列标题	Methods in Molecular Biology
作者	Marilena Aquino de Muro
年度	2023
出版社	Humana New York
DOI	https://doi.org/10.1007/978-1-0716-2895-9
序号	42
标题	**West Nile Virus**
副标题	Methods and Protocols
系列标题	Methods in Molecular Biology
作者	Fengwei Bai
年度	2023
出版社	Humana New York
DOI	https://doi.org/10.1007/978-1-0716-2760-0
序号	43

续表

标题	**World Christianity and Covid-19**
副标题	Looking Back and Looking Forward
作者	Chammah J. Kaunda
年度	2023
出版社	Palgrave Macmillan Cham
DOI	https://doi.org/10.1007/978-3-031-12570-6
序号	44
标题	**Access to Medicines and Vaccines**
副标题	Implementing Flexibilities Under Intellectual Property Law
作者	Carlos M. Correa, Reto M. Hilty
年度	2022
出版社	Springer Cham
DOI	https://doi.org/10.1007/978-3-030-83114-1
序号	45
标题	**Active Learning in Political Science for a Post-Pandemic World**
副标题	From Triage to Transformation
系列标题	Political Pedagogies
作者	Jeffrey S. Lantis
年度	2022
出版社	Palgrave Macmillan Cham
DOI	https://doi.org/10.1007/978-3-030-94713-2
序号	46
标题	**Advances in Data Science and Intelligent Data Communication Technologies for COVID-19**
副标题	Innovative Solutions Against COVID-19
系列标题	Studies in Systems, Decision and Control
作者	Aboul-Ella Hassanien, Sally M. Elghamrawy, Ivan Zelinka
年度	2022
出版社	Springer Cham
DOI	https://doi.org/10.1007/978-3-030-77302-1

续表

序号	47
标题	**Advances in Microbiology, Infectious Diseases and Public Health**
副标题	Volume 16
系列标题	Advances in Experimental Medicine and Biology
作者	Gianfranco Donelli
年度	2022
出版社	Springer Cham
DOI	https://doi.org/10.1007/978-3-031-01995-1
序号	48
标题	**African Swine Fever Virus**
副标题	Methods and Protocols
系列标题	Methods in Molecular Biology
作者	Christopher L. Netherton
年度	2022
出版社	Humana New York
DOI	https://doi.org/10.1007/978-1-0716-2333-6
序号	49
标题	**Aging with HIV in Sub-Saharan Africa**
副标题	Health and Psychosocial Perspectives
作者	Mark Brennan-Ing, Kristen E. Porter, Jennifer E. Kaufman, Catherine MacPhail, Janet Seeley
年度	2022
出版社	Springer Cham
DOI	https://doi.org/10.1007/978-3-030-96368-2
序号	50
标题	**AI for Disease Surveillance and Pandemic Intelligence**
副标题	Intelligent Disease Detection in Action
系列标题	Studies in Computational Intelligence
作者	Arash Shaban-Nejad, Martin Michalowski, Simone Bianco
年度	2022

续表

出版社	Springer Cham
DOI	https://doi.org/10.1007/978-3-030-93080-6
序号	51
标题	Artificial Intelligence and COVID Effect on Accounting
系列标题	Accounting, Finance, Sustainability, Governance & Fraud: Theory and Application
作者	Bahaaeddin Alareeni, Allam Hamdan
年度	2022
出版社	Springer Singapore
DOI	https://doi.org/10.1007/978-981-19-1036-4
序号	52
标题	Artificial Intelligence and Machine Learning Methods in COVID-19 and Related Health Diseases
系列标题	Studies in Computational Intelligence
作者	Victor Chang, Harleen Kaur, Simon James Fong
年度	2022
出版社	Springer Cham
DOI	https://doi.org/10.1007/978-3-031-04597-4
序号	53
标题	Artificial Intelligence in Covid-19
作者	Niklas Lidströmer, Yonina C. Eldar
年度	2022
出版社	Springer Cham
DOI	https://doi.org/10.1007/978-3-031-08506-2
序号	54
标题	Assessing COVID-19 and Other Pandemics and Epidemics Using Computational Modelling and Data Analysis
作者	Subhendu Kumar Pani, Sujata Dash, Wellington P. dos Santos, Syed Ahmad Chan Bukhari, Francesco Flammini
年度	2022
出版社	Springer Cham

续表

DOI	https://doi.org/10.1007/978-3-030-79753-9
序号	55
标题	**Bacterial Vaccines**
副标题	Methods and Protocols
系列标题	Methods in Molecular Biology
作者	Fadil Bidmos, Janine Bossé, Paul Langford
年度	2022
出版社	Humana New York
DOI	https://doi.org/10.1007/978-1-0716-1900-1
序号	56
标题	**Balancing the Socio-Political and Medico-Ethical Dimensions of HIV**
副标题	A Social Public Health Approach
系列标题	SpringerBriefs in Public Health
作者	Amos Laar
年度	2022
出版社	Springer Cham
DOI	https://doi.org/10.1007/978-3-031-09191-9
序号	57
标题	**Beta-Lactam Resistance in Gram-Negative Bacteria**
副标题	Threats and Challenges
作者	Mohammad Shahid, Anuradha Singh, Hiba Sami
年度	2022
出版社	Springer Singapore
DOI	https://doi.org/10.1007/978-981-16-9097-6
序号	58
标题	**Cardiovascular Complications of COVID-19**
副标题	Risk, Pathogenesis and Outcomes
作者	Umair Mallick
年度	2022
出版社	Springer Cham

续表

DOI	https://doi.org/10.1007/978-3-030-90065-6
序号	59
标题	**Cardiovascular Complications of COVID-19**
副标题	Acute and Long-Term Impacts
系列标题	Contemporary Cardiology
作者	Maciej Banach
年度	2022
出版社	Humana Cham
DOI	https://doi.org/10.1007/978-3-031-15478-2
序号	60
标题	**Caring on the Frontline During COVID-19**
副标题	Contributions from Rapid Qualitative Research
作者	Cecilia Vindrola-Padros, Ginger A. Johnson
年度	2022
出版社	Palgrave Macmillan Singapore
DOI	https://doi.org/10.1007/978-981-16-6486-1
序号	61
标题	**Chikungunya Virus**
系列标题	Current Topics in Microbiology and Immunology
作者	Mark Heise
年度	2022
出版社	Springer Cham
DOI	https://doi.org/10.1007/978-3-030-90610-8
序号	62
标题	**Children's Experience, Participation, and Rights During COVID-19**
作者	Ruby Turok-Squire
年度	2022
出版社	Palgrave Macmillan Cham
DOI	https://doi.org/10.1007/978-3-031-07099-0
序号	63

续表

标题	**Colonialism and the COVID-19 Pandemic**
副标题	Perspectives from Indigenous Psychology
系列标题	International and Cultural Psychology
作者	Arthur W. Blume
年度	2022
出版社	Springer Cham
DOI	https://doi.org/10.1007/978-3-030-92825-4
序号	64
标题	**Community, Economy and COVID-19**
副标题	Lessons from Multi-Country Analyses of a Global Pandemic
系列标题	Community Quality-of-Life and Well-Being
作者	Clifford J. Shultz, II, Don R. Rahtz, M. Joseph Sirgy
年度	2022
出版社	Springer Cham
DOI	https://doi.org/10.1007/978-3-030-98152-5
序号	65
标题	**Computational Intelligence for COVID-19 and Future Pandemics**
副标题	Emerging Applications and Strategies
系列标题	Disruptive Technologies and Digital Transformations for Society 5.0
作者	Utku Kose, Junzo Watada, Omer Deperlioglu, Jose Antonio Marmolejo Saucedo
年度	2022
出版社	Springer Singapore
DOI	https://doi.org/10.1007/978-981-16-3783-4
序号	66
标题	**Considerations for a Post-COVID-19 Technology and Innovation Ecosystem in China**
系列标题	Disaster Risk Reduction
作者	Jinling Hua, Bismark Adu Gyamfi, Rajib Shaw
年度	2022
出版社	Springer Singapore

续表

DOI	https://doi.org/10.1007/978-981-16-6959-0
序号	67
标题	**Constitutional Resilience and the COVID-19 Pandemic**
副标题	Perspectives from Sub-Saharan Africa
作者	Ebenezer Durojaye, Derek M. Powell
年度	2022
出版社	Palgrave Macmillan Cham
DOI	https://doi.org/10.1007/978-3-031-06401-2
序号	68
标题	**Contactless Healthcare Facilitation and Commodity Delivery Management During COVID 19 Pandemic**
系列标题	Advanced Technologies and Societal Change
作者	Mousmi Ajay Chaurasia, Stefan Mozar
年度	2022
出版社	Springer Singapore
DOI	https://doi.org/10.1007/978-981-16-5411-4
序号	69
标题	**Contemporary French Environmental Thought in the Post-COVID-19 Era**
系列标题	Sustainable Development Goals Series
作者	Keith Moser
年度	2022
出版社	Palgrave Macmillan Cham
DOI	https://doi.org/10.1007/978-3-030-96129-9
序号	70
标题	**Coping with COVID-19, the Mobile Way**
副标题	Experience and Expertise from China
作者	Xiaoge Xu
年度	2022
出版社	Palgrave Macmillan Singapore
DOI	https://doi.org/10.1007/978-981-19-5787-1

续表

序号	71
标题	**Coping with the Pandemic in Fragile Cities**
系列标题	SpringerBriefs in Applied Sciences and Technology
作者	Gabriele Pasqui
年度	2022
出版社	Springer Cham
DOI	https://doi.org/10.1007/978-3-030-93979-3
序号	72
标题	**Coronavirus（COVID-19）Outbreaks, Vaccination, Politics and Society**
副标题	The Continuing Challenge
作者	Rais Akhtar
年度	2022
出版社	Springer Cham
DOI	https://doi.org/10.1007/978-3-031-09432-3
序号	73
标题	**COVID 19, Containment, Life, Work and Restart**
副标题	Urban Studies
系列标题	Advances in 21st Century Human Settlements
作者	T. M. Vinod Kumar
年度	2022
出版社	Springer Singapore
DOI	https://doi.org/10.1007/978-981-19-5940-0
序号	74
标题	**COVID 19, Containment, Life, Work and Restart**
副标题	Regional Studies
系列标题	Advances in 21st Century Human Settlements
作者	T. M. Vinod Kumar
年度	2022
出版社	Springer Singapore
DOI	https://doi.org/10.1007/978-981-19-6183-0

续表

序号	75
标题	**COVID-19 and a World of Ad Hoc Geographies**
作者	Stanley D. Brunn, Donna Gilbreath
年度	2022
出版社	Springer Cham
DOI	https://doi.org/10.1007/978-3-030-94350-9
序号	76
标题	**Covid-19 and Capitalism**
副标题	Success and Failure of the Legal Methods for Dealing with a Pandemic
系列标题	Economic and Financial Law & Policy—Shifting Insights & Values
作者	Koen Byttebier
年度	2022
出版社	Springer Cham
DOI	https://doi.org/10.1007/978-3-030-92901-5
序号	77
标题	**COVID-19 and Communities**
副标题	The University of Palermo's Voices and Analyses During the Pandemic
系列标题	UNIPA Springer Series
作者	Giuseppina Campisi, Arabella Mocciaro Li Destri, Carlo Amenta
年度	2022
出版社	Springer Cham
DOI	https://doi.org/10.1007/978-3-030-88622-6
序号	78
标题	**COVID-19 and Education in the Global North**
副标题	Storytelling and Alternative Pedagogies
作者	Ruby Turok-Squire
年度	2022
出版社	Palgrave Macmillan Cham
DOI	https://doi.org/10.1007/978-3-031-02469-6
序号	79

续表

标题	**COVID-19 and Health System Segregation in the US**
副标题	Racial Health Disparities and Systemic Racism
系列标题	SpringerBriefs in Public Health
作者	Prem Misir
年度	2022
出版社	Springer Cham
DOI	https://doi.org/10.1007/978-3-030-88766-7
序号	80
标题	**COVID-19 and International Development**
作者	Elissaios Papyrakis
年度	2022
出版社	Springer Cham
DOI	https://doi.org/10.1007/978-3-030-82339-9
序号	81
标题	**COVID-19 and Marginalisation of People and Places**
副标题	Impacts, Responses and Observed Effects of COVID-19 on Geographical Marginality
系列标题	Perspectives on Geographical Marginality
作者	Borna Fuerst-Bjeliš, Etienne Nel, Stanko Pelc
年度	2022
出版社	Springer Cham
DOI	https://doi.org/10.1007/978-3-031-11139-6
序号	82
标题	**COVID-19 and Society**
副标题	Socio-Economic Perspectives on the Impact, Implications, and Challenges
系列标题	Science, Technology and Innovation Studies
作者	Mustafa Polat, Serhat Burmaoglu, Ozcan Saritas
年度	2022
出版社	Springer Cham
DOI	https://doi.org/10.1007/978-3-031-13142-4

续表

序号	83	
标题	COVID-19 and the Case Against Neoliberalism	
副标题	The United Kingdom's Political Pandemic	
作者	Mark Boyle, James Hickson, Katalin Ujhelyi Gomez	
年度	2022	
出版社	Palgrave Macmillan Cham	
DOI	https://doi.org/10.1007/978-3-031-18935-7	
序号	84	
标题	COVID-19 and the Evolving Business Environment in Asia	
副标题	The Hidden Impact on the Economy, Business and Society	
作者	Andrei O. J. Kwok, Motoki Watabe, Sharon G.M. Koh	
年度	2022	
出版社	Springer Singapore	
DOI	https://doi.org/10.1007/978-981-19-2749-2	
序号	85	
标题	COVID-19 and the Sociology of Risk and Uncertainty	
副标题	Studies of Social Phenomena and Social Theory Across 6 Continents	
系列标题	Critical Studies in Risk and Uncertainty	
作者	Patrick R. Brown, Jens O. Zinn	
年度	2022	
出版社	Palgrave Macmillan Cham	
DOI	https://doi.org/10.1007/978-3-030-95167-2	
序号	86	
标题	COVID-19 Challenges to University Information Technology Governance	
作者	Mansoor Alaali	
年度	2022	
出版社	Springer Cham	
DOI	https://doi.org/10.1007/978-3-031-13351-0	
序号	87	
标题	COVID-19 Critical and Intensive Care Medicine Essentials	
作者	Denise Battaglini, Paolo Pelosi	

续表

年度	2022
出版社	Springer Cham
DOI	https://doi.org/10.1007/978-3-030-94992-1
序号	88
标题	**COVID-19 Disinformation: A Multi-National, Whole of Society Perspective**
系列标题	Advanced Sciences and Technologies for Security Applications
作者	Ritu Gill, Rebecca Goolsby
年度	2022
出版社	Springer Cham
DOI	https://doi.org/10.1007/978-3-030-94825-2
序号	89
标题	**COVID-19 Epidemiology and Virus Dynamics**
副标题	Nonlinear Physics and Mathematical Modeling
系列标题	Understanding Complex Systems
作者	Till D. Frank
年度	2022
出版社	Springer Cham
DOI	https://doi.org/10.1007/978-3-030-97178-6
序号	90
标题	**COVID-19 Pandemic**
副标题	Research and Development Activities from Modeling to Realization
系列标题	Materials Horizons: From Nature to Nanomaterials
作者	Mamata Mohapatra, Balamati Choudhury, Suddhasatwa Basu
年度	2022
出版社	Springer Singapore
DOI	https://doi.org/10.1007/978-981-16-4372-9
序号	91
标题	**COVID-19, Society and Crime in Europe**
系列标题	Studies of Organized Crime

作者	Dina Siegel, Aleksandras Dobryninas, Stefano Becucci
年度	2022
出版社	Springer Cham
DOI	https://doi.org/10.1007/978-3-031-13562-0
序号	92
标题	**COVID-19, State-Power and Society in Europe**
副标题	Focus on Western Balkans
系列标题	European Union and Its Neighbours in a Globalized World
作者	Neven Andjelic
年度	2022
出版社	Springer Cham
DOI	https://doi.org/10.1007/978-3-030-91073-0
序号	93
标题	**Decision Sciences for COVID-19**
副标题	Learning Through Case Studies
系列标题	International Series in Operations Research & Management Science
作者	Said Ali Hassan, Ali Wagdy Mohamed, Khalid Abdulaziz Alnowibet
年度	2022
出版社	Springer Cham
DOI	https://doi.org/10.1007/978-3-030-87019-5
序号	94
标题	**Democracy After Covid**
副标题	Challenges in Europe and Beyond
作者	Kostas Chrysogonos, Anna Tsiftsoglou
年度	2022
出版社	Springer Cham
DOI	https://doi.org/10.1007/978-3-031-13901-7
序号	95
标题	**Dengue Virus**
副标题	Methods and Protocols

续表

系列标题	Methods in Molecular Biology
作者	Ronaldo Mohana-Borges
年度	2022
出版社	Humana New York
DOI	https://doi.org/10.1007/978-1-0716-1879-0
序号	96
标题	**Destigmatisation of People Living with HIV/AIDS in China**
系列标题	A Sociological View of AIDS
作者	Xiaoping Wang
年度	2022
出版社	Springer Singapore
DOI	https://doi.org/10.1007/978-981-16-8534-7
序号	97
标题	**Dispatches from Home and the Field During the COVID-19 Pandemic**
系列标题	Palgrave Studies in Literary Anthropology
作者	Robert Desjarlais, Sabina M. Perrino, Joshua O. Reno, Nicholas Bartlett, Aurora Donzelli, Margaux Fitoussi, Alexa Hagerty, Rafadi Hakim, Parthiban Muniandy, Emily Ng
年度	2022
出版社	Palgrave Macmillan Cham
DOI	https://doi.org/10.1007/978-3-031-19193-0
序号	98
标题	**Economic and Societal Transformation in Pandemic-Trapped India**
副标题	Emerging Challenges and Resilient Policy Prescriptions
系列标题	New Frontiers in Regional Science: Asian Perspectives
作者	Subrata Saha, Mukunda Mishra, Anil Bhuimali
年度	2022
出版社	Springer Singapore
DOI	https://doi.org/10.1007/978-981-16-5755-9
序号	99
标题	**Economic Challenges for Europe After the Pandemic**
副标题	Proceedings of the XXXII Villa Mondragone International Economic Seminar, Rome, Italy, 2021

续表

系列标题	Springer Proceedings in Business and Economics
作者	Luigi Paganetto
年度	2022
出版社	Springer Cham
DOI	https://doi.org/10.1007/978-3-031-10302-5
序号	100
标题	**Economists and COVID-19**
副标题	Ideas, Theories and Policies During the Pandemic
作者	Andrés Lazzarini, Denis Melnik
年度	2022
出版社	Palgrave Macmillan Cham
DOI	https://doi.org/10.1007/978-3-031-05811-0
序号	101
标题	**Emerging Adulthood in the COVID-19 Pandemic and Other Crises: Individual and Relational Resources**
系列标题	Cross-Cultural Advancements in Positive Psychology
作者	Sophie Leontopoulou, Antonella Delle Fave
年度	2022
出版社	Springer Cham
DOI	https://doi.org/10.1007/978-3-031-22288-7
序号	102
标题	**Emerging Applications of 3D Printing During CoVID 19 Pandemic**
系列标题	Lecture Notes in Bioengineering
作者	Kamalpreet Sandhu, Sunpreet Singh, Chander Prakash, Neeta Raj Sharma, Karupppasamy Subburaj
年度	2022
出版社	Springer Singapore
DOI	https://doi.org/10.1007/978-981-33-6703-6
序号	103
标题	**Emerging European Economies After the Pandemic**
副标题	Stuck in the Middle Income Trap?

续表

系列标题	Contributions to Economics
作者	László Mátyás
年度	2022
出版社	Springer Cham
DOI	https://doi.org/10.1007/978-3-030-93963-2
序号	104
标题	Epidemic Analytics for Decision Supports in COVID19 Crisis
作者	Joao Alexandre Lobo Marques, Simon James Fong
年度	2022
出版社	Springer Cham
DOI	https://doi.org/10.1007/978-3-030-95281-5
序号	105
标题	Essential Writing, Communication and Narrative Skills for Medical Scientists Before and After the COVID Era
作者	Gian Carlo Di Renzo
年度	2022
出版社	Springer Cham
DOI	https://doi.org/10.1007/978-3-030-84954-2
序号	106
标题	Ethical Failures of the COVID-19 Pandemic Response
作者	Péter Marton
年度	2022
出版社	Palgrave Macmillan Cham
DOI	https://doi.org/10.1007/978-3-031-09194-0
序号	107
标题	Ethical Public Health Policy Within Pandemics
副标题	Theory and Practice in Ethical Pandemic Administration
系列标题	The International Library of Bioethics
作者	Michael Boylan
年度	2022

续表

出版社	Springer Cham
DOI	https://doi.org/10.1007/978-3-030-99692-5
序号	108
标题	European Cities After COVID-19
副标题	Strategies for Resilient Cities and Real Estate
系列标题	Future of Business and Finance
作者	Tobias Just, Franziska Plößl
年度	2022
出版社	Springer Cham
DOI	https://doi.org/10.1007/978-3-030-89788-8
序号	109
标题	Executive Education After the Pandemic
副标题	A Vision for the Future
作者	Santiago Iñiguez, Peter Lorange
年度	2022
出版社	Palgrave Macmillan Cham
DOI	https://doi.org/10.1007/978-3-030-82343-6
序号	110
标题	Exploring Susceptible-Infectious-Recovered (SIR) Model for COVID-19 Investigation
系列标题	SpringerBriefs in Applied Sciences and Technology
作者	Rahul Saxena, Mahipal Jadeja, Vikrant Bhateja
年度	2022
出版社	Springer Singapore
DOI	https://doi.org/10.1007/978-981-19-4175-7
序号	111
标题	Extended Reality Usage During COVID 19 Pandemic
系列标题	Intelligent Systems Reference Library
作者	Anitha S. Pillai, Giuliana Guazzaroni
年度	2022

续表

出版社	Springer Cham
DOI	https://doi.org/10.1007/978-3-030-91394-6
序号	112
标题	Features and Management of Acute and Chronic Neuro-Covid
作者	Marco Cascella, Elvio De Blasio
年度	2022
出版社	Springer Cham
DOI	https://doi.org/10.1007/978-3-030-86705-8
序号	113
标题	Finance, Law, and the Crisis of COVID-19
副标题	An Interdisciplinary Perspective
系列标题	Contributions to Management Science
作者	Nadia Mansour, Lorenzo M. Bujosa Vadell
年度	2022
出版社	Springer Cham
DOI	https://doi.org/10.1007/978-3-030-89416-0
序号	114
标题	Financial Crises, Poverty and Environmental Sustainability: Challenges in the Context of the SDGs and Covid-19 Recovery
系列标题	Sustainable Development Goals Series
作者	Andreas Antoniades, Alexander S. Antonarakis, Isabell Kempf
年度	2022
出版社	Springer Cham
DOI	https://doi.org/10.1007/978-3-030-87417-9
序号	115
标题	Financial Market Dynamics After COVID 19
副标题	The Contagion Effect of the Pandemic in Finance
系列标题	Contributions to Finance and Accounting
作者	Stéphane Goutte, Khaled Guesmi, Christian Urom
年度	2022

出版社	Springer Cham
DOI	https://doi.org/10.1007/978-3-030-98542-4
序号	116
标题	**From Cogito to Covid**
副标题	Rethinking Lacan's "Science and Truth"
系列标题	The Palgrave Lacan Series
作者	Molly A. Wallace, Concetta V. Principe
年度	2022
出版社	Palgrave Macmillan Cham
DOI	https://doi.org/10.1007/978-3-030-99604-8
序号	117
标题	**From Grand Challenges to Great Solutions: Digital Transformation in the Age of COVID-19**
副标题	20th Workshop on e-Business, WeB 2021, Virtual Event, December 11, 2021, Revised Selected Papers
系列标题	Lecture Notes in Business Information Processing
作者	Shaokun Fan, Noyan Ilk, Zhe Shan, Kexin Zhao
年度	2022
出版社	Springer Cham
DOI	https://doi.org/10.1007/978-3-031-04126-6
序号	118
标题	**Frontiers of COVID-19**
副标题	Scientific and Clinical Aspects of the Novel Coronavirus 2019
作者	Sasan Adibi, Paul Griffin, Melvin Sanicas, Maryam Rashidi, Francesco Lanfranchi
年度	2022
出版社	Springer Cham
DOI	https://doi.org/10.1007/978-3-031-08045-6
序号	119
标题	**Future of Work and Business in Covid-19 Era**
副标题	Proceedings of IMC-2021

续表

系列标题	Springer Proceedings in Business and Economics
作者	Rabi Narayan Subudhi, Sumita Mishra, Abu Saleh, Dariush Khezrimotlagh
年度	2022
出版社	Springer Singapore
DOI	https://doi.org/10.1007/978-981-19-0357-1
序号	120
标题	**Gender, Internet Use, and Covid-19 in the Global South**
副标题	Multiple Causalities and Policy Options
系列标题	SpringerBriefs in Economics
作者	Jeffrey James
年度	2022
出版社	Springer Cham
DOI	https://doi.org/10.1007/978-3-031-15576-5
序号	121
标题	**Global Higher Education During and Beyond COVID-19**
副标题	Perspectives and Challenges
作者	C. Raj Kumar, Mousumi Mukherjee, Tatiana Belousova, Nisha Nair
年度	2022
出版社	Springer Singapore
DOI	https://doi.org/10.1007/978-981-16-9049-5
序号	122
标题	**Global Pandemic and Human Security**
副标题	Technology and Development Perspective
作者	Rajib Shaw, Anjula Gurtoo
年度	2022
出版社	Springer Singapore
DOI	https://doi.org/10.1007/978-981-16-5074-1
序号	123
标题	**Governance Challenges During the COVID-19 Pandemic in Africa**
作者	Nirmala Dorasamy

续表

年度	2022
出版社	Palgrave Macmillan Cham
DOI	https://doi.org/10.1007/978-3-031-11244-7
序号	124
标题	**Health Care Waste Management and COVID 19 Pandemic**
副标题	Policy, Implementation Status and Vaccine Management
作者	Sadhan Kumar Ghosh, Pariatamby Agamuthu
年度	2022
出版社	Springer Singapore
DOI	https://doi.org/10.1007/978-981-16-9336-6
序号	125
标题	**Health Dimensions of COVID-19 in India and Beyond**
作者	Saroj Pachauri, Ash Pachauri
年度	2022
出版社	Springer Singapore
DOI	https://doi.org/10.1007/978-981-16-7385-6
序号	126
标题	**Health Humanities for Quality of Care in Times of COVID-19**
系列标题	New Paradigms in Healthcare
作者	Maria Giulia Marini, Jonathan McFarland
年度	2022
出版社	Springer Cham
DOI	https://doi.org/10.1007/978-3-030-93359-3
序号	127
标题	**Healthcare Informatics for Fighting COVID-19 and Future Epidemics**
系列标题	EAI/Springer Innovations in Communication and Computing
作者	Lalit Garg, Chinmay Chakraborty, Saïd Mahmoudi, Victor S. Sohmen
年度	2022
出版社	Springer Cham
DOI	https://doi.org/10.1007/978-3-030-72752-9

续表

序号	128
标题	Higher Education and Disaster Capitalism in the Age of COVID-19
系列标题	Palgrave Critical University Studies
作者	Marina Vujnovic, Johanna E. Foster
年度	2022
出版社	Palgrave Macmillan Cham
DOI	https://doi.org/10.1007/978-3-031-12370-2
序号	129
标题	**HIV Psychiatry**
副标题	A Practical Guide for Clinicians
作者	James A. Bourgeois, Mary Ann Adler Cohen, Getrude Makurumidze
年度	2022
出版社	Springer Cham
DOI	https://doi.org/10.1007/978-3-030-80665-1
序号	130
标题	**HIV Reservoirs**
副标题	Methods and Protocols
系列标题	Methods in Molecular Biology
作者	Guido Poli, Elisa Vicenzi, Fabio Romerio
年度	2022
出版社	Humana New York
DOI	https://doi.org/10.1007/978-1-0716-1871-4
序号	131
标题	**How COVID-19 is Accelerating the Digital Revolution**
副标题	Challenges and Opportunities
作者	R. Anandan, G. Suseendran, Pushpita Chatterjee, Noor Zaman Jhanjhi, Uttam Ghosh
年度	2022
出版社	Springer Cham
DOI	https://doi.org/10.1007/978-3-030-98167-9

续表

序号	132
标题	**How COVID-19 Reshapes New World Order: Political Economy Perspective**
系列标题	Contributions to International Relations
作者	Li Sheng
年度	2022
出版社	Springer Singapore
DOI	https://doi.org/10.1007/978-981-16-6190-7
序号	133
标题	**Imaging of Tuberculosis**
系列标题	Medical Radiology
作者	Mohamed Fethi Ladeb, Wilfred C. G. Peh
年度	2022
出版社	Springer Cham
DOI	https://doi.org/10.1007/978-3-031-07040-2
序号	134
标题	**Impact of COVID-19 on Emerging Contaminants**
副标题	One Health Framework for Risk Assessment and Remediation
系列标题	Springer Transactions in Civil and Environmental Engineering
作者	Manish Kumar, Sanjeeb Mohapatra
年度	2022
出版社	Springer Singapore
DOI	https://doi.org/10.1007/978-981-19-1847-6
序号	135
标题	**Inclusive Pedagogical Practices Amidst a Global Pandemic**
副标题	Issues and Perspectives Around the Globe
系列标题	Inclusive Learning and Educational Equity
作者	Lawrence Meda, Jonathan Chitiyo
年度	2022
出版社	Springer Cham

续表

DOI	https://doi.org/10.1007/978-3-031-10642-2
序号	136
标题	Infectious Lesions of the Central Nervous System
作者	Vsevolod Zinserling
年度	2022
出版社	Springer Cham
DOI	https://doi.org/10.1007/978-3-030-96260-9
序号	137
标题	Infectious Tropical Diseases and One Health in Latin America
系列标题	Parasitology Research Monographs
作者	Heinz Mehlhorn, Jorg Heukelbach
年度	2022
出版社	Springer Cham
DOI	https://doi.org/10.1007/978-3-030-99712-0
序号	138
标题	Leadership After COVID-19
副标题	Working Together Toward a Sustainable Future
系列标题	Future of Business and Finance
作者	Satinder K. Dhiman, Joan F. Marques
年度	2022
出版社	Springer Cham
DOI	https://doi.org/10.1007/978-3-030-84867-5
序号	139
标题	Legal Education and Legal Profession During and After COVID-19
作者	C. Raj Kumar, S.G. Sreejith
年度	2022
出版社	Springer Singapore
DOI	https://doi.org/10.1007/978-981-19-2568-9
序号	140

续表

标题	Lifecycles of Pathogenic Protists in Humans
系列标题	Microbiology Monographs
作者	Wanderley de Souza
年度	2022
出版社	Springer Cham
DOI	https://doi.org/10.1007/978-3-030-80682-8
序号	141
标题	Local Government and the COVID-19 Pandemic
副标题	A Global Perspective
系列标题	Local and Urban Governance
作者	Carlos Nunes Silva
年度	2022
出版社	Springer Cham
DOI	https://doi.org/10.1007/978-3-030-91112-6
序号	142
标题	Loneliness Among Older Adults During the COVID-19 Pandemic
副标题	The Role of Family and Community Social Capital
作者	Nan LU
年度	2022
出版社	Springer Singapore
DOI	https://doi.org/10.1007/978-981-19-0611-4
序号	143
标题	Managing Sustainable Business Relationships in a Post Covid-19 Era
副标题	Towards a Dodecahedron Shaped Stakeholder Model
系列标题	SpringerBriefs in Business
作者	Vijay Pereira, Yama Temouri, Daicy Vaz
年度	2022
出版社	Springer Cham
DOI	https://doi.org/10.1007/978-3-030-96199-2
序号	144

续表

标题	**Manufacturing Government Communication on Covid-19**
副标题	A Comparative Perspective
系列标题	Springer Studies in Media and Political Communication
作者	Philippe J. Maarek
年度	2022
出版社	Springer Cham
DOI	https://doi.org/10.1007/978-3-031-09230-5
序号	145
标题	**Mechanical Ventilation Amid the COVID-19 Pandemic**
副标题	A Guide for Physicians and Engineers
作者	Amir A. Hakimi, Thomas E. Milner, Govind R. Rajan, Brian J-F Wong
年度	2022
出版社	Springer Cham
DOI	https://doi.org/10.1007/978-3-030-87978-5
序号	146
标题	**Migration and Pandemics**
副标题	Spaces of Solidarity and Spaces of Exception
系列标题	IMISCOE Research Series
作者	Anna Triandafyllidou
年度	2022
出版社	Springer Cham
DOI	https://doi.org/10.1007/978-3-030-81210-2
序号	147
标题	**Modeling and Simulation of Infectious Diseases**
副标题	Microscale Transmission, Decontamination and Macroscale Propagation
作者	Tarek I. Zohdi
年度	2022
出版社	Springer Cham
DOI	https://doi.org/10.1007/978-3-031-18053-8
序号	148

续表

标题	Modeling, Control and Drug Development for COVID-19 Outbreak Prevention
系列标题	Studies in Systems, Decision and Control
作者	Ahmad Taher Azar, Aboul Ella Hassanien
年度	2022
出版社	Springer Cham
DOI	https://doi.org/10.1007/978-3-030-72834-2
序号	149
标题	mRNA Vaccines
系列标题	Current Topics in Microbiology and Immunology
作者	Dong Yu, Benjamin Petsch
年度	2022
出版社	Springer Cham
DOI	https://doi.org/10.1007/978-3-031-18070-5
序号	150
标题	Nanotechnology for Infectious Diseases
作者	Saif Hameed, Suriya Rehman
年度	2022
出版社	Springer Singapore
DOI	https://doi.org/10.1007/978-981-16-9190-4
序号	151
标题	Navigating Through the Crisis—A Special Issue on the Covid 19 Crises
副标题	The 2020 Annual Griffiths School of Management and IT Conference (GSMAC) Vol 1
系列标题	Springer Proceedings in Business and Economics
作者	Silvia L. Fotea, Ioan Ș. Fotea, Sebastian Văduva
年度	2022
出版社	Springer Cham
DOI	https://doi.org/10.1007/978-3-030-82755-7
序号	152

续表

标题	**Nurses and COVID-19: Ethical Considerations in Pandemic Care**
作者	Connie M. Ulrich, Christine Grady
年度	2022
出版社	Springer Cham
DOI	https://doi.org/10.1007/978-3-030-82113-5
序号	153
标题	**Organizational Management in Post Pandemic Crisis**
系列标题	Management and Industrial Engineering
作者	Carolina Machado, J. Paulo Davim
年度	2022
出版社	Springer Cham
DOI	https://doi.org/10.1007/978-3-030-98052-8
序号	154
标题	**Pandemic Cities**
副标题	The COVID-19 Crisis and Australian Urban Regions
系列标题	Cities Research Series
作者	Scott Baum, Emma Baker, Amanda Davies, John Stone, Elizabeth Taylor
年度	2022
出版社	Springer Singapore
DOI	https://doi.org/10.1007/978-981-19-5884-7
序号	155
标题	**Pandemic Pedagogy**
副标题	Teaching International Relations Amid COVID-19
系列标题	Political Pedagogies
作者	Andrew A. Szarejko
年度	2022
出版社	Palgrave Macmillan Cham
DOI	https://doi.org/10.1007/978-3-030-83557-6
序号	156

续表

标题	Pandemic Police Power, Public Health and the Abolition Question
系列标题	Palgrave Studies in Race, Ethnicity, Indigeneity and Criminal Justice
作者	Tryon P. Woods
年度	2022
出版社	Palgrave Macmillan Cham
DOI	https://doi.org/10.1007/978-3-030-93031-8
序号	157
标题	Pandemic, New Normal and Implications on Business
副标题	12th Annual International Research Conference of Symbiosis Institute of Management Studies(SIMSARC21)
系列标题	Springer Proceedings in Business and Economics
作者	Arti Chandani, Rajiv Divekar, J. K. Nayak, Komal Chopra
年度	2022
出版社	Springer Singapore
DOI	https://doi.org/10.1007/978-981-19-4892-3
序号	158
标题	Pandemics and Epidemics in Cultural Representation
作者	Sathyaraj Venkatesan, Antara Chatterjee, A. David Lewis, Brian Callender
年度	2022
出版社	Springer Singapore
DOI	https://doi.org/10.1007/978-981-19-1296-2
序号	159
标题	Pandemics, Economics and Inequality
副标题	Lessons from the Spanish Flu
系列标题	Palgrave Studies in Economic History
作者	Sergi Basco, Jordi Domènech, Joan R. Rosés
年度	2022
出版社	Palgrave Macmillan Cham
DOI	https://doi.org/10.1007/978-3-031-05668-0
序号	160

续表

标题	**Pandemics: Insurance and Social Protection**
系列标题	Springer Actuarial
作者	María del Carmen Boado-Penas, Julia Eisenberg, Şule Şahin
年度	2022
出版社	Springer Cham
DOI	https://doi.org/10.1007/978-3-030-78334-1
序号	161
标题	**Pandemnomics: The Pandemic's Lasting Economic Effects**
系列标题	Accounting, Finance, Sustainability, Governance & Fraud: Theory and Application
作者	Bernur Açıkgöz, İbrahim Attila Acar
年度	2022
出版社	Springer Singapore
DOI	https://doi.org/10.1007/978-981-16-8024-3
序号	162
标题	**Pastoral Interventions During the Pandemic**
副标题	Pentecostal Perspectives on Christian Ministry in South Africa
作者	Mookgo Solomon Kgatle, Collium Banda
年度	2022
出版社	Palgrave Macmillan Cham
DOI	https://doi.org/10.1007/978-3-031-08034-0
序号	163
标题	**Point-of-Care Testing of COVID-19**
副标题	Current Status, Clinical Impact, and Future Therapeutic Perspectives
系列标题	SpringerBriefs in Applied Sciences and Technology
作者	Abilash Gangula, Brandon Kim, Benjamin Casey, Allison Hamill, Hariharan Regunath, Anandhi Upendran
年度	2022
出版社	Springer Singapore
DOI	https://doi.org/10.1007/978-981-19-4957-9
序号	164

续表

标题	**Post COVID-19 Complications and Management**
作者	Anant Mohan, Saurabh Mittal
年度	2022
出版社	Springer Singapore
DOI	https://doi.org/10.1007/978-981-19-4407-9
序号	165
标题	**Post Pandemic Facilitation of Air Transport**
副标题	Legal, Political and Economic Aspects
作者	Ruwantissa Abeyratne
年度	2022
出版社	Springer Cham
DOI	https://doi.org/10.1007/978-3-031-07373-1
序号	166
标题	**Post-COVID Economic Revival, Volume Ⅱ**
副标题	Sectors, Institutions, and Policy
作者	Vladimir S. Osipov
年度	2022
出版社	Palgrave Macmillan Cham
DOI	https://doi.org/10.1007/978-3-030-83566-8
序号	167
标题	**Post-Pandemic Realities and Growth in Eastern Europe**
副标题	The Griffiths School of Management & IT 12th Annual Conference on Business, Entrepreneurship and Ethics
系列标题	Springer Proceedings in Business and Economics
作者	Silvia L. Fotea, Ioan Ș. Fotea, Sebastian Văduva
年度	2022
出版社	Springer Cham
DOI	https://doi.org/10.1007/978-3-031-09421-7
序号	168

续表

标题	Predicting Pandemics in a Globally Connected World, Volume 1
副标题	Toward a Multiscale, Multidisciplinary Framework Through Modeling and Simulation
系列标题	Modeling and Simulation in Science, Engineering and Technology
作者	Nicola Bellomo, Mark A. J. Chaplain
年度	2022
出版社	Birkhäuser Cham
DOI	https://doi.org/10.1007/978-3-030-96562-4
序号	169
标题	**Preventing Errors and Pitfalls in Nursing with Infectious Patients**
作者	Kim Maryniak, Robbie Garrett
年度	2022
出版社	Springer Cham
DOI	https://doi.org/10.1007/978-3-030-86728-7
序号	170
标题	**Primary and Secondary Education During COVID-19**
副标题	Disruptions to Educational Opportunity During a Pandemic
作者	Fernando M. Reimers
年度	2022
出版社	Springer Cham
DOI	https://doi.org/10.1007/978-3-030-81500-4
序号	171
标题	**Principles in Nursing Practice in the Era of COVID-19**
作者	Amanda Bergeron, Russell Perkins, Emily Ingebretson, Linda Holifield
年度	2022
出版社	Springer Cham
DOI	https://doi.org/10.1007/978-3-030-94740-8
序号	172
标题	**Psycho-Social Approaches to the COVID-19 Pandemic**
副标题	Change, Crisis and Trauma

续表

作者	Athanasia Chalari, Eirini Efsevia Koutantou
年度	2022
出版社	Palgrave Macmillan Cham
DOI	https://doi.org/10.1007/978-3-031-07831-6
序号	173
标题	**Pulmonary Tuberculosis and Its Prevention**
系列标题	Respiratory Disease Series: Diagnostic Tools and Disease Managements
作者	Takefumi Saito, Masahiro Narita, Charles L. Daley
年度	2022
出版社	Springer Singapore
DOI	https://doi.org/10.1007/978-981-19-3995-2
序号	174
标题	**Quality of Work-Life During Pandemic**
副标题	Data Analysis and Mathematical Modeling
系列标题	Studies in Big Data
作者	Gitanjali Rahul Shinde, Soumi Majumder, Haribhau R. Bhapkar, Parikshit N. Mahalle
年度	2022
出版社	Springer Singapore
DOI	https://doi.org/10.1007/978-981-16-7523-2
序号	175
标题	**Radiology of Infectious and Inflammatory Diseases—Volume 2**
副标题	Head and Neck
作者	Hongjun Li, Shuang Xia, Yubo Lyu
年度	2022
出版社	Springer Singapore
DOI	https://doi.org/10.1007/978-981-16-8841-6
序号	176
标题	**Radiology of Infectious and Inflammatory Diseases—Volume 5**
副标题	Musculoskeletal System

作者	Hongjun Li, Shinong Pan, Jun Zhou
年度	2022
出版社	Springer Singapore
DOI	https://doi.org/10.1007/978-981-16-5003-1
序号	177
标题	**Real and Financial Sectors in Post-Pandemic Central and Eastern Europe**
副标题	The Impact of Economic, Monetary, and Fiscal Policy
系列标题	Contributions to Economics
作者	Bojana Olgić Draženović, Vesna Buterin, Stella Suljić Nikolaj
年度	2022
出版社	Springer Cham
DOI	https://doi.org/10.1007/978-3-030-99850-9
序号	178
标题	**Research and Teaching in a Pandemic World**
副标题	The Challenges of Establishing Academic Identities During Times of Crisis
作者	Basil Cahusac de Caux, Lynette Pretorius, Luke Macaulay
年度	2022
出版社	Springer Singapore
DOI	https://doi.org/10.1007/978-981-19-7757-2
序号	179
标题	**SARS-CoV-2**
副标题	Methods and Protocols
系列标题	Methods in Molecular Biology
作者	Justin Jang Hann Chu, Bintou Ahmadou Ahidjo, Chee Keng Mok
年度	2022
出版社	Humana New York
DOI	https://doi.org/10.1007/978-1-0716-2111-0
序号	180
标题	**Singapore's First Year of COVID-19**
副标题	Public Health, Immigration, the Neoliberal State, and Authoritarian Populism

续表

作者	Kenneth Paul Tan
年度	2022
出版社	Palgrave Macmillan Singapore
DOI	https://doi.org/10.1007/978-981-19-0368-7
序号	181
标题	Socio-Life Science and the COVID-19 Outbreak
副标题	Public Health and Public Policy
系列标题	Economics, Law, and Institutions in Asia Pacific
作者	Makoto Yano, Fumihiko Matsuda, Anavaj Sakuntabhai, Shigeru Hirota
年度	2022
出版社	Springer Singapore
DOI	https://doi.org/10.1007/978-981-16-5727-6
序号	182
标题	Studies to Combat COVID-19 Using Science and Engineering
作者	Dana Barry, Hideyuki Kanematsu
年度	2022
出版社	Springer Singapore
DOI	https://doi.org/10.1007/978-981-19-1356-3
序号	183
标题	Sustainable Development and Innovation of Digital Enterprises for Living with COVID-19
作者	Subhra R Mondal, Jana Majerova, Subhankar Das
年度	2022
出版社	Springer Singapore
DOI	https://doi.org/10.1007/978-981-19-2173-5
序号	184
标题	Sustainable Development Goals and Pandemic Planning
副标题	Role of Efficiency Based Regional Approaches
作者	Venkatachalam Anbumozhi, Kaliappa Kalirajan, Fukunari Kimura
年度	2022

续表

出版社	Springer Singapore
DOI	https://doi.org/10.1007/978-981-16-6734-3
序号	185
标题	**Technologies, Artificial Intelligence and the Future of Learning Post-COVID-19**
副标题	The Crucial Role of International Accreditation
系列标题	Studies in Computational Intelligence
作者	Allam Hamdan, Aboul Ella Hassanien, Timothy Mescon, Bahaaeddin Alareeni
年度	2022
出版社	Springer Cham
DOI	https://doi.org/10.1007/978-3-030-93921-2
序号	186
标题	**The Biological Role of a Virus**
系列标题	Advances in Environmental Microbiology
作者	Christon J. Hurst
年度	2022
出版社	Springer Cham
DOI	https://doi.org/10.1007/978-3-030-85395-2
序号	187
标题	**The Coagulation Labyrinth of COVID-19**
作者	Marco Ranucci
年度	2022
出版社	Springer Cham
DOI	https://doi.org/10.1007/978-3-030-82938-4
序号	188
标题	**The COVID Pandemic: Essays, Book Reviews, and Poems**
作者	Therese Jones, Kathleen Pachucki
年度	2022
出版社	Springer Cham

续表

DOI	https://doi.org/10.1007/978-3-031-19231-9
序号	189
标题	The COVID-19 Crisis and Entrepreneurship
副标题	Perspectives and Experiences of Researchers, Thought Leaders, and Policymakers
系列标题	International Studies in Entrepreneurship
作者	David B. Audretsch, Iris A. M. Kunadt
年度	2022
出版社	Springer Cham
DOI	https://doi.org/10.1007/978-3-031-04655-1
序号	190
标题	The COVID-19 Pandemic and Global Bioethics
系列标题	Advancing Global Bioethics
作者	Henk ten Have
年度	2022
出版社	Springer Cham
DOI	https://doi.org/10.1007/978-3-030-91491-2
序号	191
标题	The Economics of Pandemics
副标题	Exploring Globally Shared Experiences
作者	S. Niggol Seo
年度	2022
出版社	Palgrave Macmillan Cham
DOI	https://doi.org/10.1007/978-3-030-91021-1
序号	192
标题	The Eroticizing of HIV
副标题	Viral Fantasies
系列标题	Health, Technology and Society
作者	Jaime García-Iglesias
年度	2022

续表

出版社	Palgrave Macmillan Cham
DOI	https://doi.org/10.1007/978-3-031-11352-9
序号	193
标题	**The Ethical, Legal and Social Issues of Pandemics**
副标题	An Analysis from the EU Perspective
作者	Iñigo de Miguel Beriain
年度	2022
出版社	Springer Cham
DOI	https://doi.org/10.1007/978-3-031-03818-1
序号	194
标题	**The Future of the South African Political Economy Post-COVID 19**
系列标题	International Political Economy Series
作者	Mzukisi Qobo, Mills Soko, Nomfundo Xenia Ngwenya
年度	2022
出版社	Palgrave Macmillan Cham
DOI	https://doi.org/10.1007/978-3-031-10576-0
序号	195
标题	**The Geographies of COVID-19**
副标题	Geospatial Stories of a Global Pandemic
系列标题	Global Perspectives on Health Geography
作者	Melinda Laituri, Robert B. Richardson, Junghwan Kim
年度	2022
出版社	Springer Cham
DOI	https://doi.org/10.1007/978-3-031-11775-6
序号	196
标题	**The Global and Social Consequences of the COVID-19 Pandemic**
副标题	An Ethical and Philosophical Reflection
系列标题	Studies in Global Justice
作者	Gottfried Schweiger
年度	2022

续表

出版社	Springer Cham
DOI	https://doi.org/10.1007/978-3-030-97982-9
序号	197
标题	The Global, Regional and Local Politics of Institutional Responses to COVID-19
副标题	Implications for Women and Children
系列标题	Sustainable Development Goals Series
作者	Madeleine O. Hosli, Amy Blessing, Irini Iacovidou
年度	2022
出版社	Palgrave Macmillan Cham
DOI	https://doi.org/10.1007/978-3-031-09913-7
序号	198
标题	The Impact of COVID-19 on Corporations and Corporate Law in Malaysia
作者	Loganathan Krishnan, Wai Meng Chan
年度	2022
出版社	Springer Singapore
DOI	https://doi.org/10.1007/978-981-19-5519-8
序号	199
标题	The Impact of COVID-19 on Early Childhood Education and Care
副标题	International Perspectives, Challenges, and Responses
系列标题	Educating the Young Child
作者	Jyotsna Pattnaik, Mary Renck Jalongo
年度	2022
出版社	Springer Cham
DOI	https://doi.org/10.1007/978-3-030-96977-6
序号	200
标题	The Impact of COVID-19 on India and the Global Order
副标题	A Multidisciplinary Approach
作者	Mousumi Dutta, Zakir Husain, Anup Kumar Sinha
年度	2022

出版社	Springer Singapore
DOI	https://doi.org/10.1007/978-981-16-8472-2
序号	201
标题	**The Kyoto Post-COVID Manifesto For Global Economics**
副标题	Confronting Our Shattered Society
系列标题	Creative Economy
作者	Stephen Hill, Tadashi Yagi, Stomu Yamash'ta
年度	2022
出版社	Springer Singapore
DOI	https://doi.org/10.1007/978-981-16-8566-8
序号	202
标题	**The Making of a Pandemic**
副标题	Social, Political, and Psychological Perspectives on COVID-19
系列标题	SpringerBriefs in Psychology
作者	John Ehrenreich
年度	2022
出版社	Springer Cham
DOI	https://doi.org/10.1007/978-3-031-04964-4
序号	203
标题	**The Pandemic of Argumentation**
系列标题	Argumentation Library
作者	Steve Oswald, Marcin Lewiński, Sara Greco, Serena Villata
年度	2022
出版社	Springer Cham
DOI	https://doi.org/10.1007/978-3-030-91017-4
序号	204
标题	**The Political Economy of Post-COVID Life and Work in the Global South: Pandemic and Precarity**
系列标题	International Political Economy Series
作者	Sandya Hewamanne, Smytta Yadav

续表

年度	2022
出版社	Palgrave Macmillan Cham
DOI	https://doi.org/10.1007/978-3-030-93228-2
序号	205
标题	**The Post-Pandemic World**
副标题	Sustainable Living on a Wounded Planet
作者	John Erik Meyer
年度	2022
出版社	Springer Cham
DOI	https://doi.org/10.1007/978-3-030-91782-1
序号	206
标题	**The Post-Pandemic World and Global Politics**
作者	AKM Ahsan Ullah, Jannatul Ferdous
年度	2022
出版社	Springer Singapore
DOI	https://doi.org/10.1007/978-981-19-1910-7
序号	207
标题	**The Recurrence of COVID-19 in New York State and New York City**
副标题	Surfing the Second Wave
系列标题	SpringerBriefs in Public Health
作者	Deborah Wallace, Rodrick Wallace
年度	2022
出版社	Springer Cham
DOI	https://doi.org/10.1007/978-3-030-88619-6
序号	208
标题	**The Role of Digital Technologies in Shaping the Post-Pandemic World**
副标题	21st IFIP WG 6.11 Conference on e-Business, e-Services and e-Society, I3E 2022, Newcastle upon Tyne, UK, September 13–14, 2022, Proceedings
系列标题	Lecture Notes in Computer Science
作者	Savvas Papagiannidis, Eleftherios Alamanos, Suraksha Gupta, Yogesh K. Dwivedi, Matti Mäntymäki, Ilias O. Pappas

续表

年度	2022
出版社	Springer Cham
DOI	https://doi.org/10.1007/978-3-031-15342-6
序号	209
标题	The Science Behind the COVID Pandemic and Healthcare Technology Solutions
系列标题	Springer Series on Bio- and Neurosystems
作者	Sasan Adibi, Abbas Rajabifard, Sheikh Mohammed Shariful Islam, Alireza Ahmadvand
年度	2022
出版社	Springer Cham
DOI	https://doi.org/10.1007/978-3-031-10031-4
序号	210
标题	The Unequal Costs of COVID-19 on Well-being in Europe
系列标题	Human Well-Being Research and Policy Making
作者	Louise Dalingwater, Vanessa Boullet, Iside Costantini, Paul Gibbs
年度	2022
出版社	Springer Cham
DOI	https://doi.org/10.1007/978-3-031-14425-7
序号	211
标题	Tourism, Aviation and Hospitality Development During the COVID-19 Pandemic
作者	Yuhua Luo, Hongmei Zhang, Jinbo Jiang, Doubou Bi, Yujing Chu
年度	2022
出版社	Springer Singapore
DOI	https://doi.org/10.1007/978-981-19-1661-8
序号	212
标题	Transitioning Media in a Post COVID World
副标题	Digital Transformation, Immersive Technologies, and Consumer Behavior
系列标题	The Economics of Information, Communication, and Entertainment
作者	Gali Einav

续表

年度	2022
出版社	Springer Cham
DOI	https://doi.org/10.1007/978-3-030-95330-0
序号	213
标题	**Translation and Interpreting in the Age of COVID-19**
系列标题	Corpora and Intercultural Studies
作者	Kanglong Liu, Andrew K. F. Cheung
年度	2022
出版社	Springer Singapore
DOI	https://doi.org/10.1007/978-981-19-6680-4
序号	214
标题	**Tuberculosis of the Gastrointestinal System**
作者	Vishal Sharma
年度	2022
出版社	Springer Singapore
DOI	https://doi.org/10.1007/978-981-16-9053-2
序号	215
标题	**Tuberculosis of the Spine**
作者	Sarvdeep Singh Dhatt, Vishal Kumar
年度	2022
出版社	Springer Singapore
DOI	https://doi.org/10.1007/978-981-16-9495-0
序号	216
标题	**Understanding COVID-19: The Role of Computational Intelligence**
系列标题	Studies in Computational Intelligence
作者	Janmenjoy Nayak, Bighnaraj Naik, Ajith Abraham
年度	2022
出版社	Springer Cham
DOI	https://doi.org/10.1007/978-3-030-74761-9
序号	217

续表

标题	Understanding Post-COVID-19 Social and Cultural Realities
副标题	Global Context
作者	Sajal Roy, Debasish Nandy
年度	2022
出版社	Springer Singapore
DOI	https://doi.org/10.1007/978-981-19-0809-5
序号	218
标题	University and School Collaborations During a Pandemic
副标题	Sustaining Educational Opportunity and Reinventing Education
系列标题	Knowledge Studies in Higher Education
作者	Fernando M. Reimers, Francisco J. Marmolejo
年度	2022
出版社	Springer Cham
DOI	https://doi.org/10.1007/978-3-030-82159-3
序号	219
标题	Vaccine Design（Second Edition）
副标题	Methods and Protocols, Volume 1. Vaccines for Human Diseases
系列标题	Methods in Molecular Biology
作者	Sunil Thomas
年度	2022
出版社	Humana New York
DOI	https://doi.org/10.1007/978-1-0716-1884-4
序号	220
标题	Vaccine Design（Second Edition）
副标题	Methods and Protocols, Volume 2. Vaccines for Veterinary Diseases
系列标题	Methods in Molecular Biology
作者	Sunil Thomas
年度	2022
出版社	Humana New York
DOI	https://doi.org/10.1007/978-1-0716-1888-2
序号	221

标题	**Vaccine Design（Second Edition）**
副标题	Methods and Protocols, Volume 3. Resources for Vaccine Development
系列标题	Methods in Molecular Biology
作者	Sunil Thomas
年度	2022
出版社	Humana New York
DOI	https://doi.org/10.1007/978-1-0716-1892-9
序号	222
标题	**Vaccine Technologies for Veterinary Viral Diseases**
副标题	Methods and Protocols
系列标题	Methods in Molecular Biology
作者	Alejandro Brun
年度	2022
出版社	Humana New York
DOI	https://doi.org/10.1007/978-1-0716-2168-4
序号	223
标题	**Vaccines, Medicines and COVID-19**
副标题	How Can WHO Be Given a Stronger Voice?
系列标题	SpringerBriefs in Public Health
作者	Germán Velásquez
年度	2022
出版社	Springer Cham
DOI	https://doi.org/10.1007/978-3-030-89125-1
序号	224
标题	**Values for a Post-Pandemic Future**
系列标题	Philosophy of Engineering and Technology
作者	Matthew J. Dennis, Georgy Ishmaev, Steven Umbrello, Jeroen van den Hoven
年度	2022
出版社	Springer Cham
DOI	https://doi.org/10.1007/978-3-031-08424-9

续表

序号	225
标题	**Virus Entry Inhibitors**
副标题	Stopping the Enemy at the Gate
系列标题	Advances in Experimental Medicine and Biology
作者	Shibo Jiang, Lu Lu
年度	2022
出版社	Springer Singapore
DOI	https://doi.org/10.1007/978-981-16-8702-0
序号	226
标题	**Virus Host Cell Genetic Material Transport**
副标题	Computational ODE/PDE Modeling with R
作者	William E. Schiesser
年度	2022
出版社	Springer Cham
DOI	https://doi.org/10.1007/978-3-030-68865-3
序号	227
标题	**Viruses: Intimate Invaders**
作者	Van G. Wilson
年度	2022
出版社	Springer Cham
DOI	https://doi.org/10.1007/978-3-030-85487-4
序号	228
标题	**3D Printing in Medicine and Its Role in the COVID-19 Pandemic**
副标题	Personal Protective Equipment (PPE) and Other Novel Medical and Non-Medical Devices
作者	Frank J. Rybicki
年度	2021
出版社	Springer Cham
DOI	https://doi.org/10.1007/978-3-030-61993-0
序号	229

续表

标题	A Sociological Study on Emotion Regulation in People Living with HIV/AIDS in China
系列标题	A Sociological View of AIDS
作者	Rongting Hou, Translated by Leilei Liu, Zhiquan Zhang
年度	2021
出版社	Springer Singapore
DOI	https://doi.org/10.1007/978-981-16-1494-1
序号	230
标题	Advances in Host-Directed Therapies Against Tuberculosis
作者	Petros C. Karakousis, Richard Hafner, Maria Laura Gennaro
年度	2021
出版社	Springer Cham
DOI	https://doi.org/10.1007/978-3-030-56905-1
序号	231
标题	Advances in Microbiology, Infectious Diseases and Public Health
副标题	Volume 15
系列标题	Advances in Experimental Medicine and Biology
作者	Gianfranco Donelli
年度	2021
出版社	Springer Cham
DOI	https://doi.org/10.1007/978-3-030-71202-0
序号	232
标题	Alternative Medicine Interventions for COVID-19
作者	Muhammad Zia-Ul-Haq, May Nasser Bin-Jumah, Sarah I. Alothman, Hanan A. Henidi
年度	2021
出版社	Springer Cham
DOI	https://doi.org/10.1007/978-3-030-67989-7
序号	233
标题	Analysis of Infectious Disease Problems (COVID-19) and Their Global Impact
系列标题	Infosys Science Foundation Series

续表

作者	Praveen Agarwal, Juan J. Nieto, Michael Ruzhansky, Delfim F. M. Torres
年度	2021
出版社	Springer Singapore
DOI	https://doi.org/10.1007/978-981-16-2450-6
序号	234
标题	**Applications of Artificial Intelligence in COVID-19**
系列标题	Medical Virology: From Pathogenesis to Disease Control
作者	Sachi Nandan Mohanty, Shailendra K. Saxena, Suneeta Satpathy, Jyotir Moy Chatterjee
年度	2021
出版社	Springer Singapore
DOI	https://doi.org/10.1007/978-981-15-7317-0
序号	235
标题	**Arab MENA Countries: Vulnerabilities and Constraints Against Democracy on the Eve of the Global COVID-19 Crisis**
系列标题	Perspectives on Development in the Middle East and North Africa (MENA) Region
作者	Hussein Solomon, Arno Tausch
年度	2021
出版社	Springer Singapore
DOI	https://doi.org/10.1007/978-981-15-7047-6
序号	236
标题	**Artificial Intelligence and Machine Learning for COVID-19**
系列标题	Studies in Computational Intelligence
作者	Fadi Al-Turjman
年度	2021
出版社	Springer Cham
DOI	https://doi.org/10.1007/978-3-030-60188-1
序号	237
标题	**Artificial Intelligence for COVID-19**
系列标题	Studies in Systems, Decision and Control

续表

作者	Diego Oliva, Said Ali Hassan, Ali Mohamed
年度	2021
出版社	Springer Cham
DOI	https://doi.org/10.1007/978-3-030-69744-0
序号	238
标题	**Atlas of Chest Imaging in COVID-19 Patients**
作者	Jinxin Liu, Xiaoping Tang, Chunliang Lei
年度	2021
出版社	Springer Singapore
DOI	https://doi.org/10.1007/978-981-16-1082-0
序号	239
标题	**Avian Influenza in Human**
作者	Chen Qiu, Yu-Xin Shi, Pu-Xuan Lu
年度	2021
出版社	Springer Singapore
DOI	https://doi.org/10.1007/978-981-16-1429-3
序号	240
标题	**Capacity-Building and Pandemics**
副标题	Singapore's Response to COVID-19
作者	Jun Jie Woo
年度	2021
出版社	Palgrave Macmillan Singapore
DOI	https://doi.org/10.1007/978-981-15-9453-3
序号	241
标题	**Circadian Rhythms in Bacteria and Microbiomes**
作者	Carl Hirschie Johnson, Michael Joseph Rust
年度	2021
出版社	Springer Cham
DOI	https://doi.org/10.1007/978-3-030-72158-9
序号	242

标题	Clinical Image-Based Procedures, Distributed and Collaborative Learning, Artificial Intelligence for Combating COVID-19 and Secure and Privacy-Preserving Machine Learning
副标题	10th Workshop, CLIP 2021, Second Workshop, DCL 2021, First Workshop, LL-COVID19 2021, and First Workshop and Tutorial, PPML 2021, Held in Conjunction with MICCAI 2021, Strasbourg, France, September 27 and October 1, 2021, Proceedings
系列标题	Lecture Notes in Computer Science
作者	Cristina Oyarzun Laura, M. Jorge Cardoso, Michal Rosen-Zvi, et al
年度	2021
出版社	Springer Cham
DOI	https://doi.org/10.1007/978-3-030-90874-4
序号	243
标题	Clinical, Biological and Molecular Aspects of COVID-19
系列标题	Advances in Experimental Medicine and Biology
作者	Paul C. Guest
年度	2021
出版社	Springer Cham
DOI	https://doi.org/10.1007/978-3-030-59261-5
序号	244
标题	Communicating COVID-19
副标题	Interdisciplinary Perspectives
作者	Monique Lewis, Eliza Govender, Kate Holland
年度	2021
出版社	Palgrave Macmillan Cham
DOI	https://doi.org/10.1007/978-3-030-79735-5
序号	245
标题	Computational Intelligence Methods in COVID-19: Surveillance, Prevention, Prediction and Diagnosis
副标题	Khalid Raza

作者	Studies in Computational Intelligence
年度	2021
出版社	Springer Singapore
DOI	https://doi.org/10.1007/978-981-15-8534-0
序号	246
标题	**Computational Intelligence Techniques for Combating COVID-19**
系列标题	EAI/Springer Innovations in Communication and Computing
作者	Sandeep Kautish, Sheng-Lung Peng, Ahmed J. Obaid
年度	2021
出版社	Springer Cham
DOI	https://doi.org/10.1007/978-3-030-68936-0
序号	247
标题	**Coronavirus Disease—COVID-19**
系列标题	Advances in Experimental Medicine and Biology
作者	Nima Rezaei
年度	2021
出版社	Springer Cham
DOI	https://doi.org/10.1007/978-3-030-63761-3
序号	248
标题	**COVID in the Islands: A Comparative Perspective on the Caribbean and the Pacific**
作者	Yonique Campbell, John Connell
年度	2021
出版社	Palgrave Macmillan Singapore
DOI	https://doi.org/10.1007/978-981-16-5285-1
序号	249
标题	**COVID-19**
副标题	Sustainable Waste Management and Air Emission
系列标题	Environmental Footprints and Eco-design of Products and Processes
作者	Subramanian Senthilkannan Muthu

续表

年度	2021
出版社	Springer Singapore
DOI	https://doi.org/10.1007/978-981-16-3856-5
序号	250
标题	**COVID-19**
副标题	Environmental Sustainability and Sustainable Development Goals
系列标题	Environmental Footprints and Eco-design of Products and Processes
作者	Subramanian Senthilkannan Muthu
年度	2021
出版社	Springer Singapore
DOI	https://doi.org/10.1007/978-981-16-3860-2
序号	251
标题	**COVID-19**
副标题	Science to Social Impact
作者	Moones Rahmandoust, Seyed-Omid Ranaei-Siadat
年度	2021
出版社	Springer Singapore
DOI	https://doi.org/10.1007/978-981-16-3108-5
序号	252
标题	**COVID-19 and Cities**
副标题	Experiences, Responses, and Uncertainties
系列标题	The Urban Book Series
作者	Miguel A. Montoya, Aleksandra Krstikj, Johannes Rehner, Daniel Lemus-Delgado
年度	2021
出版社	Springer Cham
DOI	https://doi.org/10.1007/978-3-030-84134-8
序号	253
标题	**COVID-19 and Psychology**
副标题	People and Society in Times of Pandemic

续表

系列标题	Essentials
作者	John G. Haas
年度	2021
出版社	Springer Wiesbaden
DOI	https://doi.org/10.1007/978-3-658-34893-9
序号	254
标题	**COVID-19 and Similar Futures**
副标题	Pandemic Geographies
系列标题	Global Perspectives on Health Geography
作者	Gavin J. Andrews, Valorie A. Crooks, Jamie R. Pearce, Jane P. Messina
年度	2021
出版社	Springer Cham
DOI	https://doi.org/10.1007/978-3-030-70179-6
序号	255
标题	**COVID-19 and Social Protection**
副标题	A Study in Human Resilience and Social Solidarity
作者	Steven Ratuva, Tara Ross, Yvonne Crichton-Hill, Arindam Basu, Patrick Vakaoti, Rosemarie Martin-Neuninger
年度	2021
出版社	Palgrave Macmillan Singapore
DOI	https://doi.org/10.1007/978-981-16-2948-8
序号	256
标题	**COVID-19 in Clinical Practice**
副标题	Lessons Learned and Future Perspectives
系列标题	In Clinical Practice
作者	Flavio Tangianu, Ombretta Para, Fabio Capello
年度	2021
出版社	Springer Cham
DOI	https://doi.org/10.1007/978-3-030-78021-0
序号	257

续表

标题	COVID-19 in New York City
副标题	An Ecology of Race and Class Oppression
系列标题	SpringerBriefs in Public Health
作者	Deborah Wallace, Rodrick Wallace
年度	2021
出版社	Springer Cham
DOI	https://doi.org/10.1007/978-3-030-59624-8
序号	258
标题	COVID-19 Pandemic and Economic Development
副标题	Emerging Public Policy Lessons for Indian Punjab
作者	Sukhpal Singh, Lakhwinder Singh, Kamal Vatta
年度	2021
出版社	Palgrave Macmillan Singapore
DOI	https://doi.org/10.1007/978-981-16-4442-9
序号	259
标题	COVID-19 Pandemic Dynamics
副标题	Mathematical Simulations
作者	Igor Nesteruk
年度	2021
出版社	Springer Singapore
DOI	https://doi.org/10.1007/978-981-33-6416-5
序号	260
标题	COVID-19 Pandemic Trajectory in the Developing World
副标题	Exploring the Changing Environmental and Economic Milieus in India
系列标题	Advances in Geographical and Environmental Sciences
作者	Mukunda Mishra, R. B. Singh
年度	2021
出版社	Springer Singapore
DOI	https://doi.org/10.1007/978-981-33-6440-0
序号	261

续表

标题	COVID-19 Pandemic, Crisis Responses and the Changing World
副标题	Perspectives in Humanities and Social Sciences
作者	Simon X.B. Zhao, Johnston H.C. Wong, Charles Lowe, Edoardo Monaco, John Corbett
年度	2021
出版社	Springer Singapore
DOI	https://doi.org/10.1007/978-981-16-2430-8
序号	262
标题	COVID-19, Technology and Marketing
副标题	Moving Forward and the New Normal
作者	Vanessa Ratten, Park Thaichon
年度	2021
出版社	Palgrave Macmillan Singapore
DOI	https://doi.org/10.1007/978-981-16-1442-2
序号	263
标题	COVID-19: Paving the Way for a More Sustainable World
系列标题	World Sustainability Series
作者	Walter Leal Filho
年度	2021
出版社	Springer Cham
DOI	https://doi.org/10.1007/978-3-030-69284-1
序号	264
标题	COVID-19: Prediction, Decision-Making, and Its Impacts
系列标题	Lecture Notes on Data Engineering and Communications Technologies
作者	K.C. Santosh, Amit Joshi
年度	2021
出版社	Springer Singapore
DOI	https://doi.org/10.1007/978-981-15-9682-7
序号	265
标题	COVID-19: Systemic Risk and Resilience
系列标题	Risk, Systems and Decisions

续表

作者	Igor Linkov, Jesse M. Keenan, Benjamin D. Trump
年度	2021
出版社	Springer Cham
DOI	https://doi.org/10.1007/978-3-030-71587-8
序号	266
标题	COVID-19's Political Challenges in Latin America
系列标题	Latin American Societies
作者	Michelle Fernandez, Carlos Machado
年度	2021
出版社	Springer Cham
DOI	https://doi.org/10.1007/978-3-030-77602-2
序号	267
标题	Critical Care of COVID-19 in the Emergency Department
作者	Joseph R. Shiber
年度	2021
出版社	Springer Cham
DOI	https://doi.org/10.1007/978-3-030-85636-6
序号	268
标题	Delineating Health and Health System: Mechanistic Insights into COVID-19 Complications
作者	R. C. Sobti, Naranjan S. Dhalla, Masatoshi Watanabe, Aastha Sobti
年度	2021
出版社	Springer Singapore
DOI	https://doi.org/10.1007/978-981-16-5105-2
序号	269
标题	Detection and Enumeration of Bacteria, Yeast, Viruses, and Protozoan in Foods and Freshwater
系列标题	Methods and Protocols in Food Science
作者	Marciane Magnani
年度	2021
出版社	Humana New York

续表

DOI	https://doi.org/10.1007/978-1-0716-1932-2
序号	270
标题	**Development and Connection in the Time of COVID-19**
副标题	Corona's Call for Conscious Choices
作者	Cornelia C. Walther
年度	2021
出版社	Palgrave Macmillan Cham
DOI	https://doi.org/10.1007/978-3-030-53641-1
序号	271
标题	**Digital Responses to COVID-19**
副标题	Digital Innovation, Transformation, and Entrepreneurship During Pandemic Outbreaks
系列标题	SpringerBriefs in Information Systems
作者	Christian Hovestadt, Jan Recker, Janek Richter, Karl Werder
年度	2021
出版社	Springer Cham
DOI	https://doi.org/10.1007/978-3-030-66611-8
序号	272
标题	**Digital Transformation and Emerging Technologies for Fighting COVID-19 Pandemic: Innovative Approaches**
系列标题	Studies in Systems, Decision and Control
作者	Aboul Ella Hassanien, Ashraf Darwish
年度	2021
出版社	Springer Cham
DOI	https://doi.org/10.1007/978-3-030-63307-3
序号	273
标题	**DNA Vaccines**
副标题	Methods and Protocols
系列标题	Methods in Molecular Biology
作者	Ângela Sousa
年度	2021

续表

出版社	Humana New York
DOI	https://doi.org/10.1007/978-1-0716-0872-2
序号	274
标题	Ecology of Tuberculosis in India
系列标题	Global Perspectives on Health Geography
作者	Bikramaditya K. Choudhary
年度	2021
出版社	Springer Cham
DOI	https://doi.org/10.1007/978-3-030-64034-7
序号	275
标题	Economic Recovery After COVID-19
副标题	3rd International Conference on Economics and Social Sciences, ICESS 2020, Bucharest, Romania
系列标题	Springer Proceedings in Business and Economics
作者	Alina Mihaela Dima, Ion Anghel, Razvan Catalin Dobrea
年度	2021
出版社	Springer Cham
DOI	https://doi.org/10.1007/978-3-030-86641-9
序号	276
标题	Elimination of Infectious Diseases from the South-East Asia Region
副标题	Keeping the Promise
系列标题	SpringerBriefs in Public Health
作者	Poonam Khetrapal Singh
年度	2021
出版社	Springer Singapore
DOI	https://doi.org/10.1007/978-981-16-5566-1
序号	277
标题	Emerging Technologies During the Era of COVID-19 Pandemic
系列标题	Studies in Systems, Decision and Control
作者	Ibrahim Arpaci, Mostafa Al-Emran, Mohammed A. Al-Sharafi, Gonçalo Marques

续表

年度	2021
出版社	Springer Cham
DOI	https://doi.org/10.1007/978-3-030-67716-9
序号	278
标题	**Emerging Technologies for Battling COVID-19**
副标题	Applications and Innovations
系列标题	Studies in Systems, Decision and Control
作者	Fadi Al-Turjman, Ajantha Devi, Anand Nayyar
年度	2021
出版社	Springer Cham
DOI	https://doi.org/10.1007/978-3-030-60039-6
序号	279
标题	**Energy Transition, Climate Change, and COVID-19**
副标题	Economic Impacts of the Pandemic
作者	Fateh Belaïd, Anna Cretì
年度	2021
出版社	Springer Cham
DOI	https://doi.org/10.1007/978-3-030-79713-3
序号	280
标题	**Essential Tuberculosis**
作者	Giovanni Battista Migliori, Mario C. Raviglione
年度	2021
出版社	Springer Cham
DOI	https://doi.org/10.1007/978-3-030-66703-0
序号	281
标题	**Gendered Experiences of COVID-19 in India**
作者	Irene George, Moly Kuruvilla
年度	2021
出版社	Palgrave Macmillan Cham
DOI	https://doi.org/10.1007/978-3-030-85335-8

续表

序号	282
标题	**Gendered Perspectives on COVID-19 Recovery in Africa**
副标题	Towards Sustainable Development
作者	Ogechi Adeola
年度	2021
出版社	Palgrave Macmillan Cham
DOI	https://doi.org/10.1007/978－3－030－88152－8
序号	283
标题	**Governing the Pandemic**
副标题	The Politics of Navigating a Mega-Crisis
作者	Arjen Boin, Allan McConnell, Paul 't Hart
年度	2021
出版社	Palgrave Pivot Cham
DOI	https://doi.org/10.1007/978－3－030－72680－5
序号	284
标题	**Greek Culture After the Financial Crisis and the COVID-19 Crisis**
副标题	An Economic Analysis
系列标题	The Political Economy of Greek Growth up to 2030
作者	Panagiotis E. Petrakis, Kyriaki I. Kafka, Pantelis C. Kostis, Dionysis G. Valsamis
年度	2021
出版社	Palgrave Macmillan Cham
DOI	https://doi.org/10.1007/978－3－030－81018－4
序号	285
标题	**Hepatitis B Virus and Liver Disease**
作者	Jia-Horng Kao
年度	2021
出版社	Springer Singapore
DOI	https://doi.org/10.1007/978－981－16－3615－8
序号	286

续表

标题	**Hepatitis C: Epidemiology, Prevention and Elimination**
副标题	Volume 1
作者	Angelos Hatzakis
年度	2021
出版社	Springer Cham
DOI	https://doi.org/10.1007/978-3-030-64649-3
序号	287
标题	**Hepatitis C: Care and Treatment**
副标题	Volume 2
作者	Angelos Hatzakis
年度	2021
出版社	Springer Cham
DOI	https://doi.org/10.1007/978-3-030-67762-6
序号	288
标题	**HIV in US Communities of Color**
作者	Bisola O. Ojikutu, Valerie E. Stone
年度	2021
出版社	Springer Cham
DOI	https://doi.org/10.1007/978-3-030-48744-7
序号	289
标题	**Human Resource Management in a Post COVID-19 World**
副标题	New Distribution of Power, Individualization, Digitalization and Demographic Developments
系列标题	Future of Business and Finance
作者	Hermann Troger
年度	2021
出版社	Springer Cham
DOI	https://doi.org/10.1007/978-3-030-67470-0
序号	290
标题	**Human Viruses: Diseases, Treatments and Vaccines**
副标题	The New Insights

续表

作者	Shamim I. Ahmad
年度	2021
出版社	Springer Cham
DOI	https://doi.org/10.1007/978-3-030-71165-8
序号	291
标题	**Identification of Biomarkers, New Treatments, and Vaccines for COVID-19**
系列标题	Advances in Experimental Medicine and Biology
作者	Paul C. Guest
年度	2021
出版社	Springer Cham
DOI	https://doi.org/10.1007/978-3-030-71697-4
序号	292
标题	**Image-Guided Management of COVID-19 Lung Disease**
作者	Robert L. Bard
年度	2021
出版社	Springer Cham
DOI	https://doi.org/10.1007/978-3-030-66614-9
序号	293
标题	**Impact of AI and Data Science in Response to Coronavirus Pandemic**
系列标题	Algorithms for Intelligent Systems
作者	Sushruta Mishra, Pradeep Kumar Mallick, Hrudaya Kumar Tripathy, Gyoo-Soo Chae, Bhabani Shankar Prasad Mishra
年度	2021
出版社	Springer Singapore
DOI	https://doi.org/10.1007/978-981-16-2786-6
序号	294
标题	**Infectious Diseases and Our Planet**
系列标题	Mathematics of Planet Earth
作者	Miranda I. Teboh-Ewungkem, Gideon Akumah Ngwa
年度	2021

续表

出版社	Springer Cham
DOI	https://doi.org/10.1007/978-3-030-50826-5
序号	295
标题	**Infectious Diseases of Dromedary Camels**
副标题	A Concise Guide
作者	Abdelmalik I. Khalafalla, Mansour F. Hussein
年度	2021
出版社	Springer Cham
DOI	https://doi.org/10.1007/978-3-030-79389-0
序号	296
标题	**Infectious Pathology of the Respiratory Tract**
作者	Vsevolod Zinserling
年度	2021
出版社	Springer Cham
DOI	https://doi.org/10.1007/978-3-030-66325-4
序号	297
标题	**Influenza**
副标题	Advances in Diagnosis and Management
系列标题	Respiratory Disease Series: Diagnostic Tools and Disease Managements
作者	Jiro Fujita
年度	2021
出版社	Springer Singapore
DOI	https://doi.org/10.1007/978-981-15-9109-9
序号	298
标题	**Information Security Technologies for Controlling Pandemics**
系列标题	Advanced Sciences and Technologies for Security Applications
作者	Hamid Jahankhani, Stefan Kendzierskyj, Babak Akhgar
年度	2021
出版社	Springer Cham
DOI	https://doi.org/10.1007/978-3-030-72120-6

续表

序号	299
标题	Integrated Omics Approaches to Infectious Diseases
作者	Saif Hameed, Zeeshan Fatima
年度	2021
出版社	Springer Singapore
DOI	https://doi.org/10.1007/978-981-16-0691-5
序号	300
标题	Intelligent Data Analysis for COVID-19 Pandemic
系列标题	Algorithms for Intelligent Systems
作者	M. Niranjanamurthy, Siddhartha Bhattacharyya, Neeraj Kumar
年度	2021
出版社	Springer Singapore
DOI	https://doi.org/10.1007/978-981-16-1574-0
序号	301
标题	Internet of Things and Sensor Network for COVID-19
系列标题	SpringerBriefs in Applied Sciences and Technology
作者	Siba Kumar Udgata, Nagender Kumar Suryadevara
年度	2021
出版社	Springer Singapore
DOI	https://doi.org/10.1007/978-981-15-7654-6
序号	302
标题	Lessons from the Pandemic
副标题	Trauma-Informed Approaches to College, Crisis, Change
作者	Janice Carello, Phyllis Thompson
年度	2021
出版社	Palgrave Macmillan Cham
DOI	https://doi.org/10.1007/978-3-030-83849-2
序号	303
标题	Macroeconomic Responses to the COVID-19 Pandemic
副标题	Policies from Southeast Europe

	续表
作者	Neven Vidaković, Ivan Lovrinović
年度	2021
出版社	Palgrave Macmillan Cham
DOI	https://doi.org/10.1007/978-3-030-75444-0
序号	304
标题	**Male Same-Sex Sexuality and HIV in Sub-Saharan Africa**
系列标题	Social Aspects of HIV
作者	Theo Sandfort
年度	2021
出版社	Springer Cham
DOI	https://doi.org/10.1007/978-3-030-73726-9
序号	305
标题	**Managing Supply Chain Risk and Disruptions: Post COVID-19**
系列标题	Management and Industrial Engineering
作者	Aravind Raj Sakthivel, Jayakrishna Kandasamy, J. Paulo Davim
年度	2021
出版社	Springer Cham
DOI	https://doi.org/10.1007/978-3-030-72575-4
序号	306
标题	**Mapping COVID-19 in Space and Time**
副标题	Understanding the Spatial and Temporal Dynamics of a Global Pandemic
系列标题	Human Dynamics in Smart Cities
作者	Shih-Lung Shaw, Daniel Sui
年度	2021
出版社	Springer Cham
DOI	https://doi.org/10.1007/978-3-030-72808-3
序号	307
标题	**Mathematical Analysis for Transmission of COVID-19**
系列标题	Mathematical Engineering

续表

作者	Nita H. Shah, Mandeep Mittal
年度	2021
出版社	Springer Singapore
DOI	https://doi.org/10.1007/978-981-33-6264-2
序号	308
标题	**Mathematical Modelling and Nonstandard Schemes for the Corona Virus Pandemic**
系列标题	BestMasters
作者	Sarah Marie Treibert
年度	2021
出版社	Springer Spektrum Wiesbaden
DOI	https://doi.org/10.1007/978-3-658-35932-4
序号	309
标题	**Nanoparticles for Rational Vaccine Design**
系列标题	Current Topics in Microbiology and Immunology
作者	Harvinder Singh Gill, Richard W. Compans
年度	2021
出版社	Springer Cham
DOI	https://doi.org/10.1007/978-3-030-85067-8
序号	310
标题	**Nanotechnology-COVID-19 Interface**
系列标题	SpringerBriefs in Applied Sciences and Technology
作者	Devasena T
年度	2021
出版社	Springer Singapore
DOI	https://doi.org/10.1007/978-981-33-6300-7
序号	311
标题	**Neurocognitive Complications of HIV-Infection**
副标题	Neuropathogenesis to Implications for Clinical Practice
系列标题	Current Topics in Behavioral Neurosciences

续表

作者	Lucette A. Cysique, Sean B. Rourke
年度	2021
出版社	Springer Cham
DOI	https://doi.org/10.1007/978-3-030-80759-7
序号	312
标题	**Neuroimaging of COVID-19. First Insights Based on Clinical Cases**
作者	Simonetta Gerevini
年度	2021
出版社	Springer Cham
DOI	https://doi.org/10.1007/978-3-030-67521-9
序号	313
标题	**Neurological Complications of Infectious Diseases**
系列标题	Current Clinical Neurology
作者	Rodrigo Hasbun, Karen C. Bloch, Adarsh Bhimraj
年度	2021
出版社	Humana Cham
DOI	https://doi.org/10.1007/978-3-030-56084-3
序号	314
标题	**Nutrition and Infectious Diseases**
副标题	Shifting the Clinical Paradigm
系列标题	Nutrition and Health
作者	Debbie L. Humphries, Marilyn E. Scott, Sten H. Vermund
年度	2021
出版社	Humana Cham
DOI	https://doi.org/10.1007/978-3-030-56913-6
序号	315
标题	**Organising Care in a Time of COVID-19**
副标题	Implications for Leadership, Governance and Policy
系列标题	Organizational Behaviour in Healthcare
作者	Justin Waring, Jean-Louis Denis, Anne Reff Pedersen, Tim Tenbensel

续表

年度	2021
出版社	Palgrave Macmillan Cham
DOI	https://doi.org/10.1007/978-3-030-82696-3
序号	316
标题	Pandemic Communication and Resilience
系列标题	Risk, Systems and Decisions
作者	David M. Berube
年度	2021
出版社	Springer Cham
DOI	https://doi.org/10.1007/978-3-030-77344-1
序号	317
标题	Pandemic, Lockdown, and Digital Transformation
副标题	Challenges and Opportunities for Public Administration, NGOs, and Businesses
系列标题	Public Administration and Information Technology
作者	Saqib Saeed, Manuel Pedro Rodríguez Bolívar, Ramayah Thurasamy
年度	2021
出版社	Springer Cham
DOI	https://doi.org/10.1007/978-3-030-86274-9
序号	318
标题	Parasite Genomics
副标题	Methods and Protocols
系列标题	Methods in Molecular Biology
作者	Luis M. de Pablos, Javier Sotillo
年度	2021
出版社	Humana New York
DOI	https://doi.org/10.1007/978-1-0716-1681-9
序号	319
标题	Pediatric Vaccines and Vaccinations
副标题	A European Textbook

续表

作者	Timo Vesikari, Pierre Van Damme
年度	2021
出版社	Springer Cham
DOI	https://doi.org/10.1007/978-3-030-77173-7
序号	320
标题	**Place and Post-Pandemic Flourishing**
副标题	Disruption, Adjustment, and Healthy Behaviors
系列标题	SpringerBriefs in Psychology
作者	Victor Counted, Richard G. Cowden, Haywantee Ramkissoon
年度	2021
出版社	Springer Cham
DOI	https://doi.org/10.1007/978-3-030-82580-5
序号	321
标题	**Populism and the Politicization of the COVID-19 Crisis in Europe**
作者	Giuliano Bobba, Nicolas Hubé
年度	2021
出版社	Palgrave Macmillan Cham
DOI	https://doi.org/10.1007/978-3-030-66011-6
序号	322
标题	**Post-COVID Economic Revival, Volume Ⅰ**
副标题	Sectors, Institutions, and Policy
作者	Vladimir S. Osipov
年度	2021
出版社	Palgrave Macmillan Cham
DOI	https://doi.org/10.1007/978-3-030-83561-3
序号	323
标题	**Post-Covid Schooling**
副标题	Future Alternatives to the Global Normal
系列标题	Palgrave Studies in Alternative Education
作者	Clive Harber

一、图书

续表

年度	2021
出版社	Palgrave Macmillan Cham
DOI	https://doi.org/10.1007/978-3-030-87824-5
序号	324
标题	Predictive and Preventive Measures for COVID-19 Pandemic
系列标题	Algorithms for Intelligent Systems
作者	Praveen Kumar Khosla, Mamta Mittal, Dolly Sharma, Lalit Mohan Goyal
年度	2021
出版社	Springer Singapore
DOI	https://doi.org/10.1007/978-981-33-4236-1
序号	325
标题	Predictive Models for Decision Support in the COVID-19 Crisis
系列标题	SpringerBriefs in Applied Sciences and Technology
作者	Joao Alexandre Lobo Marques, Francisco Nauber Bernardo Gois, José Xavier-Neto, Simon James Fong
年度	2021
出版社	Springer Cham
DOI	https://doi.org/10.1007/978-3-030-61913-8
序号	326
标题	Prevention and Control of Infectious Diseases in BRI Countries
作者	Weizhong Yang
年度	2021
出版社	Springer Singapore
DOI	https://doi.org/10.1007/978-981-33-6958-0
序号	327
标题	Providing HIV Care: Lessons from the Field for Nurses and Healthcare Practitioners
作者	Michelle Croston, Ian Hodgson
年度	2021
出版社	Springer Cham

DOI	https://doi.org/10.1007/978-3-030-71295-2
序号	328
标题	**Public Secrets and Private Sufferings in the South African AIDS Epidemic**
系列标题	Social Aspects of HIV
作者	Jonathan Stadler
年度	2021
出版社	Springer Cham
DOI	https://doi.org/10.1007/978-3-030-69437-1
序号	329
标题	**Recovering Civility During COVID-19**
作者	Matteo Bonotti, Steven T. Zech
年度	2021
出版社	Palgrave Macmillan Singapore
DOI	https://doi.org/10.1007/978-981-33-6706-7
序号	330
标题	**Remaking HIV Prevention in the 21st Century**
副标题	The Promise of TasP, U=U and PrEP
系列标题	Social Aspects of HIV
作者	Sarah Bernays, Adam Bourne, Susan Kippax, Peter Aggleton, Richard Parker
年度	2021
出版社	Springer Cham
DOI	https://doi.org/10.1007/978-3-030-69819-5
序号	331
标题	**SARS-CoV-2 and Coronacrisis**
副标题	Epidemiological Challenges, Social Policies and Administrative Strategies
作者	Fr archpriest Evgeny I. Legach, Konstantin S. Sharov
年度	2021
出版社	Springer Singapore
DOI	https://doi.org/10.1007/978-981-16-2605-0

续表

序号	332
标题	**SARS-CoV-2 Spike Protein Convergent Evolution**
副标题	Impact of Virus Variants on Efficacy of COVID-19 Therapeutics and Vaccines
系列标题	SpringerBriefs in Microbiology
作者	Daniele Focosi
年度	2021
出版社	Springer Cham
DOI	https://doi.org/10.1007/978-3-030-87324-0
序号	333
标题	**Shared Trauma, Shared Resilience During a Pandemic**
副标题	Social Work in the Time of COVID-19
系列标题	Essential Clinical Social Work Series
作者	Carol Tosone
年度	2021
出版社	Springer Cham
DOI	https://doi.org/10.1007/978-3-030-61442-3
序号	334
标题	**Sociological Reflections on the COVID-19 Pandemic in India**
副标题	Redefining the Normal
作者	Gopi Devdutt Tripathy, Anurita Jalan, Mala Kapur Shankardass
年度	2021
出版社	Springer Singapore
DOI	https://doi.org/10.1007/978-981-16-2320-2
序号	335
标题	**Strategic Innovative Marketing and Tourism in the COVID-19 Era**
副标题	9th ICSIMAT Conference 2020
系列标题	Springer Proceedings in Business and Economics
作者	Androniki Kavoura, Stephen J. Havlovic, Natalya Totskaya
年度	2021
出版社	Springer Cham

续表

DOI	https://doi.org/10.1007/978-3-030-66154-0	
序号	336	
标题	Sustainability Measures for COVID-19 Pandemic	
作者	Rashmi Agrawal, Mamta Mittal, Lalit Mohan Goyal	
年度	2021	
出版社	Springer Singapore	
DOI	https://doi.org/10.1007/978-981-16-3227-3	
序号	337	
标题	The Effect of Coronavirus Disease (COVID-19) on Business Intelligence	
系列标题	Studies in Systems, Decision and Control	
作者	M.T. Alshurideh, Aboul Ella Hassanien, Ra'ed Masa'deh	
年度	2021	
出版社	Springer Cham	
DOI	https://doi.org/10.1007/978-3-030-67151-8	
序号	338	
标题	The Future of Service Post-COVID-19 Pandemic, Volume 1	
副标题	Rapid Adoption of Digital Service Technology	
系列标题	The ICT and Evolution of Work	
作者	Jungwoo Lee, Spring H. Han	
年度	2021	
出版社	Springer Singapore	
DOI	https://doi.org/10.1007/978-981-33-4126-5	
序号	339	
标题	The Future of Service Post-COVID-19 Pandemic, Volume 2	
副标题	Transformation of Services Marketing	
系列标题	The ICT and Evolution of Work	
作者	Jungwoo Lee, Spring H. Han	
年度	2021	
出版社	Springer Singapore	
DOI	https://doi.org/10.1007/978-981-33-4134-0	

续表

序号	340
标题	The Global Environmental Effects During and Beyond COVID-19
副标题	Intelligent Computing Solutions
系列标题	Studies in Systems, Decision and Control
作者	Aboul Ella Hassanien, Ashraf Darwish, Benji Gyampoh, Alaa Tharwat Abdel-Monaim, Ahmed M. Anter
年度	2021
出版社	Springer Cham
DOI	https://doi.org/10.1007/978-3-030-72933-2
序号	341
标题	The Impact of the COVID-19 Pandemic on Green Societies
副标题	Environmental Sustainability
作者	Chinmay Chakraborty, Swapnila Roy, Susmita Sharma, Tien Anh Tran
年度	2021
出版社	Springer Cham
DOI	https://doi.org/10.1007/978-3-030-66490-9
序号	342
标题	The Post-Pandemic Business Playbook
副标题	Customer-Centric Solutions to Help Your Firm Grow
作者	Ofer Mintz
年度	2021
出版社	Palgrave Macmillan Singapore
DOI	https://doi.org/10.1007/978-981-16-5868-6
序号	343
标题	The Reshaping of China-Southeast Asia Relations in Light of the COVID-19 Pandemic
作者	Nian Peng
年度	2021
出版社	Springer Singapore
DOI	https://doi.org/10.1007/978-981-33-4416-7

续表

序号	344
标题	The Role of Toll-Like Receptor 4 in Infectious and Non Infectious Inflammation
系列标题	Progress in Inflammation Research
作者	Carlo Rossetti, Francesco Peri
年度	2021
出版社	Springer Cham
DOI	https://doi.org/10.1007/978-3-030-56319-6
序号	345
标题	The Science and Politics of COVID-19
副标题	How Scientists Should Tackle Global Crises
作者	Michel Claessens
年度	2021
出版社	Springer Cham
DOI	https://doi.org/10.1007/978-3-030-77864-4
序号	346
标题	The Social Construction of AIDS Issues
系列标题	A Sociological View of AIDS
作者	Suiming Pan, Translated by Hulin Zhao
年度	2021
出版社	Springer Singapore
DOI	https://doi.org/10.1007/978-981-16-7519-5
序号	347
标题	Transforming Nations After the COVID-19 Pandemic
副标题	A Humanitarian and Planetary Systems Perspective
系列标题	Management, Change, Strategy and Positive Leadership
作者	Denis H. J. Caro
年度	2021
出版社	Springer Cham
DOI	https://doi.org/10.1007/978-3-030-61810-0

续表

序号	348
标题	**Tuberculosis in Clinical Practice**
作者	Onn Min Kon
年度	2021
出版社	Springer Cham
DOI	https://doi.org/10.1007/978-3-030-75509-6
序号	349
标题	**Utilizing Effective Risk Communication in COVID-19**
副标题	Highlighting the BRCT
作者	Andy Lazris, Erik Rifkin
年度	2021
出版社	Springer Cham
DOI	https://doi.org/10.1007/978-3-030-74521-9
序号	350
标题	**Vaccine Delivery Technology**
副标题	Methods and Protocols
系列标题	Methods in Molecular Biology
作者	Blaine A. Pfeifer, Andrew Hill
年度	2021
出版社	Humana New York
DOI	https://doi.org/10.1007/978-1-0716-0795-4
序号	351
标题	**Vaccines**
副标题	A Clinical Overview and Practical Guide
作者	Joseph Domachowske, Manika Suryadevara
年度	2021
出版社	Springer Cham
DOI	https://doi.org/10.1007/978-3-030-58414-6
序号	352
标题	**Viral Vectors in Veterinary Vaccine Development**
副标题	A Textbook

续表

作者	Thiru Vanniasinkam, Suresh K. Tikoo, Siba K. Samal
年度	2021
出版社	Springer Cham
DOI	https://doi.org/10.1007/978-3-030-51927-8
序号	353
标题	**Viruses and Human Cancer**
副标题	From Basic Science to Clinical Prevention
系列标题	Recent Results in Cancer Research
作者	T.-C. Wu, Mei-Hwei Chang, Kuan-Teh Jeang
年度	2021
出版社	Springer Cham
DOI	https://doi.org/10.1007/978-3-030-57362-1
序号	354
标题	**Viruses as Therapeutics**
副标题	Methods and Protocols
系列标题	Methods in Molecular Biology
作者	Alexandra R. Lucas
年度	2021
出版社	Humana New York
DOI	https://doi.org/10.1007/978-1-0716-1012-1
序号	355
标题	**Working with Excluded Populations in HIV**
副标题	Hard to Reach or Out of Sight?
系列标题	Social Aspects of HIV
作者	Carmen Logie
年度	2021
出版社	Springer Cham
DOI	https://doi.org/10.1007/978-3-030-77048-8
序号	356

续表

标题	Advances in Microbiology, Infectious Diseases and Public Health
副标题	Volume 14
系列标题	Advances in Experimental Medicine and Biology
作者	Gianfranco Donelli
年度	2020
出版社	Springer Cham
DOI	https://doi.org/10.1007/978-3-030-53647-3
序号	357
标题	Animal Influenza Virus（Third Edition）
副标题	Methods and Protocols
系列标题	Methods in Molecular Biology
作者	Erica Spackman
年度	2020
出版社	Humana New York
DOI	https://doi.org/10.1007/978-1-0716-0346-8
序号	358
标题	Big Data Analytics and Artificial Intelligence Against COVID-19: Innovation Vision and Approach
系列标题	Studies in Big Data
作者	Aboul-Ella Hassanien, Nilanjan Dey, Sally Elghamrawy
年度	2020
出版社	Springer Cham
DOI	https://doi.org/10.1007/978-3-030-55258-9
序号	359
标题	Clinical Infectious Diseases Study Guide
副标题	A Problem-Based Approach
作者	Joseph Domachowske, Manika Suryadevara
年度	2020
出版社	Springer Cham
DOI	https://doi.org/10.1007/978-3-030-50873-9

续表

序号	360
标题	**Clinical Synopsis of COVID-19**
副标题	Evolving and Challenging
作者	Hemanshu Prabhakar, Indu Kapoor, Charu Mahajan
年度	2020
出版社	Springer Singapore
DOI	https://doi.org/10.1007/978-981-15-8681-1
序号	361
标题	**Contact Tracing in Post-Covid World**
副标题	A Cryptologic Approach
系列标题	Indian Statistical Institute Series
作者	Pranab Chakraborty, Subhamoy Maitra, Mridul Nandi, Suprita Talnikar
年度	2020
出版社	Springer Singapore
DOI	https://doi.org/10.1007/978-981-15-9727-5
序号	362
标题	**Coronavirus Disease 2019（COVID-19）**
副标题	Epidemiology, Pathogenesis, Diagnosis, and Therapeutics
系列标题	Medical Virology: From Pathogenesis to Disease Control
作者	Shailendra K. Saxena
年度	2020
出版社	Springer Singapore
DOI	https://doi.org/10.1007/978-981-15-4814-7
序号	363
标题	**Counting the Cost of COVID-19 on the Global Tourism Industry**
作者	Godwell Nhamo, Kaitano Dube, David Chikodzi
年度	2020
出版社	Springer Cham
DOI	https://doi.org/10.1007/978-3-030-56231-1
序号	364

续表

标题	COVID-19
副标题	Proportionality, Public Policy and Social Distancing
作者	Peter Murphy
年度	2020
出版社	Palgrave Pivot Singapore
DOI	https://doi.org/10.1007/978-981-15-7514-3
序号	365
标题	COVID-19 Airway Management and Ventilation Strategy for Critically Ⅲ Older Patients
作者	Nicola Vargas, Antonio M. Esquinas
年度	2020
出版社	Springer Cham
DOI	https://doi.org/10.1007/978-3-030-55621-1
序号	366
标题	Current Trends and Concerns in Infectious Diseases
系列标题	Emerging Infectious Diseases of the 21st Century
作者	I. W. Fong
年度	2020
出版社	Springer Cham
DOI	https://doi.org/10.1007/978-3-030-36966-8
序号	367
标题	Diagnostic Strategies for COVID-19 and Other Coronaviruses
系列标题	Medical Virology: From Pathogenesis to Disease Control
作者	Pranjal Chandra, Sharmili Roy
年度	2020
出版社	Springer Singapore
DOI	https://doi.org/10.1007/978-981-15-6006-4
序号	368
标题	Emerging and Transboundary Animal Viruses
系列标题	Livestock Diseases and Management

作者	Yashpal Singh Malik, Raj Kumar Singh, Mahendra Pal Yadav
年度	2020
出版社	Springer Singapore
DOI	https://doi.org/10.1007/978-981-15-0402-0
序号	369
标题	**Encyclopedia of AIDS**
作者	Thomas J. Hope, Douglas Richman, Mario Stevenson
年度	2020
出版社	Springer New York
DOI	https://doi.org/10.1007/978-1-4614-9610-6
序号	370
标题	**Hepatitis B Virus Infection**
副标题	Molecular Virology to Antiviral Drugs
系列标题	Advances in Experimental Medicine and Biology
作者	Hong Tang
年度	2020
出版社	Springer Singapore
DOI	https://doi.org/10.1007/978-981-13-9151-4
序号	371
标题	**Herpes Simplex Virus**
副标题	Methods and Protocols
系列标题	Methods in Molecular Biology
作者	Russell J. Diefenbach, Cornel Fraefel
年度	2020
出版社	Humana New York
DOI	https://doi.org/10.1007/978-1-4939-9814-2
序号	372
标题	**Highly Infectious Diseases in Critical Care**
副标题	A Comprehensive Clinical Guide
作者	Jorge Hidalgo, Laila Woc-Colburn

续表

年度	2020
出版社	Springer Cham
DOI	https://doi.org/10.1007/978-3-030-33803-9
序号	373
标题	**HIV and Gay Men**
副标题	Clinical, Social and Psychological Aspects
作者	Rusi Jaspal, Jake Bayley
年度	2020
出版社	Palgrave Macmillan Singapore
DOI	https://doi.org/10.1007/978-981-15-7226-5
序号	374
标题	**HIV Infection in Children and Adolescents**
作者	Raziya Bobat
年度	2020
出版社	Springer Cham
DOI	https://doi.org/10.1007/978-3-030-35433-6
序号	375
标题	**HIV Transmission**
副标题	Statistical Modelling
作者	D. M. Basavarajaiah, Bhamidipati Narasimha Murthy
年度	2020
出版社	Springer Singapore
DOI	https://doi.org/10.1007/978-981-15-0151-7
序号	376
标题	**HIV/AIDS in Bangladesh**
副标题	Stigmatized People, Policy and Place
系列标题	Global Perspectives on Health Geography
作者	Alak Paul
年度	2020
出版社	Springer Cham

续表

DOI	https://doi.org/10.1007/978-3-030-57650-9
序号	377
标题	**HIV/AIDS in China**
副标题	Epidemiology, Prevention and Treatment
作者	Zunyou Wu, Yu Wang, Roger Detels, Marc Bulterys, Jennifer M. McGoogan
年度	2020
出版社	Springer Singapore
DOI	https://doi.org/10.1007/978-981-13-8518-6
序号	378
标题	**Infectious Diseases in the Intensive Care Unit**
作者	Manish Soneja, Puneet Khanna
年度	2020
出版社	Springer Singapore
DOI	https://doi.org/10.1007/978-981-15-4039-4
序号	379
标题	**Infectious Diseases in the New Millennium**
副标题	Legal and Ethical Challenges
系列标题	International Library of Ethics, Law, and the New Medicine
作者	Mark Eccleston-Turner, Iain Brassington
年度	2020
出版社	Springer Cham
DOI	https://doi.org/10.1007/978-3-030-39819-4
序号	380
标题	**Inflammatory and Infectious Ocular Disorders**
系列标题	Retina Atlas
作者	Hyeong Gon Yu
年度	2020
出版社	Springer Singapore
DOI	https://doi.org/10.1007/978-981-13-8546-9
序号	381

续表

标题	Integrated Risk of Pandemic: COVID-19 Impacts, Resilience and Recommendations
系列标题	Disaster Resilience and Green Growth
作者	Manish Kumar Goyal, Anil Kumar Gupta
年度	2020
出版社	Springer Singapore
DOI	https://doi.org/10.1007/978-981-15-7679-9
序号	382
标题	Mathematical Modelling and Analysis of Infectious Diseases
系列标题	Studies in Systems, Decision and Control
作者	Khalid Hattaf, Hemen Dutta
年度	2020
出版社	Springer Cham
DOI	https://doi.org/10.1007/978-3-030-49896-2
序号	383
标题	Mucocutaneous Manifestations of HIV/AIDS
副标题	Early Diagnostic Clues
作者	Yu-Ye Li, Kun-Hua Wang, Li He
年度	2020
出版社	Springer Singapore
DOI	https://doi.org/10.1007/978-981-15-5467-4
序号	384
标题	Nuclear Medicine in Infectious Diseases
作者	Alberto Signore, Andor W. J. M. Glaudemans
年度	2020
出版社	Springer Cham
DOI	https://doi.org/10.1007/978-3-030-25494-0
序号	385
标题	Oncolytic Viruses
系列标题	Methods in Molecular Biology

续表

作者	Christine E. Engeland
年度	2020
出版社	Humana New York
DOI	https://doi.org/10.1007/978-1-4939-9794-7
序号	386
标题	**Order and Fluctuations in Collective Dynamics of Swimming Bacteria**
副标题	Experimental Exploration of Active Matter Physics
系列标题	Springer Theses
作者	Daiki Nishiguchi
年度	2020
出版社	Springer Singapore
DOI	https://doi.org/10.1007/978-981-32-9998-6
序号	387
标题	**Pandemic Risk Management in Operations and Finance**
副标题	Modeling the Impact of COVID-19
系列标题	Computational Risk Management
作者	Desheng Dash Wu, David L. Olson
年度	2020
出版社	Springer Cham
DOI	https://doi.org/10.1007/978-3-030-52197-4
序号	388
标题	**Preventing Occupational Exposures to Infectious Disease in Health Care**
副标题	A Practical Guide
作者	Amber Hogan Mitchell
年度	2020
出版社	Springer Cham
DOI	https://doi.org/10.1007/978-3-030-56039-3
序号	389
标题	**Rabies and Rabies Vaccines**
作者	Hildegund C.J. Ertl

续表

年度	2020
出版社	Springer Cham
DOI	https://doi.org/10.1007/978-3-030-21084-7
序号	390
标题	**Self-Restoration of People Living with HIV/AIDS in China**
作者	Rongting Hou, Translated by Hulin Zhao
年度	2020
出版社	Springer Singapore
DOI	https://doi.org/10.1007/978-981-15-7413-9
序号	391
标题	**Statistics in Clinical and Observational Vaccine Studies**
系列标题	Springer Series in Pharmaceutical Statistics
作者	Jozef Nauta
年度	2020
出版社	Springer Cham
DOI	https://doi.org/10.1007/978-3-030-37693-2
序号	392
标题	**Trans Women and HIV**
副标题	Social Psychological Perspectives
作者	Rusi Jaspal
年度	2020
出版社	Palgrave Macmillan Cham
DOI	https://doi.org/10.1007/978-3-030-57545-8
序号	393
标题	**Tuberculosis Control in Migrating Population**
作者	Wei-Ye Yu, Pu-Xuan Lu, Wei-Guo Tan
年度	2020
出版社	Springer Singapore
DOI	https://doi.org/10.1007/978-981-32-9763-0
序号	394

续表

标题	Water-Associated Infectious Diseases
作者	Shailendra K. Saxena
年度	2020
出版社	Springer Singapore
DOI	https://doi.org/10.1007/978-981-13-9197-2
序号	395
标题	Zika Virus
副标题	Methods and Protocols
系列标题	Methods in Molecular Biology
作者	Gary Kobinger, Trina Racine
年度	2020
出版社	Humana New York
DOI	https://doi.org/10.1007/978-1-0716-0581-3
序号	396
标题	Acute Exacerbation of Chronic Hepatitis B
副标题	Volume 1. Definition, Research Technology, Virology, Genetics and Immunology
作者	Qin Ning
年度	2019
出版社	Springer Dordrecht
DOI	https://doi.org/10.1007/978-94-024-1606-0
序号	397
标题	Acute Exacerbation of Chronic Hepatitis B
副标题	Volume 2. Diagnosis and Management
作者	Qin Ning
年度	2019
出版社	Springer Dordrecht
DOI	https://doi.org/10.1007/978-94-024-1603-9
序号	398
标题	Adeno-Associated Virus Vectors
副标题	Design and Delivery

续表

系列标题	Methods in Molecular Biology
作者	Michael J. Castle
年度	2019
出版社	Humana New York
DOI	https://doi.org/10.1007/978-1-4939-9139-6
序号	399
标题	**Advances in Microbiology, Infectious Diseases and Public Health**
副标题	Volume 13
系列标题	Advances in Experimental Medicine and Biology
作者	Gianfranco Donelli
年度	2019
出版社	Springer Cham
DOI	https://doi.org/10.1007/978-3-030-35469-5
序号	400
标题	**Antibiotic Resistant Bacteria: A Challenge to Modern Medicine**
作者	Sadhana Sagar, Shilpa Kaistha, Amar Jyoti Das, Rajesh Kumar
年度	2019
出版社	Springer Singapore
DOI	https://doi.org/10.1007/978-981-13-9879-7
序号	401
标题	**Cancer and AIDS**
副标题	Part Ⅰ: An Historical Perspective
作者	Christopher Kwesi O. Williams
年度	2019
出版社	Springer Cham
DOI	https://doi.org/10.1007/978-3-319-99359-1
序号	402
标题	**Cancer and AIDS**
副标题	Part Ⅱ: Cancer Pathogenesis and Epidemiology
作者	Christopher Kwesi O. Williams

续表

年度	2019
出版社	Springer Cham
DOI	https://doi.org/10.1007/978-3-319-99235-8
序号	403
标题	**Cancer and AIDS**
副标题	Part Ⅲ: Presentation and Management
作者	Christopher Kwesi O. Williams
年度	2019
出版社	Springer Cham
DOI	https://doi.org/10.1007/978-3-319-99362-1
序号	404
标题	**Cancer and AIDS**
副标题	Part Ⅳ: Future Perspectives
作者	Christopher Kwesi O. Williams
年度	2019
出版社	Springer Cham
DOI	https://doi.org/10.1007/978-3-319-99238-9
序号	405
标题	**Cardiovascular Care in Patients with HIV**
作者	Merle Myerson, Marshall J. Glesby
年度	2019
出版社	Springer Cham
DOI	https://doi.org/10.1007/978-3-030-10451-1
序号	406
标题	**Charting the Next Pandemic**
副标题	Modeling Infectious Disease Spreading in the Data Science Age
作者	Ana Pastore y Piontti, Nicola Perra, Luca Rossi, Nicole Samay, Alessandro Vespignani
年度	2019
出版社	Springer Cham
DOI	https://doi.org/10.1007/978-3-319-93290-3

续表

序号	407
标题	**Chlamydia Trachomatis**
副标题	Methods and Protocols
系列标题	Methods in Molecular Biology
作者	Amanda Claire Brown
年度	2019
出版社	Humana New York
DOI	https://doi.org/10.1007/978-1-4939-9694-0
序号	408
标题	**Development, Sexual Cultural Practices and HIV/AIDS in Africa**
作者	Samantha Page
年度	2019
出版社	Palgrave Macmillan Cham
DOI	https://doi.org/10.1007/978-3-030-04119-9
序号	409
标题	**Extrapulmonary Tuberculosis**
作者	Alper Sener, Hakan Erdem
年度	2019
出版社	Springer Cham
DOI	https://doi.org/10.1007/978-3-030-04744-3
序号	410
标题	**Hepatitis C Virus Protocols**
系列标题	Methods in Molecular Biology
作者	Mansun Law
年度	2019
出版社	Humana New York
DOI	https://doi.org/10.1007/978-1-4939-8976-8
序号	411
标题	**HIV and GI Tract Complications**
副标题	A Comprehensive Clinical Guide

续表

系列标题	Clinical Gastroenterology
作者	Lisa M. Chirch, Jurate Ivanaviciene
年度	2019
出版社	Humana Cham
DOI	https://doi.org/10.1007/978-3-030-13377-1
序号	412
标题	**HIV and Tuberculosis**
副标题	A Formidable Alliance
作者	Irini Sereti, Gregory P. Bisson, Graeme Meintjes
年度	2019
出版社	Springer Cham
DOI	https://doi.org/10.1007/978-3-030-29108-2
序号	413
标题	**HIV Survivors in Sydney**
副标题	Memories of the Epidemic
系列标题	Palgrave Studies in Oral History
作者	Cheryl Ware
年度	2019
出版社	Palgrave Macmillan Cham
DOI	https://doi.org/10.1007/978-3-030-05102-0
序号	414
标题	**HIV/AIDS and Adolescents**
副标题	South Pacific and Caribbean
作者	Prem Misir
年度	2019
出版社	Palgrave Macmillan Singapore
DOI	https://doi.org/10.1007/978-981-13-5989-7
序号	415
标题	**HIV/AIDS: Immunochemistry, Reductionism and Vaccine Design**
副标题	A Review of 20 Years of Research

续表

作者	Marc H V Van Regenmortel
年度	2019
出版社	Springer Cham
DOI	https://doi.org/10.1007/978-3-030-32459-9
序号	416
标题	**HIV/AIDS-Associated Viral Oncogenesis（Second Edition）**
系列标题	Cancer Treatment and Research
作者	Craig Meyers
年度	2019
出版社	Springer Cham
DOI	https://doi.org/10.1007/978-3-030-03502-0
序号	417
标题	**Infectious Diseases in Solid-Organ Transplant Recipients**
副标题	A practical approach
作者	Oriol Manuel，Michael G Ison
年度	2019
出版社	Springer Cham
DOI	https://doi.org/10.1007/978-3-030-15394-6
序号	418
标题	**Introduction to Clinical Infectious Diseases**
副标题	A Problem-Based Approach
作者	Joseph Domachowske
年度	2019
出版社	Springer Cham
DOI	https://doi.org/10.1007/978-3-319-91080-2
序号	419
标题	**Mycobacterium Tuberculosis: Molecular Infection Biology, Pathogenesis, Diagnostics and New Interventions**
作者	Seyed Ehtesham Hasnain，Nasreen Z. Ehtesham，Sonam Grover
年度	2019

出版社	Springer Singapore
DOI	https://doi.org/10.1007/978-981-32-9413-4
序号	420
标题	**Pandemics, Publics, and Politics**
副标题	Staging Responses to Public Health Crises
作者	Kristian Bjørkdahl, Benedicte Carlsen
年度	2019
出版社	Palgrave Pivot Singapore
DOI	https://doi.org/10.1007/978-981-13-2802-2
序号	421
标题	**Parasite and Disease Spread by Major Rivers on Earth**
副标题	Past and Future Perspectives
系列标题	Parasitology Research Monographs
作者	Heinz Mehlhorn, Sven Klimpel
年度	2019
出版社	Springer Cham
DOI	https://doi.org/10.1007/978-3-030-29061-0
序号	422
标题	**Pathogenic Yersinia**
副标题	Methods and Protocols
系列标题	Methods in Molecular Biology
作者	Viveka Vadyvaloo, Matthew B. Lawrenz
年度	2019
出版社	Humana New York
DOI	https://doi.org/10.1007/978-1-4939-9541-7
序号	423
标题	**Persister Cells and Infectious Disease**
作者	Kim Lewis
年度	2019
出版社	Springer Cham

续表

DOI	https://doi.org/10.1007/978-3-030-25241-0
序号	424
标题	**Pertussis Infection and Vaccines**
副标题	Advances in Microbiology, Infectious Diseases and Public Health Volume 12
系列标题	Advances in Experimental Medicine and Biology
作者	Giorgio Fedele, Clara Maria Ausiello
年度	2019
出版社	Springer Cham
DOI	https://doi.org/10.1007/978-3-030-33249-5
序号	425
标题	**Pregnant in the Time of Ebola**
副标题	Women and Their Children in the 2013—2015 West African Epidemic
系列标题	Global Maternal and Child Health
作者	David A. Schwartz, Julienne Ngoundoung Anoko, Sharon A. Abramowitz
年度	2019
出版社	Springer Cham
DOI	https://doi.org/10.1007/978-3-319-97637-2
序号	426
标题	**Principles and Practice of Transplant Infectious Diseases**
作者	Amar Safdar
年度	2019
出版社	Springer New York
DOI	https://doi.org/10.1007/978-1-4939-9034-4
序号	427
标题	**Psychiatry of Pandemics**
副标题	A Mental Health Response to Infection Outbreak
作者	Damir Huremović
年度	2019
出版社	Springer Cham
DOI	https://doi.org/10.1007/978-3-030-15346-5

续表

序号	428
标题	**Quantitative Methods for Investigating Infectious Disease Outbreaks**
系列标题	Texts in Applied Mathematics
作者	Ping Yan, Gerardo Chowell
年度	2019
出版社	Springer Cham
DOI	https://doi.org/10.1007/978-3-030-21923-9
序号	429
标题	**Socio-Cultural Dimensions of Emerging Infectious Diseases in Africa**
副标题	An Indigenous Response to Deadly Epidemics
作者	Godfrey B. Tangwa, Akin Abayomi, Samuel J. Ujewe, Nchangwi Syntia Munung
年度	2019
出版社	Springer Cham
DOI	https://doi.org/10.1007/978-3-030-17474-3
序号	430
标题	**Spatiotemporal Modeling of Influenza**
副标题	Partial Differential Equation Analysis in R
系列标题	Synthesis Lectures on Biomedical Engineering
作者	William E. Schiesser
年度	2019
出版社	Springer Cham
DOI	https://doi.org/10.1007/978-3-031-01665-3
序号	431
标题	**Teaching AIDS**
副标题	The Cultural Politics of HIV Disease in India
作者	Dilip K. Das
年度	2019
出版社	Springer Singapore
DOI	https://doi.org/10.1007/978-981-13-6120-3

续表

序号	432
标题	**The Role of Bacteria in Urology**
作者	Dirk Lange, Kymora B. Scotland
年度	2019
出版社	Springer Cham
DOI	https://doi.org/10.1007/978-3-030-17542-9
序号	433
标题	**Therapeutic Vaccines as Novel Immunotherapy**
副标题	Biological and Clinical Concepts
作者	Hironori Nakagami
年度	2019
出版社	Springer Singapore
DOI	https://doi.org/10.1007/978-981-32-9628-2
序号	434
标题	**Tuberculosis Host-Pathogen Interactions**
作者	Jeffrey D. Cirillo, Ying Kong
年度	2019
出版社	Springer Cham
DOI	https://doi.org/10.1007/978-3-030-25381-3
序号	435
标题	**Tuberculosis in Animals: An African Perspective**
作者	Asseged B. Dibaba, Nicolaas P. J. Kriek, Charles O. Thoen
年度	2019
出版社	Springer Cham
DOI	https://doi.org/10.1007/978-3-030-18690-6
序号	436
标题	**Vaccinia Virus**
副标题	Methods and Protocols
系列标题	Methods in Molecular Biology
作者	Jason Mercer

续表

年度	2019
出版社	Humana New York
DOI	https://doi.org/10.1007/978-1-4939-9593-6
序号	437
标题	**Viral Hepatitis in Children**
副标题	Prevention and Management
作者	Mei-Hwei Chang, Kathleen B. Schwarz
年度	2019
出版社	Springer Singapore
DOI	https://doi.org/10.1007/978-981-13-0050-9
序号	438
标题	**Viral Hepatitis: Acute Hepatitis**
作者	Resat Ozaras, Joop E. Arends
年度	2019
出版社	Springer Cham
DOI	https://doi.org/10.1007/978-3-030-03535-8
序号	439
标题	**Viral Hepatitis: Chronic Hepatitis C**
作者	Resat Ozaras, Dominique Salmon-Ceron
年度	2019
出版社	Springer Cham
DOI	https://doi.org/10.1007/978-3-030-03757-4
序号	440
标题	**Virus Infection and Tumorigenesis**
副标题	Hints from Marine Hosts' Stress Responses
作者	Xiaobo Zhang
年度	2019
出版社	Springer Singapore
DOI	https://doi.org/10.1007/978-981-13-6198-2
序号	441

标题	A Day-by-Day Chronicle of the 2013—2016 Ebola Outbreak	
作者	Stephan Gregory Bullard	
年度	2018	
出版社	Springer Cham	
DOI	https://doi.org/10.1007/978-3-319-76565-5	
序号	442	
标题	Activation of Viruses by Host Proteases	
作者	Eva Böttcher-Friebertshäuser, Wolfgang Garten, Hans Dieter Klenk	
年度	2018	
出版社	Springer Cham	
DOI	https://doi.org/10.1007/978-3-319-75474-1	
序号	443	
标题	Advances in Microbiology, Infectious Diseases and Public Health	
副标题	Volume 9	
系列标题	Advances in Experimental Medicine and Biology	
作者	Gianfranco Donelli	
年度	2018	
出版社	Springer Cham	
DOI	https://doi.org/10.1007/978-3-319-79017-6	
序号	444	
标题	AIDS in Pakistan	
副标题	Bureaucracy, Public Goods and NGOs	
作者	Ayaz Qureshi	
年度	2018	
出版社	Palgrave Macmillan Singapore	
DOI	https://doi.org/10.1007/978-981-10-6220-9	
序号	445	
标题	An Introduction to Mathematical Modeling of Infectious Diseases	
系列标题	Mathematics of Planet Earth	
作者	Michael Y. Li	

续表

年度	2018
出版社	Springer Cham
DOI	https://doi.org/10.1007/978-3-319-72122-4
序号	446
标题	**Biology of Chlamydia**
系列标题	Current Topics in Microbiology and Immunology
作者	Georg Häcker
年度	2018
出版社	Springer Cham
DOI	https://doi.org/10.1007/978-3-319-71232-1
序号	447
标题	**Communicable Diseases of the Developing World**
系列标题	Topics in Medicinal Chemistry
作者	Anil Kumar Saxena
年度	2018
出版社	Springer Cham
DOI	https://doi.org/10.1007/978-3-319-78254-6
序号	448
标题	**Copper and Bacteria**
副标题	Evolution, Homeostasis and Toxicity
系列标题	SpringerBriefs in Molecular Science
作者	Marc Solioz
年度	2018
出版社	Springer Cham
DOI	https://doi.org/10.1007/978-3-319-94439-5
序号	449
标题	**Drug Interactions in Infectious Diseases: Antimicrobial Drug Interactions (Fourth Edition)**
系列标题	Infectious Disease
作者	Manjunath P. Pai, Jennifer J. Kiser, Paul O. Gubbins, Keith A. Rodvold
年度	2018

续表

出版社	Humana Cham
DOI	https://doi.org/10.1007/978-3-319-72416-4
序号	450
标题	**Drug Interactions in Infectious Diseases: Mechanisms and Models of Drug Interactions（Fourth Edition）**
系列标题	Infectious Disease
作者	Manjunath P. Pai, Jennifer J. Kiser, Paul O. Gubbins, Keith A. Rodvold
年度	2018
出版社	Humana Cham
DOI	https://doi.org/10.1007/978-3-319-72422-5
序号	451
标题	**Ebola Virus Disease**
副标题	A Manual for EVD Management
作者	Marta Lado
年度	2018
出版社	Springer Cham
DOI	https://doi.org/10.1007/978-3-319-94854-6
序号	452
标题	**Encyclopedia of AIDS**
作者	Thomas J. Hope, Douglas D. Richman, Mario Stevenson
年度	2018
出版社	Springer New York
DOI	https://doi.org/10.1007/978-1-4939-7101-5
序号	453
标题	**Escherichia Coli, a Versatile Pathogen**
系列标题	Current Topics in Microbiology and Immunology
作者	Gad Frankel, Eliora Z Ron
年度	2018
出版社	Springer Cham
DOI	https://doi.org/10.1007/978-3-319-99664-6

续表

序号	454
标题	**Frugal Innovation in Bioengineering for the Detection of Infectious Diseases**
作者	Arvind K. Chavali, Ramesh Ramji
年度	2018
出版社	Springer Cham
DOI	https://doi.org/10.1007/978-3-319-66647-1
序号	455
标题	**Gender and HIV in South Africa**
副标题	Advancing Women's Health and Capabilities
系列标题	Global Research in Gender, Sexuality and Health
作者	Courtenay Sprague
年度	2018
出版社	Palgrave Macmillan London
DOI	https://doi.org/10.1057/978-1-137-55997-5
序号	456
标题	**Hemorrhagic Fever Viruses**
副标题	Methods and Protocols
系列标题	Methods in Molecular Biology
作者	Maria S. Salvato
年度	2018
出版社	Humana New York
DOI	https://doi.org/10.1007/978-1-4939-6981-4
序号	457
标题	**Hepatitis B Virus and Liver Disease**
作者	Jia-Horng Kao, Ding-Shinn Chen
年度	2018
出版社	Springer Singapore
DOI	https://doi.org/10.1007/978-981-10-4843-2
序号	458

续表

标题	**HIV Vaccines and Cure**
副标题	The Path Towards Finding an Effective Cure and Vaccine
系列标题	Advances in Experimental Medicine and Biology
作者	Linqi Zhang, Sharon R. Lewin
年度	2018
出版社	Springer Singapore
DOI	https://doi.org/10.1007/978-981-13-0484-2
序号	459
标题	**HIV-1 Latency**
系列标题	Current Topics in Microbiology and Immunology
作者	Guido Silvestri, Mathias Lichterfeld
年度	2018
出版社	Springer Cham
DOI	https://doi.org/10.1007/978-3-030-02816-9
序号	460
标题	**Host-Pathogen Interactions**
副标题	Methods and Protocols
系列标题	Methods in Molecular Biology
作者	Carlos Medina, Francisco Javier López-Baena
年度	2018
出版社	Humana New York
DOI	https://doi.org/10.1007/978-1-4939-7604-1
序号	461
标题	**Infectious Diseases and Arthropods(Third Edition)**
系列标题	Infectious Disease
作者	Jerome Goddard
年度	2018
出版社	Humana Cham
DOI	https://doi.org/10.1007/978-3-319-75874-9
序号	462

续表

标题	**Infectious Diseases and Nanomedicine Ⅲ**
副标题	Second International Conference(ICIDN-2015), Dec. 15-18, 2015, Kathmandu, Nepal
系列标题	Advances in Experimental Medicine and Biology
作者	Rameshwar Adhikari, Santosh Thapa
年度	2018
出版社	Springer Singapore
DOI	https://doi.org/10.1007/978-981-10-7572-8
序号	463
标题	**Infectious Diseases and Your Health**
作者	Prati Pal Singh
年度	2018
出版社	Springer Singapore
DOI	https://doi.org/10.1007/978-981-13-1577-0
序号	464
标题	**Influenza Virus**
副标题	Methods and Protocols
系列标题	Methods in Molecular Biology
作者	Yohei Yamauchi
年度	2018
出版社	Humana New York
DOI	https://doi.org/10.1007/978-1-4939-8678-1
序号	465
标题	**Islam and Health Policies Related to HIV Prevention in Malaysia**
系列标题	SpringerBriefs in Public Health
作者	Sima Barmania, Michael J. Reiss
年度	2018
出版社	Springer Cham
DOI	https://doi.org/10.1007/978-3-319-68909-8
序号	466

续表

标题	Mathematical Immunology of Virus Infections
作者	Gennady Bocharov, Vitaly Volpert, Burkhard Ludewig, Andreas Meyerhans
年度	2018
出版社	Springer Cham
DOI	https://doi.org/10.1007/978-3-319-72317-4
序号	467
标题	Roles of Host Gene and Non-Coding RNA Expression in Virus Infection
系列标题	Current Topics in Microbiology and Immunology
作者	Ralph A. Tripp, S. Mark Tompkins
年度	2018
出版社	Springer Cham
DOI	https://doi.org/10.1007/978-3-030-05369-7
序号	468
标题	Structural Dynamics of HIV
副标题	Risk, Resilience and Response
系列标题	Social Aspects of HIV
作者	Deanna Kerrigan, Clare Barrington
年度	2018
出版社	Springer Cham
DOI	https://doi.org/10.1007/978-3-319-63522-4
序号	469
标题	The AIDS Pandemic
副标题	Searching for a Global Response
作者	Michael Merson, Stephen Inrig
年度	2018
出版社	Springer Cham
DOI	https://doi.org/10.1007/978-3-319-47133-4
序号	470
标题	The Clinician's Vaccine Safety Resource Guide
副标题	Optimizing Prevention of Vaccine-Preventable Diseases Across the Lifespan

续表

作者	Matthew Z. Dudley, Daniel A. Salmon, Neal A. Halsey, Walter A. Orenstein, Rupali J. Limaye, Sean T. O'Leary, Saad B. Omer
年度	2018
出版社	Springer Cham
DOI	https://doi.org/10.1007/978-3-319-94694-8
序号	471
标题	**The Connections Between Ecology and Infectious Disease**
系列标题	Advances in Environmental Microbiology
作者	Christon J. Hurst
年度	2018
出版社	Springer Cham
DOI	https://doi.org/10.1007/978-3-319-92373-4
序号	472
标题	**The Infectious Disease Diagnosis**
副标题	A Case Approach
作者	Michael David, Jean-Luc Benoit
年度	2018
出版社	Springer Cham
DOI	https://doi.org/10.1007/978-3-319-64906-1
序号	473
标题	**Tuberculosis and Disabled Identity in Nineteenth Century Literature**
副标题	Invalid Lives
系列标题	Literary Disability Studies
作者	Alex Tankard
年度	2018
出版社	Palgrave Macmillan Cham
DOI	https://doi.org/10.1007/978-3-319-71446-2
序号	474
标题	**Understanding the Host Immune Response Against Mycobacterium Tuberculosis Infection**
作者	Vishwanath Venketaraman

续表

年度	2018
出版社	Springer Cham
DOI	https://doi.org/10.1007/978-3-319-97367-8
序号	475
标题	**Vaccines: Are They Worth a Shot?**
作者	Andrea Grignolio, Translated by Joan Rundo
年度	2018
出版社	Copernicus Cham
DOI	https://doi.org/10.1007/978-3-319-68106-1
序号	476
标题	**Vibrio Cholerae**
副标题	Methods and Protocols
系列标题	Methods in Molecular Biology
作者	Aleksandra E. Sikora
年度	2018
出版社	Humana New York
DOI	https://doi.org/10.1007/978-1-4939-8685-9
序号	477
标题	**Viral Hepatitis: Chronic Hepatitis B**
作者	Resat Ozaras, Veysel Tahan
年度	2018
出版社	Springer Cham
DOI	https://doi.org/10.1007/978-3-319-93449-5
序号	478
标题	**Virus Protein and Nucleoprotein Complexes**
系列标题	Subcellular Biochemistry
作者	J. Robin Harris, David Bhella
年度	2018
出版社	Springer Singapore
DOI	https://doi.org/10.1007/978-981-10-8456-0

续表

序号	479
标题	**Virus-Derived Nanoparticles for Advanced Technologies**
副标题	Methods and Protocols
系列标题	Methods in Molecular Biology
作者	Christina Wege, George P. Lomonossoff
年度	2018
出版社	Humana New York
DOI	https://doi.org/10.1007/978-1-4939-7808-3
序号	480
标题	**Yersinia Pestis Protocols**
系列标题	Springer Protocols Handbooks
作者	Ruifu Yang
年度	2018
出版社	Springer Singapore
DOI	https://doi.org/10.1007/978-981-10-7947-4
序号	481
标题	**Advances in Microbiology, Infectious Diseases and Public Health**
副标题	Volume 7
系列标题	Advances in Experimental Medicine and Biology
作者	Gianfranco Donelli
年度	2017
出版社	Springer Cham
DOI	https://doi.org/10.1007/978-3-319-60765-8
序号	482
标题	**AIDS Activism, Science and Community Across Three Continents**
系列标题	Social Aspects of HIV
作者	Robert Lorway
年度	2017
出版社	Springer Cham
DOI	https://doi.org/10.1007/978-3-319-42199-5

续表

序号	483
标题	**Atlas of Infectious Disease Pathology**
系列标题	Atlas of Anatomic Pathology
作者	Bryan H. Schmitt
年度	2017
出版社	Springer Cham
DOI	https://doi.org/10.1007/978-3-319-54702-2
序号	484
标题	**Cancer Vaccines**
系列标题	Current Topics in Microbiology and Immunology
作者	Natalia Savelyeva, Christian Ottensmeier
年度	2017
出版社	Springer Cham
DOI	https://doi.org/10.1007/978-3-319-23910-1
序号	485
标题	**Cell Biology of Herpes Viruses**
系列标题	Advances in Anatomy, Embryology and Cell Biology
作者	Klaus Osterrieder
年度	2017
出版社	Springer Cham
DOI	https://doi.org/10.1007/978-3-319-53168-7
序号	486
标题	**Cross-Cultural Perspectives on Couples with Mixed HIV Status: Beyond Positive/Negative**
系列标题	Social Aspects of HIV
作者	Asha Persson, Shana D. Hughes
年度	2017
出版社	Springer Cham
DOI	https://doi.org/10.1007/978-3-319-42725-6
序号	487

续表

标题	Cyclospora Cayetanensis as a Foodborne Pathogen
系列标题	SpringerBriefs in Food, Health, and Nutrition
作者	Ynés R. Ortega, Lucy J. Robertson
年度	2017
出版社	Springer Cham
DOI	https://doi.org/10.1007/978-3-319-53587-6
序号	488
标题	Drug Resistance in Bacteria, Fungi, Malaria, and Cancer
作者	Gunjan Arora, Andaleeb Sajid, Vipin Chandra Kalia
年度	2017
出版社	Springer Cham
DOI	https://doi.org/10.1007/978-3-319-48683-3
序号	489
标题	Emerging and Re-Emerging Infectious Diseases of Livestock
作者	Jagadeesh Bayry
年度	2017
出版社	Springer Cham
DOI	https://doi.org/10.1007/978-3-319-47426-7
序号	490
标题	Emerging Infectious Uveitis
作者	Soon-Phaik Chee, Moncef Khairallah
年度	2017
出版社	Springer Cham
DOI	https://doi.org/10.1007/978-3-319-23416-8
序号	491
标题	Epigenetics of Infectious Diseases
系列标题	Epigenetics and Human Health
作者	Walter Doerfler, Josep Casadesús
年度	2017
出版社	Springer Cham

续表

DOI	https://doi.org/10.1007/978-3-319-55021-3
序号	492
标题	**Epstein Barr Virus**
副标题	Methods and Protocols
系列标题	Methods in Molecular Biology
作者	Janos Minarovits, Hans Helmut Niller
年度	2017
出版社	Humana New York
DOI	https://doi.org/10.1007/978-1-4939-6655-4
序号	493
标题	**Global Virology Ⅱ—HIV and NeuroAIDS**
作者	Paul Shapshak, Andrew J. Levine, Brian T. Foley, Charurut Somboonwit, Elyse Singer, Francesco Chiappelli, John T. Sinnott
年度	2017
出版社	Springer New York
DOI	https://doi.org/10.1007/978-1-4939-7290-6
序号	494
标题	**Handbook of Global Tuberculosis Control**
副标题	Practices and Challenges
作者	Yichen Lu, Lixia Wang, Hongjin Duanmu, Chris Chanyasulkit, Amie J. Strong, Hui Zhang
年度	2017
出版社	Springer New York
DOI	https://doi.org/10.1007/978-1-4939-6667-7
序号	495
标题	**Handbook of Tuberculosis**
作者	Jacques H. Grosset, Richard E. Chaisson
年度	2017
出版社	Adis Cham
DOI	https://doi.org/10.1007/978-3-319-26273-4

续表

序号	496
标题	**Hepatitis B Virus**
副标题	Methods and Protocols
系列标题	Methods in Molecular Biology
作者	Haitao Guo, Andrea Cuconati
年度	2017
出版社	Humana New York
DOI	https://doi.org/10.1007/978-1-4939-6700-1
序号	497
标题	**Hepatitis C Virus Treatment**
副标题	Highly Effective Therapy with Direct Acting Antivirals and Associated Viral Resistance
作者	Kazuaki Chayama
年度	2017
出版社	Springer Singapore
DOI	https://doi.org/10.1007/978-981-10-2416-0
序号	498
标题	**HIV/AIDS in China**
副标题	Beyond the Numbers
系列标题	Public Health in China
作者	Zunyou Wu
年度	2017
出版社	Springer Singapore
DOI	https://doi.org/10.1007/978-981-10-3746-7
序号	499
标题	**HIV/AIDS in Rural Communities**
副标题	Research, Education, and Advocacy
作者	Fayth M. Parks, Gregory S. Felzien, Sally Jue
年度	2017
出版社	Springer Cham

续表

DOI	https://doi.org/10.1007/978-3-319-56239-1
序号	500
标题	**Human Fungal Pathogen Identification**
副标题	Methods and Protocols
系列标题	Methods in Molecular Biology
作者	Thomas Lion
年度	2017
出版社	Humana New York
DOI	https://doi.org/10.1007/978-1-4939-6515-1
序号	501
标题	**Human T-Lymphotropic Viruses**
副标题	Methods and Protocols
系列标题	Methods in Molecular Biology
作者	Claudio Casoli
年度	2017
出版社	Humana New York
DOI	https://doi.org/10.1007/978-1-4939-6872-5
序号	502
标题	**Infectious Agents Associated Cancers: Epidemiology and Molecular Biology**
系列标题	Advances in Experimental Medicine and Biology
作者	Qiliang Cai, Zhenghong Yuan, Ke Lan
年度	2017
出版社	Springer Singapore
DOI	https://doi.org/10.1007/978-981-10-5765-6
序号	503
标题	**Infectious Disease Modeling**
副标题	A Hybrid System Approach
系列标题	Nonlinear Systems and Complexity
作者	Xinzhi Liu, Peter Stechlinski

续表

年度	2017
出版社	Springer Cham
DOI	https://doi.org/10.1007/978-3-319-53208-0
序号	504
标题	**Influenza and Respiratory Care**
系列标题	Advances in Experimental Medicine and Biology
作者	Mieczyslaw Pokorski
年度	2017
出版社	Springer Cham
DOI	https://doi.org/10.1007/978-3-319-51712-4
序号	505
标题	**Modeling the Transmission and Prevention of Infectious Disease**
系列标题	Advances in Environmental Microbiology
作者	Christon J. Hurst
年度	2017
出版社	Springer Cham
DOI	https://doi.org/10.1007/978-3-319-60616-3
序号	506
标题	**Tuberculosis of the Central Nervous System**
副标题	Pathogenesis, Imaging, and Management
作者	Mehmet Turgut, Ali Akhaddar, Ahmet T. Turgut, Ravindra K. Garg
年度	2017
出版社	Springer Cham
DOI	https://doi.org/10.1007/978-3-319-50712-5
序号	507
标题	**Pediatric Vaccines and Vaccinations**
副标题	A European Textbook
作者	Timo Vesikari, Pierre Van Damme
年度	2017
出版社	Springer Cham
DOI	https://doi.org/10.1007/978-3-319-59952-6

续表

序号	508
标题	**Protein and Sugar Export and Assembly in Gram-Positive Bacteria**
系列标题	Current Topics in Microbiology and Immunology
作者	Fabio Bagnoli, Rino Rappuoli
年度	2017
出版社	Springer Cham
DOI	https://doi.org/10.1007/978-3-319-56014-4
序号	509
标题	**Recombinant Antibodies for Infectious Diseases**
系列标题	Advances in Experimental Medicine and Biology
作者	Theam Soon Lim
年度	2017
出版社	Springer Cham
DOI	https://doi.org/10.1007/978-3-319-72077-7
序号	510
标题	**Recombinant Virus Vaccines**
副标题	Methods and Protocols
系列标题	Methods in Molecular Biology
作者	Maureen C. Ferran, Gary R. Skuse
年度	2017
出版社	Humana New York
DOI	https://doi.org/10.1007/978-1-4939-6869-5
序号	511
标题	**Reverse Genetics of RNA Viruses**
副标题	Methods and Protocols
系列标题	Methods in Molecular Biology
作者	Daniel R. Perez
年度	2017
出版社	Humana New York
DOI	https://doi.org/10.1007/978-1-4939-6964-7

续表

序号	512
标题	**RNA Vaccines**
副标题	Methods and Protocols
系列标题	Methods in Molecular Biology
作者	Thomas Kramps, Knut Elbers
年度	2017
出版社	Humana New York
DOI	https://doi.org/10.1007/978-1-4939-6481-9
序号	513
标题	**Sexually Transmitted Infections in HIV-Infected Adults and Special Populations**
副标题	A Clinical Guide
作者	Laura Hinkle Bachmann
年度	2017
出版社	Springer Cham
DOI	https://doi.org/10.1007/978-3-319-56694-8
序号	514
标题	**The CAPRISA Clinical Trials: HIV Treatment and Prevention**
作者	Quarraisha Abdool Karim, Salim S. Abdool Karim, Cheryl Baxter
年度	2017
出版社	Springer Cham
DOI	https://doi.org/10.1007/978-3-319-47518-9
序号	515
标题	**The Ebola Pandemic in Sierra Leone**
副标题	Representations, Actors, Interventions and the Path to Recovery
作者	John Idriss Lahai
年度	2017
出版社	Palgrave Macmillan Cham
DOI	https://doi.org/10.1007/978-3-319-45904-2
序号	516

一、图书

续表

标题	The Parasite Chronicles
副标题	My Lifelong Odyssey Among the Parasites that Cause Human Disease
作者	Boo H. Kwa
年度	2017
出版社	Springer Cham
DOI	https://doi.org/10.1007/978-3-319-74923-5
序号	517
标题	The Politics of Global AIDS
副标题	Institutionalization of Solidarity, Exclusion of Context
系列标题	Social Aspects of HIV
作者	Hakan Seckinelgin
年度	2017
出版社	Springer Cham
DOI	https://doi.org/10.1007/978-3-319-46013-0
序号	518
标题	Type IV Secretion in Gram-Negative and Gram-Positive Bacteria
系列标题	Current Topics in Microbiology and Immunology
作者	Steffen Backert, Elisabeth Grohmann
年度	2017
出版社	Springer Cham
DOI	https://doi.org/10.1007/978-3-319-75241-9
序号	519
标题	Understanding Prevention for HIV Positive Gay Men
副标题	Innovative Approaches in Addressing the AIDS Epidemic
作者	Leo Wilton
年度	2017
出版社	Springer New York
DOI	https://doi.org/10.1007/978-1-4419-0203-0
序号	520
标题	Vaccine Adjuvants
副标题	Methods and Protocols

续表

系列标题	Methods in Molecular Biology
作者	Christopher B. Fox
年度	2017
出版社	Humana New York
DOI	https://doi.org/10.1007/978-1-4939-6445-1
序号	521
标题	**Vaccine Science and Immunization Guideline**
副标题	A Practical Guide for Primary Care
作者	Pamela G. Rockwell
年度	2017
出版社	Springer Cham
DOI	https://doi.org/10.1007/978-3-319-60471-8
序号	522
标题	**Vaccines for Invasive Fungal Infections**
副标题	Methods and Protocols
系列标题	Methods in Molecular Biology
作者	Markus Kalkum, Margarita Semis
年度	2017
出版社	Humana New York
DOI	https://doi.org/10.1007/978-1-4939-7104-6
序号	523
标题	**Viruses, Genes, and Cancer**
系列标题	Current Topics in Microbiology and Immunology
作者	Eric Hunter, Klaus Bister
年度	2017
出版社	Springer Cham
DOI	https://doi.org/10.1007/978-3-319-61804-3
序号	524
标题	**Zika Virus Infection**
副标题	Risk of Spreading in Europe

续表

系列标题	SpringerBriefs in Immunology
作者	Marta Díaz-Menéndez, Clara Crespillo-Andújar
年度	2017
出版社	Springer Cham
DOI	https://doi.org/10.1007/978-3-319-59406-4
序号	525
标题	**A Clinical Guide to Pediatric HIV**
副标题	Bridging the Gaps Between Research and Practice
作者	Tiffany Chenneville
年度	2016
出版社	Springer Cham
DOI	https://doi.org/10.1007/978-3-319-49704-4
序号	526
标题	**Advances in Microbiology, Infectious Diseases and Public Health**
副标题	Volume 1
系列标题	Advances in Experimental Medicine and Biology
作者	Gianfranco Donelli
年度	2016
出版社	Springer Cham
DOI	https://doi.org/10.1007/978-3-319-26320-5
序号	527
标题	**Advances in Microbiology, Infectious Diseases and Public Health**
副标题	Volume 2
系列标题	Advances in Experimental Medicine and Biology
作者	Gianfranco Donelli
年度	2016
出版社	Springer Cham
DOI	https://doi.org/10.1007/978-3-319-27935-0
序号	528
标题	**Advances in Microbiology, Infectious Diseases and Public Health**
副标题	Volume 4

续表

系列标题	Advances in Experimental Medicine and Biology
作者	Gianfranco Donelli
年度	2016
出版社	Springer Cham
DOI	https://doi.org/10.1007/978-3-319-43207-6
序号	529
标题	**Assisted Reproductive Technologies and Infectious Diseases**
副标题	A Guide to Management
作者	Andrea Borini, Maria Valeria Savasi
年度	2016
出版社	Springer Cham
DOI	https://doi.org/10.1007/978-3-319-30112-9
序号	530
标题	**Chikungunya Virus**
副标题	Methods and Protocols
系列标题	Methods in Molecular Biology
作者	Justin Jang Hann Chu, Swee Kim Ang
年度	2016
出版社	Humana New York
DOI	https://doi.org/10.1007/978-1-4939-3618-2
序号	531
标题	**Chikungunya Virus**
副标题	Advances in Biology, Pathogenesis, and Treatment
作者	Chioma M. Okeoma
年度	2016
出版社	Springer Cham
DOI	https://doi.org/10.1007/978-3-319-42958-8
序号	532
标题	**Children and Young People Living with HIV/AIDS**
副标题	A Cross-Cultural Perspective

系列标题	Cross-Cultural Research in Health, Illness and Well-Being
作者	Pranee Liamputtong
年度	2016
出版社	Springer Cham
DOI	https://doi.org/10.1007/978-3-319-29936-5
序号	533
标题	**Diagnostic Imaging of Emerging Infectious Diseases**
作者	Pu-Xuan Lu, Bo-Ping Zhou
年度	2016
出版社	Springer Dordrecht
DOI	https://doi.org/10.1007/978-94-017-7363-8
序号	534
标题	**Efflux-Mediated Antimicrobial Resistance in Bacteria**
副标题	Mechanisms, Regulation and Clinical Implications
作者	Xian-Zhi Li, Christopher A. Elkins, Helen I. Zgurskaya
年度	2016
出版社	Adis Cham
DOI	https://doi.org/10.1007/978-3-319-39658-3
序号	535
标题	**Handbook of Hepatitis C**
作者	Nicolas Goossens, Sophie Clément, Francesco Negro
年度	2016
出版社	Adis Cham
DOI	https://doi.org/10.1007/978-3-319-28053-0
序号	536
标题	**Hepatitis B Virus in Human Diseases**
系列标题	Molecular and Translational Medicine
作者	Yun-Fan Liaw, Fabien Zoulim
年度	2016
出版社	Humana Cham

DOI	https://doi.org/10.1007/978-3-319-22330-8
序号	537
标题	**Hepatitis C Virus Ⅰ**
副标题	Cellular and Molecular Virology
作者	Tatsuo Miyamura, Stanley M. Lemon, Christopher M. Walker, Takaji Wakita
年度	2016
出版社	Springer Tokyo
DOI	https://doi.org/10.1007/978-4-431-56098-2
序号	538
标题	**Hepatitis C Virus Ⅱ**
副标题	Infection and Disease
作者	Tatsuo Miyamura, Stanley M. Lemon, Christopher M. Walker, Takaji Wakita
年度	2016
出版社	Springer Tokyo
DOI	https://doi.org/10.1007/978-4-431-56101-9
序号	539
标题	**Hepatitis E Virus**
系列标题	Advances in Experimental Medicine and Biology
作者	Youchun Wang
年度	2016
出版社	Springer Dordrecht
DOI	https://doi.org/10.1007/978-94-024-0942-0
序号	540
标题	**HIV and Young People**
副标题	Risk and Resilience in the Urban Slum
系列标题	SpringerBriefs in Public Health
作者	Gary Jones
年度	2016
出版社	Springer Cham
DOI	https://doi.org/10.1007/978-3-319-26814-9

续表

序号	541
标题	**HIV Protocols（Third Edition）**
系列标题	Methods in Molecular Biology
作者	Vinayaka R. Prasad, Ganjam V. Kalpana
年度	2016
出版社	Humana New York
DOI	https://doi.org/10.1007/978-1-4939-3046-3
序号	542
标题	**HIV-1 Proteomics**
副标题	From Discovery to Clinical Application
作者	David R. M. Graham, David E. Ott
年度	2016
出版社	Springer New York
DOI	https://doi.org/10.1007/978-1-4939-6542-7
序号	543
标题	**HIV-Associated Hematological Malignancies**
作者	Marcus Hentrich, Stefan K. Barta
年度	2016
出版社	Springer Cham
DOI	https://doi.org/10.1007/978-3-319-26857-6
序号	544
标题	**Holding Hands with Bacteria**
副标题	The Life and Work of Marjory Stephenson
系列标题	SpringerBriefs in Molecular Science
作者	Soňa Štrbáňová
年度	2016
出版社	Springer Berlin, Heidelberg
DOI	https://doi.org/10.1007/978-3-662-49736-4
序号	545
标题	**Human Respiratory Syncytial Virus**
副标题	Methods and Protocols

续表

系列标题	Methods in Molecular Biology
作者	Ralph A. Tripp, Patricia A. Jorquera
年度	2016
出版社	Humana New York
DOI	https://doi.org/10.1007/978-1-4939-3687-8
序号	546
标题	**Infectious Disease and Parasites**
系列标题	Encyclopedia of Pathology
作者	Paul Hofman
年度	2016
出版社	Springer Cham
DOI	https://doi.org/10.1007/978-3-319-30009-2
序号	547
标题	**Infectious Diseases and Rural Livelihood in Developing Countries**
作者	Fingani Annie Mphande
年度	2016
出版社	Springer Singapore
DOI	https://doi.org/10.1007/978-981-10-0428-5
序号	548
标题	**Infectious Diseases in Pediatric Otolaryngology**
副标题	A Practical Guide
作者	Tulio Valdez, Jesus Vallejo
年度	2016
出版社	Springer Cham
DOI	https://doi.org/10.1007/978-3-319-21744-4
序号	549
标题	**Managing the Older Adult Patient with HIV**
作者	Giovanni Guaraldi, Julian Falutz, Chiara Mussi, Ana Rita Silva
年度	2016
出版社	Adis Cham

续表

DOI	https://doi.org/10.1007/978-3-319-20131-3
序号	550
标题	**Mathematical and Statistical Modeling for Emerging and Re-Emerging Infectious Diseases**
作者	Gerardo Chowell, James M. Hyman
年度	2016
出版社	Springer Cham
DOI	https://doi.org/10.1007/978-3-319-40413-4
序号	551
标题	**Microbial Endocrinology: Interkingdom Signaling in Infectious Disease and Health（Second Edition）**
系列标题	Advances in Experimental Medicine and Biology
作者	Mark Lyte
年度	2016
出版社	Springer Cham
DOI	https://doi.org/10.1007/978-3-319-20215-0
序号	552
标题	**Neoliberal Ebola**
副标题	Modeling Disease Emergence from Finance to Forest and Farm
作者	Robert G. Wallace, Rodrick Wallace
年度	2016
出版社	Springer Cham
DOI	https://doi.org/10.1007/978-3-319-40940-5
序号	553
标题	**Novel Polymeric Biochips for Enhanced Detection of Infectious Diseases**
系列标题	SpringerBriefs in Applied Sciences and Technology
作者	Samira Hosseini, Fatimah Ibrahim
年度	2016
出版社	Springer Singapore
DOI	https://doi.org/10.1007/978-981-10-0107-9

续表

序号	554
标题	Patho-Epigenetics of Infectious Disease
系列标题	Advances in Experimental Medicine and Biology
作者	Janos Minarovits, Hans Helmut Niller
年度	2016
出版社	Springer Cham
DOI	https://doi.org/10.1007/978-3-319-24738-0
序号	555
标题	Politics in the Making of HIV/AIDS in South Africa
作者	Kiran Pienaar
年度	2016
出版社	Palgrave Macmillan London
DOI	https://doi.org/10.1007/978-1-137-50507-1
序号	556
标题	Presidents, Pandemics, and Politics
系列标题	The Evolving American Presidency
作者	Max J. Skidmore
年度	2016
出版社	Palgrave Macmillan New York
DOI	https://doi.org/10.1057/978-1-137-59959-9
序号	557
标题	Radiology of Influenza
副标题	A Practical Approach
作者	Hongjun Li
年度	2016
出版社	Springer Dordrecht
DOI	https://doi.org/10.1007/978-94-024-0908-6
序号	558
标题	The Role of Bacteria in Urology
作者	Dirk Lange, Ben Chew

续表

年度	2016
出版社	Springer Cham
DOI	https://doi.org/10.1007/978-3-319-17732-8
序号	559
标题	**Understanding the HIV/AIDS Epidemic in the United States**
副标题	The Role of Syndemics in the Production of Health Disparities
系列标题	Social Disparities in Health and Health Care
作者	Eric R. Wright, Neal Carnes
年度	2016
出版社	Springer Cham
DOI	https://doi.org/10.1007/978-3-319-34004-3
序号	560
标题	**Vaccine Design**
副标题	Methods and Protocols: Volume 1: Vaccines for Human Diseases
系列标题	Methods in Molecular Biology
作者	Sunil Thomas
年度	2016
出版社	Humana New York
DOI	https://doi.org/10.1007/978-1-4939-3387-7
序号	561
标题	**Vaccine Design**
副标题	Methods and Protocols, Volume 2: Vaccines for Veterinary Diseases
系列标题	Methods in Molecular Biology
作者	Sunil Thomas
年度	2016
出版社	Humana New York
DOI	https://doi.org/10.1007/978-1-4939-3389-1
序号	562
标题	**Vaccine Technologies for Veterinary Viral Diseases**
副标题	Methods and Protocols

续表

系列标题	Methods in Molecular Biology
作者	Alejandro Brun
年度	2016
出版社	Humana New York
DOI	https://doi.org/10.1007/978-1-4939-3008-1
序号	563
标题	**Viruses in Foods(Second Edition)**
系列标题	Food Microbiology and Food Safety
作者	Sagar M. Goyal, Jennifer L. Cannon
年度	2016
出版社	Springer Cham
DOI	https://doi.org/10.1007/978-3-319-30723-7
序号	564
标题	**West Nile Virus**
副标题	Methods and Protocols
系列标题	Methods in Molecular Biology
作者	Tonya M. Colpitts
年度	2016
出版社	Humana New York
DOI	https://doi.org/10.1007/978-1-4939-3670-0
序号	565
标题	**Yersinia pestis: Retrospective and Perspective**
系列标题	Advances in Experimental Medicine and Biology
作者	Ruifu Yang, Andrey Anisimov
年度	2016
出版社	Springer Dordrecht
DOI	https://doi.org/10.1007/978-94-024-0890-4
序号	566
标题	**Bacteria-Metal Interactions**
作者	Daad Saffarini

续表

年度	2015
出版社	Springer Cham
DOI	https://doi.org/10.1007/978-3-319-18570-5
序号	567
标题	**Carbohydrate-Based Vaccines**
副标题	Methods and Protocols
系列标题	Methods in Molecular Biology
作者	Bernd Lepenies
年度	2015
出版社	Humana New York
DOI	https://doi.org/10.1007/978-1-4939-2874-3
序号	568
标题	**Detection and Typing Strategies for Pathogenic Escherichia Coli**
系列标题	SpringerBriefs in Food, Health, and Nutrition
作者	Lucia Rivas, Glen E. Mellor, Kari Gobius, Narelle Fegan
年度	2015
出版社	Springer New York
DOI	https://doi.org/10.1007/978-1-4939-2346-5
序号	569
标题	**Epstein Barr Virus Volume 1**
副标题	One Herpes Virus: Many Diseases
系列标题	Current Topics in Microbiology and Immunology
作者	Christian Münz
年度	2015
出版社	Springer Cham
DOI	https://doi.org/10.1007/978-3-319-22822-8
序号	570
标题	**Epstein Barr Virus Volume 2**
副标题	One Herpes Virus: Many Diseases
系列标题	Current Topics in Microbiology and Immunology

续表

作者	Christian Münz
年度	2015
出版社	Springer Cham
DOI	https://doi.org/10.1007/978-3-319-22834-1
序号	571
标题	**Faith in the Time of AIDS**
副标题	Religion, Biopolitics and Modernity in South Africa
系列标题	Non-Governmental Public Action
作者	Marian Burchardt
年度	2015
出版社	Palgrave Macmillan London
DOI	https://doi.org/10.1057/9781137477774
序号	572
标题	**Gender, HIV and Risk**
副标题	Navigating Structural Violence
系列标题	Gender and Politics
作者	Emma-Louise Anderson
年度	2015
出版社	Palgrave Macmillan London
DOI	https://doi.org/10.1057/9781137316127
序号	573
标题	**Gene Therapy for HIV and Chronic Infections**
系列标题	Advances in Experimental Medicine and Biology
作者	Ben Berkhout, Hildegund C.J. Ertl, Marc S. Weinberg
年度	2015
出版社	Springer New York
DOI	https://doi.org/10.1007/978-1-4939-2432-5
序号	574
标题	**HIV/AIDS in China and India**
副标题	Governing Health Security

续表

作者	Catherine Yuk-ping Lo
年度	2015
出版社	Palgrave Macmillan New York
DOI	https://doi.org/10.1057/9781137504210
序号	575
标题	**Host Manipulations by Parasites and Viruses**
系列标题	Parasitology Research Monographs
作者	Heinz Mehlhorn
年度	2015
出版社	Springer Cham
DOI	https://doi.org/10.1007/978-3-319-22936-2
序号	576
标题	**Influenza Pathogenesis and Control—Volume Ⅱ**
系列标题	Current Topics in Microbiology and Immunology
作者	Michael B. A. Oldstone, Richard W. Compans
年度	2015
出版社	Springer Cham
DOI	https://doi.org/10.1007/978-3-319-11158-2
序号	577
标题	**Lyophilized Biologics and Vaccines**
副标题	Modality-Based Approaches
作者	Dushyant Varshney, Manmohan Singh
年度	2015
出版社	Springer New York
DOI	https://doi.org/10.1007/978-1-4939-2383-0
序号	578
标题	**Malaria Vaccines**
副标题	Methods and Protocols
系列标题	Methods in Molecular Biology
作者	Ashley Vaughan

续表

年度	2015
出版社	Humana New York
DOI	https://doi.org/10.1007/978-1-4939-2815-6
序号	579
标题	**Mathematical Models for Therapeutic Approaches to Control HIV Disease Transmission**
系列标题	Industrial and Applied Mathematics
作者	Priti Kumar Roy
年度	2015
出版社	Springer Singapore
DOI	https://doi.org/10.1007/978-981-287-852-6
序号	580
标题	**Pandemics, Science and Policy**
副标题	H1N1 and the World Health Organisation
系列标题	Palgrave Studies in Science, Knowledge and Policy
作者	Sudeepa Abeysinghe
年度	2015
出版社	Palgrave Macmillan London
DOI	https://doi.org/10.1057/9781137467201
序号	581
标题	**Parasite Genomics Protocols**
系列标题	Methods in Molecular Biology
作者	Christopher Peacock
年度	2015
出版社	Humana New York
DOI	https://doi.org/10.1007/978-1-4939-1438-8
序号	582
标题	**Pathogen-Host Interactions: Antigenic Variation v. Somatic Adaptations**
系列标题	Results and Problems in Cell Differentiation
作者	Ellen Hsu, Louis Du Pasquier

续表

年度	2015
出版社	Springer Cham
DOI	https://doi.org/10.1007/978-3-319-20819-0
序号	583
标题	**Pediatric Infectious Disease**
副标题	A Practically Painless Review
作者	Christine M. Houser
年度	2015
出版社	Springer New York
DOI	https://doi.org/10.1007/978-1-4939-1329-9
序号	584
标题	**Perspectives on Youth, HIV/AIDS and Indigenous Knowledges**
系列标题	Youth, Media, & Culture Series
作者	Anders Breidlid, Austin M. Cheyeka, Alawia Ibrahim Farag
年度	2015
出版社	SensePublishers Rotterdam
DOI	https://doi.org/10.1007/978-94-6300-196-0
序号	585
标题	**Prison Inmates Living with HIV in India**
副标题	Case Studies from Prisons in Maharashtra
系列标题	SpringerBriefs in Criminology
作者	Sayantani Guin
年度	2015
出版社	Springer Cham
DOI	https://doi.org/10.1007/978-3-319-15566-1
序号	586
标题	**Radiology of Infectious Diseases: Volume 1**
作者	Hongjun Li
年度	2015
出版社	Springer Dordrecht

DOI	https://doi.org/10.1007/978-94-017-9882-2	
序号	587	
标题	Radiology of Infectious Diseases: Volume 2	
作者	Hongjun Li	
年度	2015	
出版社	Springer Dordrecht	
DOI	https://doi.org/10.1007/978-94-017-9876-1	
序号	588	
标题	Sex and Gender Differences in Infection and Treatments for Infectious Diseases	
作者	Sabra L. Klein, Craig W. Roberts	
年度	2015	
出版社	Springer Cham	
DOI	https://doi.org/10.1007/978-3-319-16438-0	
序号	589	
标题	Socio-Ecological Dimensions of Infectious Diseases in Southeast Asia	
作者	Serge Morand, Jean-Pierre Dujardin, Régine Lefait-Robin, Chamnarn Apiwathnasorn	
年度	2015	
出版社	Springer Singapore	
DOI	https://doi.org/10.1007/978-981-287-527-3	
序号	590	
标题	Structure Determination of HIV-1 Tat/Fluid Phase Membranes and DMPC Ripple Phase Using X-Ray Scattering	
系列标题	Springer Theses	
作者	Kiyotaka Akabori	
年度	2015	
出版社	Springer Cham	
DOI	https://doi.org/10.1007/978-3-319-22210-3	
序号	591	
标题	**Subunit Vaccine Delivery**	
系列标题	Advances in Delivery Science and Technology	

续表

作者	Camilla Foged, Thomas Rades, Yvonne Perrie, Sarah Hook
年度	2015
出版社	Springer New York
DOI	https://doi.org/10.1007/978-1-4939-1417-3
序号	592
标题	**The Future of HIV-1 Therapeutics**
副标题	Resistance Is Futile?
系列标题	Current Topics in Microbiology and Immunology
作者	Bruce E. Torbett, David S. Goodsell, Douglas D. Richman
年度	2015
出版社	Springer Cham
DOI	https://doi.org/10.1007/978-3-319-18518-7
序号	593
标题	**Trypanosoma Cruzi as a Foodborne Pathogen**
系列标题	SpringerBriefs in Food, Health, and Nutrition
作者	Belkisyolé de Noya, Oscar González, Lucy J. Robertson
年度	2015
出版社	Springer Cham
DOI	https://doi.org/10.1007/978-3-319-23410-6
序号	594
标题	**Vaccine Analysis: Strategies, Principles, and Control**
作者	Brian K. Nunnally, Vincent E. Turula, Robert D. Sitrin
年度	2015
出版社	Springer Berlin, Heidelberg
DOI	https://doi.org/10.1007/978-3-662-45024-6
序号	595
标题	**Animal Influenza Virus**
系列标题	Methods in Molecular Biology
作者	Erica Spackman
年度	2014

续表

出版社	Humana New York
DOI	https://doi.org/10.1007/978-1-4939-0758-8
序号	596
标题	**Antiblack Racism and the AIDS Epidemic**
副标题	State Intimacies
作者	Adam M. Geary
年度	2014
出版社	Palgrave Macmillan New York
DOI	https://doi.org/10.1057/9781137438034
序号	597
标题	**Asian Immigrants in North America with HIV/AIDS**
副标题	Stigma, Vulnerabilities and Human Rights
作者	AKM Ahsan Ullah, Ahmed Shafiqul Huque
年度	2014
出版社	Springer Singapore
DOI	https://doi.org/10.1007/978-981-287-119-0
序号	598
标题	**Biomedical Advances in HIV Prevention**
副标题	Social and Behavioral Perspectives
作者	Lisa A. Eaton, Seth C. Kalichman
年度	2014
出版社	Springer New York
DOI	https://doi.org/10.1007/978-1-4614-8845-3
序号	599
标题	**Cancer Vaccines**
副标题	Methods and Protocols
系列标题	Methods in Molecular Biology
作者	Michael J.P. Lawman, Patricia D. Lawman
年度	2014
出版社	Humana New York
DOI	https://doi.org/10.1007/978-1-4939-0345-0

续表

序号	600
标题	**Cancers in People with HIV and AIDS**
副标题	Progress and Challenges
作者	Robert Yarchoan
年度	2014
出版社	Springer New York
DOI	https://doi.org/10.1007/978-1-4939-0859-2
序号	601
标题	**Collective Dynamics from Bacteria to Crowds**
副标题	An Excursion Through Modeling, Analysis and Simulation
系列标题	CISM International Centre for Mechanical Sciences
作者	Adrian Muntean, Federico Toschi
年度	2014
出版社	Springer Vienna
DOI	https://doi.org/10.1007/978-3-7091-1785-9
序号	602
标题	**Communicable Diseases in Developing Countries**
副标题	Stopping the Global Epidemics of HIV/AIDS, Tuberculosis, Malaria and Diarrhea
作者	John Malcolm Dowling, Chin-Fang Yap
年度	2014
出版社	Palgrave Macmillan London
DOI	https://doi.org/10.1057/9781137354785
序号	603
标题	**Cryptosporidium as a Foodborne Pathogen**
系列标题	SpringerBriefs in Food, Health, and Nutrition
作者	Lucy J. Robertson
年度	2014
出版社	Springer New York
DOI	https://doi.org/10.1007/978-1-4614-9378-5
序号	604

续表

标题	**Cryptosporidium: Parasite and Disease**
作者	Simone M. Cacciò, Giovanni Widmer
年度	2014
出版社	Springer Vienna
DOI	https://doi.org/10.1007/978-3-7091-1562-6
序号	605
标题	**DNA Vaccines (Third Edition)**
副标题	Methods and Protocols
系列标题	Methods in Molecular Biology
作者	Monica Rinaldi, Daniela Fioretti, Sandra Iurescia
年度	2014
出版社	Humana New York
DOI	https://doi.org/10.1007/978-1-4939-0410-5
序号	606
标题	**Gene Therapy for HIV**
副标题	From Inception to a Possible Cure
系列标题	SpringerBriefs in Biochemistry and Molecular Biology
作者	Gerhard Bauer, Joseph S. Anderson
年度	2014
出版社	Springer New York
DOI	https://doi.org/10.1007/978-1-4939-0434-1
序号	607
标题	**Hepatitis C Virus and Liver Transplantation**
作者	Marina Berenguer
年度	2014
出版社	Springer New York
DOI	https://doi.org/10.1007/978-1-4614-8438-7
序号	608
标题	**Herpes Simplex Virus**
副标题	Methods and Protocols

续表

系列标题	Methods in Molecular Biology
作者	Russell J. Diefenbach, Cornel Fraefel
年度	2014
出版社	Humana New York
DOI	https://doi.org/10.1007/978-1-4939-0428-0
序号	609
标题	**HIV Glycans in Infection and Immunity**
作者	Ralph Pantophlet
年度	2014
出版社	Springer New York
DOI	https://doi.org/10.1007/978-1-4614-8872-9
序号	610
标题	**HIV/AIDS Communication in South Africa**
副标题	Are You Human?
作者	Colin Chasi
年度	2014
出版社	Palgrave Pivot London
DOI	https://doi.org/10.1057/9781137491299
序号	611
标题	**Host-Bacteria Interactions**
副标题	Methods and Protocols
系列标题	Methods in Molecular Biology
作者	Annette C. Vergunst, David O'Callaghan
年度	2014
出版社	Humana New York
DOI	https://doi.org/10.1007/978-1-4939-1261-2
序号	612
标题	**Humanized Mice for HIV Research**
作者	Larisa Y. Poluektova, J. Victor Garcia, Yoshio Koyanagi, Markus G. Manz, Andrew M. Tager

续表

年度	2014
出版社	Springer New York
DOI	https://doi.org/10.1007/978-1-4939-1655-9
序号	613
标题	**Infectious Complications in Cancer Patients**
系列标题	Cancer Treatment and Research
作者	Valentina Stosor, Teresa R. Zembower
年度	2014
出版社	Springer Cham
DOI	https://doi.org/10.1007/978-3-319-04220-6
序号	614
标题	**Infectious Diseases and Nanomedicine Ⅰ**
副标题	First International Conference(ICIDN-2012), Dec. 15-18, 2012, Kathmandu, Nepal
系列标题	Advances in Experimental Medicine and Biology
作者	Rameshwar Adhikari, Santosh Thapa
年度	2014
出版社	Springer New Delhi
DOI	https://doi.org/10.1007/978-81-322-1777-0
序号	615
标题	**Infectious Diseases and Nanomedicine Ⅱ**
副标题	First International Conference(ICIDN-2012), Dec. 15-18, 2012, Kathmandu, Nepal
系列标题	Advances in Experimental Medicine and Biology
作者	Rameshwar Adhikari, Santosh Thapa
年度	2014
出版社	Springer New Delhi
DOI	https://doi.org/10.1007/978-81-322-1774-9
序号	616
标题	**Infectious Microecology**
副标题	Theory and Applications

一、图书

续表

系列标题	Advanced Topics in Science and Technology in China
作者	Lanjuan Li
年度	2014
出版社	Springer Berlin, Heidelberg
DOI	https://doi.org/10.1007/978-3-662-43883-1
序号	617
标题	Influenza Pathogenesis and Control—Volume Ⅰ
系列标题	Current Topics in Microbiology and Immunology
作者	Richard W. Compans, Michael B. A. Oldstone
年度	2014
出版社	Springer Cham
DOI	https://doi.org/10.1007/978-3-319-11155-1
序号	618
标题	Innovations in HIV Prevention Research and Practice through Community Engagement
作者	Scott D. Rhodes
年度	2014
出版社	Springer New York
DOI	https://doi.org/10.1007/978-1-4939-0900-1
序号	619
标题	Insight into Influenza Viruses of Animals and Humans
作者	Sanjay Kapoor, Kuldeep Dhama
年度	2014
出版社	Springer Cham
DOI	https://doi.org/10.1007/978-3-319-05512-1
序号	620
标题	Microbicides for Prevention of HIV Infection
系列标题	Current Topics in Microbiology and Immunology
作者	Jeremy Nuttall
年度	2014

续表

出版社	Springer Berlin, Heidelberg
DOI	https://doi.org/10.1007/978-3-662-44596-9
序号	621
标题	**Molecular Vaccines**
副标题	From Prophylaxis to Therapy—Volume 2
作者	Matthias Giese
年度	2014
出版社	Springer Cham
DOI	https://doi.org/10.1007/978-3-319-00978-0
序号	622
标题	**Novel Technologies for Vaccine Development**
作者	Igor S Lukashevich, Haval Shirwan
年度	2014
出版社	Springer Vienna
DOI	https://doi.org/10.1007/978-3-7091-1818-4
序号	623
标题	**People Living with HIV in the USA and Germany**
副标题	A Comparative Study of Biographical Experiences of Chronic Illness
作者	Lauren Kaplan
年度	2014
出版社	Springer VS Wiesbaden
DOI	https://doi.org/10.1007/978-3-658-05267-6
序号	624
标题	**Radiology of HIV/AIDS**
副标题	A Practical Approach
作者	Hongjun Li
年度	2014
出版社	Springer Dordrecht
DOI	https://doi.org/10.1007/978-94-007-7823-8
序号	625

续表

标题	Sphingosine-1-Phosphate Signaling in Immunology and Infectious Diseases
系列标题	Current Topics in Microbiology and Immunology
作者	Michael B. A. Oldstone, Hugh Rosen
年度	2014
出版社	Springer Cham
DOI	https://doi.org/10.1007/978-3-319-05879-5
序号	626
标题	The Parasite-Stress Theory of Values and Sociality
副标题	Infectious Disease, History and Human Values Worldwide
作者	Randy Thornhill, Corey L. Fincher
年度	2014
出版社	Springer Cham
DOI	https://doi.org/10.1007/978-3-319-08040-6
序号	627
标题	The Role of Microbes in Common Non-Infectious Diseases
系列标题	Emerging Infectious Diseases of the 21st Century
作者	I.W. Fong
年度	2014
出版社	Springer New York
DOI	https://doi.org/10.1007/978-1-4939-1670-2
序号	628
标题	Understanding and Managing Vaccine Concerns
系列标题	SpringerBriefs in Public Health
作者	Julie A. Boom, Rachel M. Cunningham
年度	2014
出版社	Springer Cham
DOI	https://doi.org/10.1007/978-3-319-07563-1
序号	629
标题	Virus Hybrids as Nanomaterials
副标题	Methods and Protocols

续表

系列标题	Methods in Molecular Biology
作者	Baochuan Lin, Banahalli Ratna
年度	2014
出版社	Humana Totowa
DOI	https://doi.org/10.1007/978-1-62703-751-8
序号	630
标题	**Viruses and Human Cancer**
作者	S. David Hudnall
年度	2014
出版社	Springer New York
DOI	https://doi.org/10.1007/978-1-4939-0870-7
序号	631
标题	**Viruses and Human Cancer**
副标题	From Basic Science to Clinical Prevention
系列标题	Recent Results in Cancer Research
作者	Mei Hwei Chang, Kuan-Teh Jeang
年度	2014
出版社	Springer Berlin, Heidelberg
DOI	https://doi.org/10.1007/978-3-642-38965-8
序号	632
标题	**Viruses and Man: A History of Interactions**
作者	Milton W. Taylor
年度	2014
出版社	Springer Cham
DOI	https://doi.org/10.1007/978-3-319-07758-1
序号	633
标题	**Viruses and the Lung**
副标题	Infections and Non-Infectious Viral-Linked Lung Disorders
作者	Armando E. Fraire, Bruce A. Woda, Raymond M. Welsh, Richard L. Kradin
年度	2014

续表

出版社	Springer Berlin, Heidelberg
DOI	https://doi.org/10.1007/978-3-642-40605-8
序号	634
标题	**Advances in HIV-1 Assembly and Release**
作者	Eric O. Freed
年度	2013
出版社	Springer New York
DOI	https://doi.org/10.1007/978-1-4614-7729-7
序号	635
标题	**Best Evidence Structural Interventions for HIV Prevention**
作者	Rachel E. Golden, Charles B. Collins, Shayna D. Cunningham, Emily N. Newman, Josefina J. Card
年度	2013
出版社	Springer New York
DOI	https://doi.org/10.1007/978-1-4614-7013-7
序号	636
标题	**Challenges and Opportunities for Respiratory Syncytial Virus Vaccines**
系列标题	Current Topics in Microbiology and Immunology
作者	Larry J. Anderson, Barney S. Graham
年度	2013
出版社	Springer Berlin, Heidelberg
DOI	https://doi.org/10.1007/978-3-642-38919-1
序号	637
标题	**Challenges in Infectious Diseases**
系列标题	Emerging Infectious Diseases of the 21st Century
作者	I.W. Fong
年度	2013
出版社	Springer New York
DOI	https://doi.org/10.1007/978-1-4614-4496-1
序号	638

续表

标题	Crime, HIV and Health: Intersections of Criminal Justice and Public Health Concerns
作者	Bill Sanders, Yonette F. Thomas, Bethany Griffin Deeds
年度	2013
出版社	Springer Dordrecht
DOI	https://doi.org/10.1007/978-90-481-8921-2
序号	639
标题	Development of Novel Anti-HIV Pyrimidobenzothiazine Derivatives
系列标题	Springer Theses
作者	Tsukasa Mizuhara
年度	2013
出版社	Springer Tokyo
DOI	https://doi.org/10.1007/978-4-431-54445-6
序号	640
标题	Diabetes and Viruses
作者	Keith Taylor, Heikki Hyöty, Antonio Toniolo, Arie J. Zuckerman
年度	2013
出版社	Springer New York
DOI	https://doi.org/10.1007/978-1-4614-4051-2
序号	641
标题	Diversity, Biomineralization and Rock Magnetism of Magnetotactic Bacteria
系列标题	Springer Theses
作者	Wei Lin
年度	2013
出版社	Springer Berlin, Heidelberg
DOI	https://doi.org/10.1007/978-3-642-38262-8
序号	642
标题	Dynamic Models of Infectious Diseases
副标题	Volume 1: Vector-Borne Diseases
作者	Vadrevu Sree Hari Rao, Ravi Durvasula

续表

年度	2013
出版社	Springer New York
DOI	https://doi.org/10.1007/978-1-4614-3961-5
序号	643
标题	**Dynamic Models of Infectious Diseases**
副标题	Volume 2：Non Vector-Borne Diseases
作者	V. Sree Hari Rao，Ravi Durvasula
年度	2013
出版社	Springer New York
DOI	https://doi.org/10.1007/978-1-4614-9224-5
序号	644
标题	**EBNA1 and Epstein-Barr Virus Associated Tumours**
系列标题	SpringerBriefs in Cancer Research
作者	Lori Frappier
年度	2013
出版社	Springer New York
DOI	https://doi.org/10.1007/978-1-4614-6886-8
序号	645
标题	**Ecology of Parasite-Vector Interactions**
系列标题	Ecology and Control of Vector-Borne Diseases
作者	Willem Takken，Constantianus J. M. Koenraadt
年度	2013
出版社	Wageningen Academic Publishers Wageningen
DOI	https://doi.org/10.3920/978-90-8686-744-8
序号	646
标题	**Female Prisoners，AIDS，and Peer Programs**
副标题	How Female Offenders Transform Their Lives
系列标题	SpringerBriefs in Psychology
作者	Kimberly Collica
年度	2013

续表

出版社	Springer New York
DOI	https://doi.org/10.1007/978-1-4614-5110-5
序号	647
标题	**Folklore, Gender, and AIDS in Malawi**
副标题	No Secret Under the Sun
系列标题	Gender and Cultural Studies in Africa and the Diaspora
作者	Anika Wilson
年度	2013
出版社	Palgrave Macmillan New York
DOI	https://doi.org/10.1057/9781137322456
序号	648
标题	**Genetics of Bacteria**
作者	Sheela Srivastava
年度	2013
出版社	Springer New Delhi
DOI	https://doi.org/10.1007/978-81-322-1090-0
序号	649
标题	**Genome-Wide Prediction and Analysis of Protein-Protein Functional Linkages in Bacteria**
系列标题	SpringerBriefs in Systems Biology
作者	Vijaykumar Yogesh Muley, Vishal Acharya
年度	2013
出版社	Springer New York
DOI	https://doi.org/10.1007/978-1-4614-4705-4
序号	650
标题	**Giardia as a Foodborne Pathogen**
系列标题	SpringerBriefs in Food, Health, and Nutrition
作者	Lucy J. Robertson
年度	2013
出版社	Springer New York

DOI	https://doi.org/10.1007/978-1-4614-7756-3
序号	651
标题	**Hepatitis A Virus in Food**
副标题	Detection and Inactivation Methods
系列标题	SpringerBriefs in Food, Health, and Nutrition
作者	Glòria Sánchez
年度	2013
出版社	Springer New York
DOI	https://doi.org/10.1007/978-1-4614-7104-2
序号	652
标题	**Hepatitis C Virus: From Molecular Virology to Antiviral Therapy**
系列标题	Current Topics in Microbiology and Immunology
作者	Ralf Bartenschlager
年度	2013
出版社	Springer Berlin, Heidelberg
DOI	https://doi.org/10.1007/978-3-642-27340-7
序号	653
标题	**Hepatitis E Virus**
副标题	An Emerging Zoonotic and Foodborne Pathogen
系列标题	SpringerBriefs in Food, Health, and Nutrition
作者	Franco Maria Ruggeri, Ilaria Di Bartolo, Fabio Ostanello, Marcello Trevisani
年度	2013
出版社	Springer New York
DOI	https://doi.org/10.1007/978-1-4614-7522-4
序号	654
标题	**HIV Interactions with Dendritic Cells**
副标题	Infection and Immunity
作者	Li Wu, Olivier Schwartz
年度	2013
出版社	Springer New York

续表

DOI	https://doi.org/10.1007/978-1-4614-4433-6
序号	655
标题	**HIV Treatments as Prevention (TasP)**
副标题	Primer for Behavior-Based Implementation
系列标题	SpringerBriefs in Public Health
作者	Seth C. Kalichman
年度	2013
出版社	Springer New York
DOI	https://doi.org/10.1007/978-1-4614-5119-8
序号	656
标题	**HIV/AIDS Treatment in Resource Poor Countries**
副标题	Public Health Challenges
作者	Yichen Lu, Max Essex, Chris Chanyasulkit
年度	2013
出版社	Springer New York
DOI	https://doi.org/10.1007/978-1-4614-4520-3
序号	657
标题	**Host-Pathogen Interactions in Streptococcal Diseases**
系列标题	Current Topics in Microbiology and Immunology
作者	G. Singh Chhatwal
年度	2013
出版社	Springer Berlin, Heidelberg
DOI	https://doi.org/10.1007/978-3-642-36340-5
序号	658
标题	**Human Immunodeficiency Virus Reverse Transcriptase**
作者	Stuart LeGrice, Matthias Gotte
年度	2013
出版社	Springer New York
DOI	https://doi.org/10.1007/978-1-4614-7291-9
序号	659

续表

标题	Immunomic Discovery of Adjuvants and Candidate Subunit Vaccines
系列标题	Immunomics Reviews
作者	Darren R. Flower, Yvonne Perrie
年度	2013
出版社	Springer New York
DOI	https://doi.org/10.1007/978-1-4614-5070-2
序号	660
标题	**Infectious Agents and Cancer**
作者	Anton G. Kutikhin, Arseniy E. Yuzhalin, Elena B. Brusina
年度	2013
出版社	Springer Dordrecht
DOI	https://doi.org/10.1007/978-94-007-5955-8
序号	661
标题	**Infectious Diseases**
副标题	Selected Entries from the Encyclopedia of Sustainability Science and Technology
作者	Phyllis Kanki, Darrell Jay Grimes
年度	2013
出版社	Springer New York
DOI	https://doi.org/10.1007/978-1-4614-5719-0
序号	662
标题	**Iron Uptake in Bacteria with Emphasis on E. Coli and Pseudomonas**
系列标题	SpringerBriefs in Molecular Science
作者	Ranjan Chakraborty, Volkmar Braun, Klaus Hantke, Pierre Cornelis
年度	2013
出版社	Springer Dordrecht
DOI	https://doi.org/10.1007/978-94-007-6088-2
序号	663
标题	**Living with HIV and ARVs**
副标题	Three-Letter Lives

续表

作者	Corinne Squire
年度	2013
出版社	Palgrave Macmillan London
DOI	https://doi.org/10.1057/9781137313676
序号	664
标题	**Mental Health Practitioner's Guide to HIV/AIDS**
作者	Sana Loue
年度	2013
出版社	Springer New York
DOI	https://doi.org/10.1007/978-1-4614-5283-6
序号	665
标题	**Modeling the Interplay Between Human Behavior and the Spread of Infectious Diseases**
作者	Piero Manfredi, Alberto D'Onofrio
年度	2013
出版社	Springer New York
DOI	https://doi.org/10.1007/978-1-4614-5474-8
序号	666
标题	**Molecular Vaccines**
副标题	From Prophylaxis to Therapy—Volume 1
作者	Matthias Giese
年度	2013
出版社	Springer Vienna
DOI	https://doi.org/10.1007/978-3-7091-1419-3
序号	667
标题	**Mosquito Vectors of Japanese Encephalitis Virus from Northern India**
副标题	Role of BPD hop cage method
系列标题	SpringerBriefs in Animal Sciences
作者	Bina Pani Das
年度	2013

一、图书

续表

出版社	Springer New Delhi
DOI	https://doi.org/10.1007/978-81-322-0861-7
序号	668
标题	**Novel Immune Potentiators and Delivery Technologies for Next Generation Vaccines**
作者	Manmohan Singh
年度	2013
出版社	Springer New York
DOI	https://doi.org/10.1007/978-1-4614-5380-2
序号	669
标题	**One Health: The Human-Animal-Environment Interfaces in Emerging Infectious Diseases**
副标题	Food Safety and Security, and International and National Plans for Implementation of One Health Activities
系列标题	Current Topics in Microbiology and Immunology
作者	John S. Mackenzie, Martyn Jeggo, Peter Daszak, Juergen A. Richt
年度	2013
出版社	Springer Berlin, Heidelberg
DOI	https://doi.org/10.1007/978-3-642-35846-3
序号	670
标题	**One Health: The Human-Animal-Environment Interfaces in Emerging Infectious Diseases**
副标题	The Concept and Examples of a One Health Approach
系列标题	Current Topics in Microbiology and Immunology
作者	John S. Mackenzie, Martyn Jeggo, Peter Daszak, Juergen A. Richt
年度	2013
出版社	Springer Berlin, Heidelberg
DOI	https://doi.org/10.1007/978-3-642-36889-9
序号	671
标题	**Radiology of Influenza A (H1N1)**
作者	Hongjun Li, Ning Li

续表

年度	2013
出版社	Springer Dordrecht
DOI	https://doi.org/10.1007/978-94-007-6162-9
序号	672
标题	**Sendai Virus Vector**
副标题	Advantages and Applications
作者	Yoshiyuki Nagai
年度	2013
出版社	Springer Tokyo
DOI	https://doi.org/10.1007/978-4-431-54556-9
序号	673
标题	**Stigma, Discrimination and Living with HIV/AIDS**
副标题	A Cross-Cultural Perspective
作者	Pranee Liamputtong
年度	2013
出版社	Springer Dordrecht
DOI	https://doi.org/10.1007/978-94-007-6324-1
序号	674
标题	**Structure and Physics of Viruses**
副标题	An Integrated Textbook
系列标题	Subcellular Biochemistry
作者	Mauricio G. Mateu
年度	2013
出版社	Springer Dordrecht
DOI	https://doi.org/10.1007/978-94-007-6552-8
序号	675
标题	**Swine Influenza**
系列标题	Current Topics in Microbiology and Immunology
作者	Jürgen A. Richt, Richard J. Webby
年度	2013

续表

出版社	Springer Berlin, Heidelberg
DOI	https://doi.org/10.1007/978-3-642-36871-4
序号	676
标题	The New Public Health and STD/HIV Prevention
副标题	Personal, Public and Health Systems Approaches
作者	Sevgi O. Aral, Kevin A. Fenton, Judith A. Lipshutz
年度	2013
出版社	Springer New York
DOI	https://doi.org/10.1007/978-1-4614-4526-5
序号	677
标题	Vaccinophobia and Vaccine Controversies of the 21st Century
作者	Archana Chatterjee
年度	2013
出版社	Springer New York
DOI	https://doi.org/10.1007/978-1-4614-7438-8
序号	678
标题	Viruses and Atherosclerosis
系列标题	SpringerBriefs in Immunology
作者	Anton Kutikhin, Elena Brusina, Arseniy E. Yuzhalin
年度	2013
出版社	Springer New York
DOI	https://doi.org/10.1007/978-1-4614-8863-7
序号	679
标题	Virus-Host Interactions
副标题	Methods and Protocols
系列标题	Methods in Molecular Biology
作者	Susanne M. Bailer, Diana Lieber
年度	2013
出版社	Humana Totowa
DOI	https://doi.org/10.1007/978-1-62703-601-6

续表

序号	680
标题	**Virus-Induced Gene Silencing**
副标题	Methods and Protocols
系列标题	Methods in Molecular Biology
作者	Annette Becker
年度	2013
出版社	Humana Totowa
DOI	https://doi.org/10.1007/978-1-62703-278-0
序号	681
标题	**Vulnerabilities, Impacts, and Responses to HIV/AIDS in Sub-Saharan Africa**
作者	Getnet Tadele, Helmut Kloos
年度	2013
出版社	Palgrave Macmillan London
DOI	https://doi.org/10.1057/9781137009951
序号	682
标题	**Women, Motherhood and Living with HIV/AIDS**
副标题	A Cross-Cultural Perspective
作者	Pranee Liamputtong
年度	2013
出版社	Springer Dordrecht
DOI	https://doi.org/10.1007/978-94-007-5887-2
序号	683
标题	**Bacteria and Cancer**
作者	Abdul Arif Khan
年度	2012
出版社	Springer Dordrecht
DOI	https://doi.org/10.1007/978-94-007-2585-0
序号	684
标题	**Blastocystis: Pathogen or Passenger?**
副标题	An Evaluation of 101 Years of Research

续表

系列标题	Parasitology Research Monographs
作者	Heinz Mehlhorn, Kevin S. W. Tan, Hisao Yoshikawa
年度	2012
出版社	Springer Berlin, Heidelberg
DOI	https://doi.org/10.1007/978-3-642-32738-4
序号	685
标题	**Cancer Associated Viruses**
系列标题	Current Cancer Research
作者	Erle S. Robertson
年度	2012
出版社	Springer New York
DOI	https://doi.org/10.1007/978-1-4614-0016-5
序号	686
标题	**Chronic Hepatitis C Virus**
副标题	Advances in Treatment, Promise for the Future
作者	Mitchell L. Shiffman
年度	2012
出版社	Springer New York
DOI	https://doi.org/10.1007/978-1-4614-1192-5
序号	687
标题	**Control of Innate and Adaptive Immune Responses During Infectious Diseases**
作者	Julio Aliberti
年度	2012
出版社	Springer New York
DOI	https://doi.org/10.1007/978-1-4614-0484-2
序号	688
标题	**Cytopathology of Infectious Diseases**
系列标题	Essentials in Cytopathology
作者	Liron Pantanowitz, Pam Michelow, Walid E. Khalbuss
年度	2012

		续表
出版社	Springer New York	
DOI	https://doi.org/10.1007/978-1-4614-0242-8	
序号	689	
标题	**Development of Novel Vaccines**	
副标题	Skills, Knowledge and Translational Technologies	
作者	Alexander von Gabain, Christoph Klade	
年度	2012	
出版社	Springer Vienna	
DOI	https://doi.org/10.1007/978-3-7091-0709-6	
序号	690	
标题	**Family and HIV/AIDS**	
副标题	Cultural and Contextual Issues in Prevention and Treatment	
作者	Willo Pequegnat, Carl C. Bell	
年度	2012	
出版社	Springer New York	
DOI	https://doi.org/10.1007/978-1-4614-0439-2	
序号	691	
标题	**Feminisms, HIV and AIDS**	
副标题	Subverting Power, Reducing Vulnerability	
作者	Vicci Tallis	
年度	2012	
出版社	Palgrave Macmillan London	
DOI	https://doi.org/10.1057/9781137005793	
序号	692	
标题	**Gene Vaccines**	
作者	Josef Thalhamer, Richard Weiss, Sandra Scheiblhofer	
年度	2012	
出版社	Springer Vienna	
DOI	https://doi.org/10.1007/978-3-7091-0439-2	
序号	693	

续表

标题	HIV and Liver Disease
作者	Kenneth E. Sherman
年度	2012
出版社	Springer New York
DOI	https://doi.org/10.1007/978-1-4419-1712-6
序号	694
标题	Human Immunodeficiency Virus Type 1（HIV-1）and Breastfeeding
副标题	Science, Research Advances, and Policy
系列标题	Advances in Experimental Medicine and Biology
作者	Athena P. Kourtis, Marc Bulterys
年度	2012
出版社	Springer New York
DOI	https://doi.org/10.1007/978-1-4614-2251-8
序号	695
标题	Infectious Disease in India, 1892—1940
副标题	Policy-Making and the Perception of Risk
系列标题	Cambridge Imperial and Post-Colonial Studies
作者	Sandhya L. Polu
年度	2012
出版社	Palgrave Macmillan London
DOI	https://doi.org/10.1057/9781137009326
序号	696
标题	Influenza Virus
副标题	Methods and Protocols
系列标题	Methods in Molecular Biology
作者	Yoshihiro Kawaoka, Gabriele Neumann
年度	2012
出版社	Humana Totowa
DOI	https://doi.org/10.1007/978-1-61779-621-0
序号	697

续表

标题	Influenza Virus Sialidase—A Drug Discovery Target
系列标题	Milestones in Drug Therapy
作者	Mark Itzstein
年度	2012
出版社	Springer Basel
DOI	https://doi.org/10.1007/978-3-7643-8927-7
序号	698
标题	Maternal Fetal Transmission of Human Viruses and their Influence on Tumorigenesis
作者	György Berencsi Ⅲ
年度	2012
出版社	Springer Dordrecht
DOI	https://doi.org/10.1007/978-94-007-4216-1
序号	699
标题	Modeling Infectious Disease Parameters Based on Serological and Social Contact Data
副标题	A Modern Statistical Perspective
系列标题	Statistics for Biology and Health
作者	Niel Hens, Ziv Shkedy, Marc Aerts, Christel Faes, Pierre Van Damme, Philippe Beutels
年度	2012
出版社	Springer New York
DOI	https://doi.org/10.1007/978-1-4614-4072-7
序号	700
标题	**Mucosal Vaccines**
副标题	Modern Concepts, Strategies, and Challenges
系列标题	Current Topics in Microbiology and Immunology
作者	Pamela A. Kozlowski
年度	2012
出版社	Springer Berlin, Heidelberg
DOI	https://doi.org/10.1007/978-3-642-23693-8

续表

序号	701
标题	**New Frontiers of Molecular Epidemiology of Infectious Diseases**
作者	Serge Morand, François Beaudeau, Jacques Cabaret
年度	2012
出版社	Springer Dordrecht
DOI	https://doi.org/10.1007/978-94-007-2114-2
序号	702
标题	**Oncolytic Viruses**
副标题	Methods and Protocols
系列标题	Methods in Molecular Biology
作者	David H. Kirn, Ta-Chiang Liu, Stephen H. Thorne
年度	2012
出版社	Humana Totowa
DOI	https://doi.org/10.1007/978-1-61779-340-0
序号	703
标题	**Outer Membrane Vesicles of Bacteria**
系列标题	SpringerBriefs in Microbiology
作者	S.N. Chatterjee, Keya Chaudhuri
年度	2012
出版社	Springer Berlin, Heidelberg
DOI	https://doi.org/10.1007/978-3-642-30526-9
序号	704
标题	**Plague-Making and the AIDS Epidemic: A Story of Discrimination**
作者	Gina M. Bright
年度	2012
出版社	Palgrave Macmillan New York
DOI	https://doi.org/10.1057/9781137011220
序号	705
标题	**The Pathogenic Spirochetes: Strategies for Evasion of Host Immunity and Persistence**
作者	Monica E. Embers

续表

年度	2012
出版社	Springer New York
DOI	https://doi.org/10.1007/978-1-4614-5404-5
序号	706
标题	**Theology in the Age of Global AIDS & HIV**
副标题	Complicity and Possibility
系列标题	Content and Context in Theological Ethics
作者	Cassie J. E. H. Trentaz
年度	2012
出版社	Palgrave Macmillan New York
DOI	https://doi.org/10.1057/9781137272904
序号	707
标题	**Vaccinia Virus and Poxvirology（Second Edition）**
副标题	Methods and Protocols
系列标题	Methods in Molecular Biology
作者	Stuart N. Isaacs
年度	2012
出版社	Humana Totowa
DOI	https://doi.org/10.1007/978-1-61779-876-4
序号	708
标题	**Viruses：Essential Agents of Life**
作者	Günther Witzany
年度	2012
出版社	Springer Dordrecht
DOI	https://doi.org/10.1007/978-94-007-4899-6
序号	709
标题	**Acting on HIV**
作者	Dennis A. Francis
年度	2011
出版社	SensePublishers Rotterdam

续表

DOI	https://doi.org/10.1007/978-94-6091-594-9
序号	710
标题	**Adeno-Associated Virus**
副标题	Methods and Protocols
系列标题	Methods in Molecular Biology
作者	Richard O. Snyder, Philippe Moullier
年度	2011
出版社	Humana Totowa
DOI	https://doi.org/10.1007/978-1-61779-370-7
序号	711
标题	**Common Infectious Diseases of Insects in Culture**
副标题	Diagnostic and Prophylactic Methods
系列标题	SpringerBriefs in Animal Sciences
作者	Vladimir Gouli, Svetlana Gouli, Jose Marcelino
年度	2011
出版社	Springer Dordrecht
DOI	https://doi.org/10.1007/978-94-007-1890-6
序号	712
标题	**Community Theatre and AIDS**
系列标题	Studies in International Performance
作者	Ola Johansson
年度	2011
出版社	Palgrave Macmillan London
DOI	https://doi.org/10.1057/9780230300439
序号	713
标题	**Cysteine Proteases of Pathogenic Organisms**
系列标题	Advances in Experimental Medicine and Biology
作者	Mark W. Robinson, John P. Dalton
年度	2011
出版社	Springer New York

续表

DOI	https://doi.org/10.1007/978-1-4419-8414-2	
序号	714	
标题	Drug Interactions in Infectious Diseases（Third Edition）	
系列标题	Infectious Disease	
作者	Stephen C. Piscitelli, Keith A. Rodvold, Manjunath P. Pai	
年度	2011	
出版社	Humana Totowa	
DOI	https://doi.org/10.1007/978-1-61779-213-7	
序号	715	
标题	Generic and Specific Roles of Saccharides at Cell and Bacteria Surfaces	
副标题	Revealed by Specular and Off-Specular X-Ray and Neutron Scattering	
系列标题	Springer Theses	
作者	Emanuel Schneck	
年度	2011	
出版社	Springer Berlin, Hcidelberg	
DOI	https://doi.org/10.1007/978-3-642-15450-8	
序号	716	
标题	History of Vaccine Development	
作者	Stanley A. Plotkin	
年度	2011	
出版社	Springer New York	
DOI	https://doi.org/10.1007/978-1-4419-1339-5	
序号	717	
标题	Infectious Disease Informatics and Biosurveillance	
系列标题	Integrated Series in Information Systems	
作者	Carlos Castillo-Chavez, Hsinchun Chen, William B. Lober, Mark Thurmond, Daniel Zeng	
年度	2011	
出版社	Springer New York	
DOI	https://doi.org/10.1007/978-1-4419-6892-0	

续表

序号	718
标题	**Influenza Vaccines for the Future**
系列标题	Birkhäuser Advances in Infectious Diseases
作者	Rino Rappuoli, Giuseppe Del Giudice
年度	2011
出版社	Springer Basel
DOI	https://doi.org/10.1007/978-3-0346-0279-2
序号	719
标题	**Medico-Legal Issues in Infectious Diseases**
副标题	Guide For Physicians
系列标题	Emerging Infectious Diseases of the 21st Century
作者	I.W. Fong
年度	2011
出版社	Springer New York
DOI	https://doi.org/10.1007/978-1-4419-8053-3
序号	720
标题	**Principles and Practice of Cancer Infectious Diseases**
系列标题	Current Clinical Oncology
作者	Amar Safdar
年度	2011
出版社	Humana Totowa
DOI	https://doi.org/10.1007/978-1-60761-644-3
序号	721
标题	**Probiotic Bacteria and Enteric Infections**
副标题	Cytoprotection by Probiotic Bacteria
作者	J.J. Malago, J.F.J.G. Koninkx, R. Marinsek-Logar
年度	2011
出版社	Springer Dordrecht
DOI	https://doi.org/10.1007/978-94-007-0386-5
序号	722

续表

标题	**Replicating Vaccines**
副标题	A New Generation
系列标题	Birkhäuser Advances in Infectious Diseases
作者	Philip R. Dormitzer, Christian W. Mandl, Rino Rappuoli
年度	2011
出版社	Springer Basel
DOI	https://doi.org/10.1007/978-3-0346-0277-8
序号	723
标题	**Statistics in Clinical Vaccine Trials**
作者	Jozef Nauta
年度	2011
出版社	Springer Berlin, Heidelberg
DOI	https://doi.org/10.1007/978-3-642-14691-6
序号	724
标题	**The Springer Index of Viruses（2nd Edition）**
作者	Christian Tidona, Gholamreza Darai
年度	2011
出版社	Springer New York
DOI	https://doi.org/10.1007/978-0-387-95919-1
序号	725
标题	**Vaccines against Allergies**
系列标题	Current Topics in Microbiology and Immunology
作者	Rudolf Valenta, Robert L. Coffman
年度	2011
出版社	Springer Berlin, Heidelberg
DOI	https://doi.org/10.1007/978-3-642-20054-0
序号	726
标题	**Varicella-Zoster Virus Epithelial Keratitis in Herpes Zoster Ophthalmicus**
副标题	In Vivo Morphology in the Human Cornea
作者	Helena M. Tabery

续表

年度	2011
出版社	Springer Berlin, Heidelberg
DOI	https://doi.org/10.1007/978-3-642-14487-5
序号	727
标题	**African Americans and HIV/AIDS**
副标题	Understanding and Addressing the Epidemic
作者	Donna Hubbard McCree, Kenneth Jones, Ann O'Leary
年度	2010
出版社	Springer New York
DOI	https://doi.org/10.1007/978-0-387-78321-5
序号	728
标题	**AIDS and Aid**
副标题	A Public Good Approach
系列标题	Contributions to Economics
作者	Diana Sonntag
年度	2010
出版社	Physica Heidelberg
DOI	https://doi.org/10.1007/978-3-7908-2419-3
序号	729
标题	**AIDS Policy in Uganda**
副标题	Evidence, Ideology, and the Making of an African Success Story
作者	John Kinsman
年度	2010
出版社	Palgrave Macmillan New York
DOI	https://doi.org/10.1057/9780230112117
序号	730
标题	**Cell Entry by Non-Enveloped Viruses**
系列标题	Current Topics in Microbiology and Immunology
作者	John E. Johnson
年度	2010

续表

出版社	Springer Berlin, Heidelberg
DOI	https://doi.org/10.1007/978-3-642-13332-9
序号	731
标题	**Chronic Viral Hepatitis**
副标题	Diagnosis and Therapeutics
系列标题	Clinical Gastroenterology
作者	Kirti Shetty, George Y. Wu
年度	2010
出版社	Humana Totowa
DOI	https://doi.org/10.1007/978-1-59745-565-7
序号	732
标题	**Current Topics of Infectious Diseases in Japan and Asia**
作者	Kazuo Tanaka, Yoshihito Niki, Akatsuski Kokaze
年度	2010
出版社	Springer Tokyo
DOI	https://doi.org/10.1007/978-4-431-53875-2
序号	733
标题	**Dengue Virus**
系列标题	Current Topics in Microbiology and Immunology
作者	Alan L. Rothman
年度	2010
出版社	Springer Berlin, Heidelberg
DOI	https://doi.org/10.1007/978-3-642-02215-9
序号	734
标题	**Design and Analysis of Vaccine Studies**
系列标题	Statistics for Biology and Health
作者	M. Elizabeth Halloran, Ira M. Longini, Claudio J. Struchiner
年度	2010
出版社	Springer New York
DOI	https://doi.org/10.1007/978-0-387-68636-3

续表

序号	735
标题	**Detection of Bacteria, Viruses, Parasites and Fungi**
副标题	Bioterrorism Prevention
系列标题	NATO Science for Peace and Security Series A: Chemistry and Biology
作者	Mariapia Viola Magni
年度	2010
出版社	Springer Dordrecht
DOI	https://doi.org/10.1007/978-90-481-8544-3
序号	736
标题	**Emerging Infectious Diseases and Society**
作者	Peter Washer
年度	2010
出版社	Palgrave Macmillan London
DOI	https://doi.org/10.1057/9780230277182
序号	737
标题	**Herpes Simplex Virus Epithelial Keratitis**
副标题	In Vivo Morphology in the Human Cornea
作者	Helen Tabery
年度	2010
出版社	Springer Berlin, Heidelberg
DOI	https://doi.org/10.1007/978-3-642-01012-5
序号	738
标题	**HIV Treatment and Prevention Technologies in International Perspective**
作者	Mark Davis, Corinne Squire
年度	2010
出版社	Palgrave Macmillan London
DOI	https://doi.org/10.1057/9780230297050
序号	739
标题	**Infectious Disease Informatics**
作者	Vitali Sintchenko
年度	2010

续表

出版社	Springer New York
DOI	https://doi.org/10.1007/978-1-4419-1327-2
序号	740
标题	**Infectious Disease Informatics**
副标题	Syndromic Surveillance for Public Health and Bio-Defense
系列标题	Integrated Series in Information Systems
作者	Hsinchun Chen, Daniel Zeng, Ping Yan
年度	2010
出版社	Springer New York
DOI	https://doi.org/10.1007/978-1-4419-1278-7
序号	741
标题	**Management of Antimicrobials in Infectious Diseases**
副标题	Impact of Antibiotic Resistance
系列标题	Infectious Disease
作者	Arch G. Mainous Ⅲ, Claire Pomeroy
年度	2010
出版社	Humana Totowa
DOI	https://doi.org/10.1007/978-1-60327-239-1
序号	742
标题	**Modelling Parasite Transmission and Control**
系列标题	Advances in Experimental Medicine and Biology
作者	Edwin Michael, Robert C. Spear
年度	2010
出版社	Springer New York
DOI	https://doi.org/10.1007/978-1-4419-6064-1
序号	743
标题	**Modern Infectious Disease Epidemiology**
副标题	Concepts, Methods, Mathematical Models, and Public Health
系列标题	Statistics for Biology and Health
作者	Alexander Krämer, Mirjam Kretzschmar, Klaus Krickeberg

一、图书

续表

年度	2010
出版社	Springer New York
DOI	https://doi.org/10.1007/978-0-387-93835-6
序号	744
标题	Molecular Basis for Therapy of AIDS-Defining Cancers
作者	Dirk P. Dittmer, Susan E. Krown
年度	2010
出版社	Springer New York
DOI	https://doi.org/10.1007/978-1-4419-1513-9
序号	745
标题	Molecular Biology of the SARS-Coronavirus
作者	Sunil K. Lal
年度	2010
出版社	Springer Berlin, Heidelberg
DOI	https://doi.org/10.1007/978-3-642-03683-5
序号	746
标题	Neuropeptide Systems as Targets for Parasite and Pest Control
作者	Timothy G. Geary, Aaron G. Maule
年度	2010
出版社	Springer New York
DOI	https://doi.org/10.1007/978-1-4419-6902-6
序号	747
标题	Pathogenic Yeasts
系列标题	The Yeast Handbook
作者	Ruth Ashbee, Elaine M. Bignell
年度	2010
出版社	Springer Berlin, Heidelberg
DOI	https://doi.org/10.1007/978-3-642-03150-2
序号	748
标题	Prokaryotic and Eukaryotic Heat Shock Proteins in Infectious Disease
系列标题	Heat Shock Proteins

续表

作者	A. Graham Pockley, Stuart K. Calderwood, M. Gabriella Santoro
年度	2010
出版社	Springer Dordrecht
DOI	https://doi.org/10.1007/978-90-481-2976-8
序号	749
标题	**Structures and Organelles in Pathogenic Protists**
系列标题	Microbiology Monographs
作者	W. de Souza
年度	2010
出版社	Springer Berlin, Heidelberg
DOI	https://doi.org/10.1007/978-3-642-12863-9
序号	750
标题	**The Challenge of Highly Pathogenic Microorganisms**
副标题	Mechanisms of Virulence and Novel Medical Countermeasures
作者	Avigdor Shafferman, Arie Ordentlich, Baruch Velan
年度	2010
出版社	Springer Dordrecht
DOI	https://doi.org/10.1007/978-90-481-9054-6
序号	751
标题	**Vaccine Adjuvants**
副标题	Methods and Protocols
系列标题	Methods in Molecular Biology
作者	Gwyn Davies
年度	2010
出版社	Humana Totowa
DOI	https://doi.org/10.1007/978-1-60761-585-9
序号	752
标题	**Vaccines: A Biography**
作者	Andrew W. Artenstein
年度	2010

续表

出版社	Springer New York
DOI	https://doi.org/10.1007/978-1-4419-1108-7
序号	753
标题	**Varicella-Zoster Virus**
系列标题	Current Topics in Microbiology and Immunology
作者	Allison Abendroth, Ann M. Arvin, Jennifer F. Moffat
年度	2010
出版社	Springer Berlin, Heidelberg
DOI	https://doi.org/10.1007/978-3-642-12728-1
序号	754
标题	**Viral Hepatitis in Children**
副标题	Unique Features and Opportunities
系列标题	Clinical Gastroenterology
作者	Maureen M. Jonas
年度	2010
出版社	Humana Totowa
DOI	https://doi.org/10.1007/978-1-60761-373-2
序号	755

ScienceDirect

标题	Advances in Epidemiological Modeling and Control of Viruses
作者	Hemen Dutta, Khalid Hattaf
年度	2023
出版社	Academic Press
DOI	https://doi.org/10.1016/C2021-0-02192-1
序号	1
标题	Autoimmunity, COVID-19, Post-COVID19 Syndrome and COVID-19 Vaccination
作者	Yehuda Shoenfeld, Arad Dotan
年度	2023
出版社	Academic Press
DOI	https://doi.org/10.1016/C2021-0-03491-X
序号	2
标题	Big Data Analytics in Chemoinformatics and Bioinformatics
副标题	With Applications to Computer-Aided Drug Design, Cancer Biology, Emerging Pathogens and Computational Toxicology
作者	Subhash C. Basak, Marjan Vračko
年度	2023
出版社	Elsevier
DOI	https://doi.org/10.1016/C2020-0-02815-X
序号	3
标题	Clinical Management of Pediatric COVID-19
副标题	An International Perspective and Practical Guide
作者	Char Leung
年度	2023
出版社	Academic Press
DOI	https://doi.org/10.1016/C2021-0-02344-0
序号	4

续表

标题	Comprehensive Guide to Hepatitis Advances
作者	Wai-Kay Seto, Mohammed Eslam
年度	2023
出版社	Academic Press
DOI	https://doi.org/10.1016/C2021-0-01029-4
序号	5
标题	Computational Modeling of Infectious Disease
副标题	With Applications in Python
作者	Chris von Csefalvay
年度	2023
出版社	Academic Press
DOI	https://doi.org/10.1016/C2021-0-02868-6
序号	6
标题	Conceptual Development of Industrial Biotechnology for Commercial Production of Vaccines and Biopharmaceuticals
作者	Basanta Kumara Behera
年度	2023
出版社	Academic Press
DOI	https://doi.org/10.1016/C2022-0-00343-3
序号	7
标题	COVID-19 and Vaccine Nationalism
副标题	Managing the Politics of Global Pandemics
作者	Eric E. Otenyo
年度	2023
出版社	Academic Press
DOI	https://doi.org/10.1016/C2022-0-00438-4
序号	8
标题	Degradation of Antibiotics and Antibiotic-Resistant Bacteria from Various Sources
作者	Pardeep Singh, Mika Sillanpää

续表

年度	2023	
出版社	Academic Press	
DOI	https://doi.org/10.1016/C2021-0-00226-1	
序号	9	
标题	**Emerging Aquatic Contaminants**	
副标题	One Health Framework for Risk Assessment and Remediation in the Post COVID-19 Anthropocene	
作者	Manish Kumar, Sanjeeb Mohapatra, Karrie Weber	
年度	2023	
出版社	Elsevier	
DOI	https://doi.org/10.1016/C2021-0-02438-X	
序号	10	
标题	**Healthcare Systems Design of Intelligent Testing Centers**	
副标题	Latest Technologies to Battle Pandemics Such as COVID-19	
作者	Tawanda Mushiri, Marvellous Moyo	
年度	2023	
出版社	Academic Press	
DOI	https://doi.org/10.1016/C2021-0-02263-X	
序号	11	
标题	**Mathematical Modelling, Simulations, and AI for Emergent Pandemic Diseases**	
副标题	Lessons Learned from COVID-19	
作者	Esteban A. Hernandez-Vargas, Jorge X. Velasco-Hernández	
年度	2023	
出版社	Academic Press	
DOI	https://doi.org/10.1016/C2021-0-02691-2	
序号	12	
标题	**Omics Approaches and Technologies in COVID-19**	
作者	Debmalya Barh, Vasco Azevedo	
年度	2023	

一、图书

续表

出版社	Academic Press
DOI	https://doi.org/10.1016/C2021-0-00367-9
序号	13
标题	**Oncogenic Viruses**
副标题	Volume 1: Fundamentals of Oncoviruses
作者	Moulay Mustapha Ennaji
年度	2023
出版社	Academic Press
DOI	https://doi.org/10.1016/C2020-0-01595-1
序号	14
标题	**Oncogenic Viruses**
副标题	Volume 2: Medical Applications of Viral Oncology Research
作者	Moulay Mustapha Ennaji
年度	2023
出版社	Academic Press
DOI	https://doi.org/10.1016/C2020-0-01600-2
序号	15
标题	**Outbreaks, Epidemics, and Health Security**
副标题	COVID-19 and Ensuring Future Pandemic Preparedness in Ireland and the World
作者	Sebastian Kevany, Aoife Kirk
年度	2023
出版社	Academic Press
DOI	https://doi.org/10.1016/C2021-0-00988-3
序号	16
标题	**Textbook of SARS-CoV-2 and COVID-19**
副标题	Epidemiology, Etiopathogenesis, Immunology, Clinical Manifestations, Treatment, Complications, and Preventive Measures
作者	Subramani Mani, Jorn-Hendrik Weitkamp
年度	2023
出版社	Elsevier

续表

DOI	https://doi.org/10.1016/C2021-0-00062-6
序号	17
标题	**Viral, Parasitic, Bacterial, and Fungal Infections**
副标题	Antimicrobial, Host Defense, and Therapeutic Strategies
作者	Debasis Bagchi, Amitava Das, Bernard William Downs
年度	2023
出版社	Academic Press
DOI	https://doi.org/10.1016/C2020-0-02784-2
序号	18
标题	**Viruses(Second Edition)**
副标题	From Understanding to Investigation
作者	Susan Payne
年度	2023
出版社	Academic Press
DOI	https://doi.org/10.1016/C2020-0-03715-1
序号	19
标题	**A New History of Vaccines for Infectious Diseases**
副标题	Immunization—Chance and Necessity
作者	Anthony R. Rees
年度	2022
出版社	Academic Press
DOI	https://doi.org/10.1016/C2016-0-01809-0
序号	20
标题	**Academic Voices**
副标题	A Conversation on New Approaches to Teaching and Learning in the post-COVID World
作者	Upasana Gitanjali Singh, Chenicheri Sid Nair, Craig Blewett, Timothy Shea
年度	2022
出版社	Chandos Publishing
DOI	https://doi.org/10.1016/C2020-0-04518-4

续表

序号	21
标题	Advanced Biosensors for Virus Detection
副标题	Smart Diagnostics to Combat SARS-CoV-2
作者	Raju Khan, Arpana Parihar, Ajeet Kaushik, Ashok Kumar
年度	2022
出版社	Academic Press
DOI	https://doi.org/10.1016/C2020-0-01961-4
序号	22
标题	Application of Natural Products in SARS-CoV-2
作者	Kamal Niaz
年度	2022
出版社	Academic Press
DOI	https://doi.org/10.1016/C2021-0-01633-3
序号	23
标题	Artificial Intelligence, Machine Learning, and Mental Health in Pandemics
副标题	A Computational Approach
作者	Shikha Jain, Kavita Pandey, Princi Jain, Kah Phooi Seng
年度	2022
出版社	Academic Press
DOI	https://doi.org/10.1016/C2020-0-04085-5
序号	24
标题	Bacterial Physiology and Biochemistry
作者	Ivan Kushkevych
年度	2022
出版社	Academic Press
DOI	https://doi.org/10.1016/C2022-0-00345-7
序号	25
标题	Bacterial Survival in the Hostile Environment
作者	Ashutosh Kumar, Shivendra Tenguria
年度	2022

续表

出版社	Academic Press
DOI	https://doi.org/10.1016/C2021-0-01218-9
序号	26
标题	**Biology of Mycobacterial Lipids**
作者	Zeeshan Fatima, Stéphane Canaan
年度	2022
出版社	Academic Press
DOI	https://doi.org/10.1016/C2021-0-00081-X
序号	27
标题	**Biomedical Engineering Applications for People with Disabilities and the Elderly in the COVID-19 Pandemic and Beyond**
作者	Valentina Emilia Balas, Oana Geman
年度	2022
出版社	Academic Press
DOI	https://doi.org/10.1016/C2020-0-02408-4
序号	28
标题	**Biosensors for Emerging and Re-Emerging Infectious Diseases**
作者	Jayashankar Das, Sushma Dave, S. Radhakrishnan, Padmaja Mohanty
年度	2022
出版社	Academic Press
DOI	https://doi.org/10.1016/C2020-0-03552-8
序号	29
标题	**Cancer Vaccines as Immunotherapy of Cancer**
作者	Luigi Buonaguro, Sjoerd Van Der Burg
年度	2022
出版社	Academic Press
DOI	https://doi.org/10.1016/C2020-0-00683-3
序号	30

续表

标题	Computational Approaches for Novel Therapeutic and Diagnostic Designing to Mitigate SARS-CoV2 Infection
副标题	Revolutionary Strategies to Combat Pandemics
作者	Arpana Parihar, Raju Khan, Ashok Kumar, Ajeet Kumar Kaushik, Hardik Gohel
年度	2022
出版社	Academic Press
DOI	https://doi.org/10.1016/C2020-0-04145-9
序号	31
标题	**Coronavirus Drug Discovery**
副标题	Volume 1：SARS-CoV-2（COVID-19）Prevention, Diagnosis, and Treatment
作者	Chukwuebuka Egbuna
年度	2022
出版社	Elsevier
DOI	https://doi.org/10.1016/C2020-0-01736-6
序号	32
标题	**Coronavirus Drug Discovery**
副标题	Volume 2：Antiviral Agents from Natural Products and Nanotechnological Applications
作者	Chukwuebuka Egbuna
年度	2022
出版社	Elsevier
DOI	https://doi.org/10.1016/C2020-0-04144-7
序号	33
标题	**Coronavirus Drug Discovery**
副标题	Volume 3：Druggable Targets and in Silico Update
作者	Chukwuebuka Egbuna
年度	2022
出版社	Elsevier
DOI	https://doi.org/10.1016/C2020-0-04195-2
序号	34

续表

标题	**COVID-19 and the Sustainable Development Goals**
作者	Mohammad Hadi Dehghani, Rama Rao Karri, Sharmili Roy
年度	2022
出版社	Elsevier
DOI	https://doi.org/10.1016/C2021-0-00555-1
序号	35
标题	**Cyber-Physical Systems**
副标题	AI and COVID-19
作者	Ramesh Chandra Poonia, Basant Agarwal, Sandeep Kumar, Mohammad S. Khan, Gonçalo Marques, Janmenjoy Nayak
年度	2022
出版社	Academic Press
DOI	https://doi.org/10.1016/C2020-0-02352-2
序号	36
标题	**Data Science for COVID-19**
副标题	Volume 2: Societal and Medical Perspectives
作者	Utku Kose, Deepak Gupta, Victor Hugo C. de Albuquerque, Ashish Khanna
年度	2022
出版社	Academic Press
DOI	https://doi.org/10.1016/C2020-0-03702-3
序号	37
标题	**Digital Innovation for Healthcare in COVID-19 Pandemic**
副标题	Strategies and Solutions
作者	Patricia Ordóñez de Pablos, Kwok Tai Chui, Miltiadis D. Lytras
年度	2022
出版社	Academic Press
DOI	https://doi.org/10.1016/C2019-0-00357-3
序号	38
标题	**Human Pathogenic Microbes**
副标题	Diseases and Concerns

作者	Manzoor Ahmad Mir
年度	2022
出版社	Academic Press
DOI	https://doi.org/10.1016/C2021-0-02174-X
序号	39
标题	Innovative Data Integration and Conceptual Space Modeling for COVID, Cancer, and Cardiac Care
作者	Amy Neustein and Nathaniel Christen
年度	2022
出版社	Academic Press
DOI	https://doi.org/10.1016/C2020-0-02302-9
序号	40
标题	Lessons from COVID-19
副标题	Impact on Healthcare Systems and Technology
作者	Arturas Kaklauskas, Ajith Abraham, Kingsley Okoye, Shankru Guggari
年度	2022
出版社	Academic Press
DOI	https://doi.org/10.1016/C2021-0-00397-7
序号	41
标题	Mathematical Analysis of Infectious Diseases
作者	Praveen Agarwal, Juan J. Nieto, Delfim F.M. Torres
年度	2022
出版社	Academic Press
DOI	https://doi.org/10.1016/C2020-0-03443-2
序号	42
标题	Methods of Mathematical Modeling
副标题	Infectious Diseases
作者	Harendra Singh, Hari Mohan Srivastava, Dumitru Baleanu
年度	2022
出版社	Academic Press

续表

DOI	https://doi.org/10.1016/C2021-0-00445-4
序号	43
标题	Nanotheranostics for Treatment and Diagnosis of Infectious Diseases
作者	Keerti Jain, Javed Ahmad
年度	2022
出版社	Academic Press
DOI	https://doi.org/10.1016/C2020-0-03819-3
序号	44
标题	Novel AI and Data Science Advancements for Sustainability in the Era of COVID-19
作者	Victor Chang, Mohamed Abdel-Basset, Muthu Ramachandran, Nicolas G. Green, Gary Wills
年度	2022
出版社	Academic Press
DOI	https://doi.org/10.1016/C2020-0-03031-8
序号	45
标题	Pandemic Risk, Response, and Resilience
副标题	COVID-19 Responses in Cities Around the World
作者	Rajib Shaw, Indrajit Pal
年度	2022
出版社	Elsevier
DOI	https://doi.org/10.1016/C2021-0-00474-0
序号	46
标题	Pathogenic Coronaviruses of Humans and Animals
副标题	SARS, MERS, COVID-19, and Animal Coronaviruses with Zoonotic Potential
作者	Lisa A. Beltz
年度	2022
出版社	Academic Press
DOI	https://doi.org/10.1016/C2021-0-01541-8
序号	47

续表

标题	Principles and Practice of Pediatric Infectious Diseases (Sixth Edition)
作者	Sarah S. Long
年度	2022
出版社	Elsevier
DOI	https://doi.org/10.1016/C2019-0-00075-1
序号	48
标题	Sensing Tools and Techniques for COVID-19
副标题	Developments and Challenges in Analysis and Detection of Coronavirus
作者	Chaudhery Mustansar Hussain, Sudheesh K. Shukla
年度	2022
出版社	Elsevier
DOI	https://doi.org/10.1016/C2020-0-03440-7
序号	49
标题	Stem Cells and COVID-19
作者	Chandra P. Sharma, Devendra K. Agrawal, Finosh G. Thankam
年度	2022
出版社	Academic Press
DOI	https://doi.org/10.1016/C2020-0-03301-3
序号	50
标题	Techno-Economics and Life Cycle Assessment of Bioreactors
副标题	Post-Covid19 Waste Management Approach
作者	Puranjan Mishra, Lakhveer Singh, Pooja Ghosh
年度	2022
出版社	Elsevier
DOI	https://doi.org/10.1016/C2020-0-02993-2
序号	51
标题	The COVID-19 Pandemic
副标题	A Global High-Tech Challenge at the Interface of Science, Politics, and Illusions
作者	Klaus Rose
年度	2022

续表

出版社	Academic Press
DOI	https://doi.org/10.1016/C2021-0-01877-0
序号	52
标题	**The COVID-19 Response**
副标题	The Vital Role of the Public Health Professional
作者	Jennifer A. Horney
年度	2022
出版社	Academic Press
DOI	https://doi.org/10.1016/C2021-0-01543-1
序号	53
标题	**The Inequality of COVID-19**
副标题	Immediate Health Communication, Governance and Response in Four Indigenous Regions
作者	Eric E. Otenyo, Lisa J. Hardy
年度	2022
出版社	Academic Press
DOI	https://doi.org/10.1016/C2021-0-00231-5
序号	54
标题	**The Paradox of the Immune System**
副标题	Protection, Chronic Inflammation, Autoimmune Disease, Cancer, and Pandemics: The Enemy Within Us
作者	Louis J. Catania
年度	2022
出版社	Academic Press
DOI	https://doi.org/10.1016/C2021-0-02530-X
序号	55
标题	**Transportation Amid Pandemics**
副标题	Lessons Learned from COVID-19
作者	Junyi Zhang, Yoshitsugu Hayashi
年度	2022
出版社	Elsevier

续表

DOI	https://doi.org/10.1016/C2020-0-04079-X
序号	56
标题	**Vaccinology and Methods in Vaccine Research**
作者	Rebecca Ashfield, Angus Nnamdi Oli, Charles Esimone, Linda Anagu
年度	2022
出版社	Academic Press
DOI	https://doi.org/10.1016/C2020-0-04049-1
序号	57
标题	**Viruses, Bacteria and Fungi in the Built Environment**
副标题	Designing Healthy Indoor Environments
作者	Fernando Pacheco-Torgal, Volodymyr Ivanov, Joseph O. Falkinham
年度	2022
出版社	Woodhead Publishing
DOI	https://doi.org/10.1016/C2020-0-02035-9
序号	58
标题	**A Mechanistic Approach to Medicines for Tuberculosis Nanotherapy**
作者	Mariappan Rajan
年度	2021
出版社	Academic Press
DOI	https://doi.org/10.1016/C2019-0-01024-2
序号	59
标题	**A Rational Approach to Clinical Infectious Diseases**
副标题	A Manual for House Officers and Other Non-Infectious Diseases Clinicians
作者	Zelalem Temesgen
年度	2021
出版社	Elsevier
DOI	https://doi.org/10.1016/C2018-0-02478-0
序号	60

续表

标题	**Biomedical Engineering Tools for Management for Patients with COVID-19**
作者	Valentina E. Balas, Oana Geman, Guojun Wang, Muhammad Arif, Octavian Postolache
年度	2021
出版社	Academic Press
DOI	https://doi.org/10.1016/C2020-0-01980-8
序号	61
标题	**Biomedical Innovations to Combat COVID-19**
作者	Sergio Rosales-Mendoza, Mauricio Comas-Garcia, Omar Gonzalez-Ortega
年度	2021
出版社	Academic Press
DOI	https://doi.org/10.1016/C2020-0-03061-6
序号	62
标题	**Coronavirus Disease**
副标题	From Origin to Outbreak
作者	Adnan I.Adnan I. Qureshi, Omar Saeed and Uzma Syed Qureshi, Omar Saeed, Uzma Syed
年度	2021
出版社	Academic Press
DOI	https://doi.org/10.1016/C2020-0-01739-1
序号	63
标题	**COVID-19 in the Environment**
副标题	Impact, Concerns, and Management of Coronavirus
作者	Deepak Rawtani, Chaudhery Mustansar Hussain, Nitasha Khatri
年度	2021
出版社	Elsevier
DOI	https://doi.org/10.1016/C2020-0-03518-8
序号	64
标题	**COVID-19 Infections and Pregnancy**
作者	Ahmed M. Maged EL-GOLY

续表

年度	2021
出版社	Academic Press
DOI	https://doi.org/10.1016/C2020-0-03990-3
序号	65
标题	COVID-19 Pandemic
副标题	Lessons from the Frontline
作者	Jorge Hidalgo, Gloria Rodríguez-Vega, Javier Pérez-Fernández
年度	2021
出版社	Elsevier
DOI	https://doi.org/10.1016/C2020-0-02438-2
序号	66
标题	COVID-19: Tackling Global Pandemics Through Scientific and Social Tools
作者	Saptarshi Chatterjee
年度	2021
出版社	Academic Press
DOI	https://doi.org/10.1016/C2020-0-02335-2
序号	67
标题	Data Science for COVID-19
副标题	Computational Perspectives
作者	Utku Kose, Deepak Gupta, Victor Hugo C. de Albuquerque, Ashish Khanna
年度	2021
出版社	Academic Press
DOI	https://doi.org/10.1016/C2020-0-01677-4
序号	68
标题	Environmental and Health Management of Novel Coronavirus Disease (COVID-19)
作者	Mohammad Hadi Dehghani, Rama Rao Karri, Sharmili Roy
年度	2021
出版社	Academic Press
DOI	https://doi.org/10.1016/C2020-0-02837-9

续表

序号	69
标题	**Environmental Resilience and Transformation in Times of COVID-19**
副标题	Climate Change Effects on Environmental Functionality
作者	A.L. Ramanathan, Chidambaram Sabarathinam, Francisco Arriola, M.V. Prasanna, Pankaj Kumar, M.P. Jonathan
年度	2021
出版社	Elsevier
DOI	https://doi.org/10.1016/C2020-0-02703-9
序号	70
标题	**Genome Stability（Second Edition）**
副标题	From Virus to Human Application
作者	Igor Kovalchuk, Olga Kovalchuk
年度	2021
出版社	Academic Press
DOI	https://doi.org/10.1016/C2020-0-00641-9
序号	71
标题	**Inoculating Cities**
副标题	Case Studies of Urban Pandemic Preparedness
作者	Rebecca Katz, Matthew Boyce
年度	2021
出版社	Academic Press
DOI	https://doi.org/10.1016/C2019-0-01018-7
序号	72
标题	**iPSCs for Studying Infectious Diseases**
作者	Alexander Birbrair
年度	2021
出版社	Academic Press
DOI	https://doi.org/10.1016/C2020-0-00475-5
序号	73
标题	**Libraries, Digital Information, and COVID**
副标题	Practical Applications and Approaches to Challenge and Change

续表

作者	David Baker, Lucy Ellis
年度	2021
出版社	Chandos Publishing
DOI	https://doi.org/10.1016/C2020-0-03590-5
序号	74
标题	**Mental Health Effects of COVID-19**
作者	Ahmed A. Moustafa
年度	2021
出版社	Academic Press
DOI	https://doi.org/10.1016/C2020-0-02010-4
序号	75
标题	**Neglected Tropical Diseases and Other Infectious Diseases Affecting the Heart**
作者	Clara Saldarriaga, Adrian Baranchuk
年度	2021
出版社	Academic Press
DOI	https://doi.org/10.1016/C2020-0-03608-X
序号	76
标题	**Neurological Care and the COVID-19 Pandemic**
作者	Ahmad Riad Ramadan, Gamaleldin Osman
年度	2021
出版社	Elsevier
DOI	https://doi.org/10.1016/C2020-0-01927-4
序号	77
标题	**Pandemic Outbreaks in the 21st Century**
副标题	Epidemiology, Pathogenesis, Prevention, and Treatment
作者	Buddolla Viswanath
年度	2021
出版社	Academic Press
DOI	https://doi.org/10.1016/C2020-0-02063-3
序号	78

续表

标题	Pathogenesis, Treatment and Prevention of Leishmaniasis
作者	Mukesh Samant, Satish Chandra Pandey
年度	2021
出版社	Academic Press
DOI	https://doi.org/10.1016/C2019-0-04690-0
序号	79
标题	Practical Aspects of Vaccine Development
作者	Parag Kolhe, Satoshi Ohtake
年度	2021
出版社	Academic Press
DOI	https://doi.org/10.1016/C2017-0-01489-1
序号	80
标题	Researches and Applications of Artificial Intelligence to Mitigate Pandemics
副标题	History, Diagnostic Tools, Epidemiology, Healthcare, and Technology
作者	Kauser Hameed, Surbhi Bhatia, Syed Tousif Ahmed
年度	2021
出版社	Academic Press
DOI	https://doi.org/10.1016/C2020-0-03006-9
序号	81
标题	The Design and Development of Novel Drugs and Vaccines
副标题	Principles and Protocols
作者	Tarun Kumar Bhatt, Surendra Nimesh
年度	2021
出版社	Academic Press
DOI	https://doi.org/10.1016/C2019-0-03291-8
序号	82
标题	Visceral Leishmaniasis
副标题	Therapeutics and Vaccines
作者	Awanish Kumar

续表

年度	2021
出版社	Academic Press
DOI	https://doi.org/10.1016/C2020-0-03820-X
序号	83
标题	**Zika and Other Neglected and Emerging Flaviviruses**
副标题	The Continuing Threat to Human Health
作者	Lisa A. Beltz
年度	2021
出版社	Elsevier
DOI	https://doi.org/10.1016/C2020-0-01482-9
序号	84
标题	**Zika Virus Biology, Transmission, and Pathology**
副标题	Volume 1: The Neuroscience of Zika
作者	Colin R. Martin, Caroline J. Hollins Martin, Victor R. Preedy, Rajkumar Rajendram
年度	2021
出版社	Academic Press
DOI	https://doi.org/10.1016/C2019-0-01146-6
序号	85
标题	**Zika Virus Impact, Diagnosis, Control, and Models**
副标题	Volume 2: The Neuroscience of Zika
作者	Colin R. Martin, Caroline J. Hollins Martin, Victor R. Preedy, Rajkumar Rajendram
年度	2021
出版社	Academic Press
DOI	https://doi.org/10.1016/C2019-0-01147-8
序号	86
标题	**Colorectal Neoplasia and the Colorectal Microbiome**
副标题	Dysplasia, Probiotics, and Fusobacteria
作者	Martin H. Floch
年度	2020

续表

出版社	Academic Press
DOI	https://doi.org/10.1016/C2019-0-00354-8
序号	87
标题	**COVID-19**
副标题	The Essentials of Prevention and Treatment
作者	Jie-Ming Qu, Bin Cao, Rong-Chang Chen
年度	2020
出版社	Elsevier
DOI	https://doi.org/10.1016/C2020-0-01584-7
序号	88
标题	**Dengue Virus Disease**
副标题	From Origin to Outbreak
作者	Adnan I. Qureshi, Omar Saeed
年度	2020
出版社	Academic Press
DOI	https://doi.org/10.1016/C2018-0-01619-9
序号	89
标题	**Drug Discovery Targeting Drug-Resistant Bacteria**
作者	Prashant Kesharwani, Sidharth Chopra, Arunava Dasgupta
年度	2020
出版社	Academic Press
DOI	https://doi.org/10.1016/C2018-0-03400-3
序号	90
标题	**Emerging and Reemerging Viral Pathogens**
副标题	Volume 1: Fundamental and Basic Virology Aspects of Human, Animal and Plant Pathogens
作者	Moulay Mustapha Ennaji
年度	2020
出版社	Academic Press
DOI	https://doi.org/10.1016/C2018-0-04146-8

续表

序号	91
标题	Emerging and Reemerging Viral Pathogens
副标题	Volume 2: Applied Virology Approaches Related to Human, Animal and Environmental Pathogens
作者	Moulay Mustapha Ennaji
年度	2020
出版社	Academic Press
DOI	https://doi.org/10.1016/C2017-0-02031-1
序号	92
标题	Hunter's Tropical Medicine and Emerging Infectious Diseases(Tenth Edition)
作者	Edward T. Ryan, David R. Hill, Tom Solomon, Naomi E. Aronson, Timothy P. Endy
年度	2020
出版社	Elsevier
DOI	https://doi.org/10.1016/C2016-0-01879-X
序号	93
标题	Mucosal Vaccines(Second Edition)
副标题	Innovation for Preventing Infectious Diseases
作者	Hiroshi Kiyono, David W. Pascual
年度	2020
出版社	Academic Press
DOI	https://doi.org/10.1016/C2016-0-00017-7
序号	94
标题	Nanotechnology Based Approaches for Tuberculosis Treatment
作者	Prashant Kesharwani
年度	2020
出版社	Academic Press
DOI	https://doi.org/10.1016/C2019-0-00687-5
序号	95

续表

标题	**Nanotoxicity**
副标题	Prevention and Antibacterial Applications of Nanomaterials
作者	Susai Rajendran, Anita Mukherjee, Tuan Anh Nguyen, Chandraiah Godugu, Ritesh K. Shukla
年度	2020
出版社	Elsevier
DOI	https://doi.org/10.1016/C2018-0-05517-6
序号	96
标题	**Parasiticide Screening, Volume 1**
副标题	In Vitro and in Vivo Tests with Relevant Parasite Rearing and Host Infection/Infestation Methods
作者	Alan A. Marchiondo, Larry R. Cruthers, Josephus J. Fourie
年度	2020
出版社	Academic Press
DOI	https://doi.org/10.1016/C2016-0-02287-8
序号	97
标题	**Parasiticide Screening, Volume 2**
副标题	In Vitro and in Vivo Tests with Relevant Parasite Rearing and Host Infection/Infestation Methods
作者	Alan A. Marchiondo, Larry R. Cruthers, Josephus J. Fourie
年度	2020
出版社	Academic Press
DOI	https://doi.org/10.1016/C2018-0-00597-6
序号	98
标题	**Pediatric Transplant and Oncology Infectious Diseases**
作者	William J. Steinbach, Michael D. Green, Marian G. Michaels, Lara A. Danziger-Isakov, Brian T. Fisher
年度	2020
出版社	Elsevier
DOI	https://doi.org/10.1016/C2017-0-02892-6
序号	99

续表

标题	**Surveying the COVID-19 Pandemic and its Implications**
副标题	Urban Health, Data Technology and Political Economy
作者	Zaheer Allam
年度	2020
出版社	Elsevier
DOI	https://doi.org/10.1016/C2020-0-01743-3
序号	100
标题	**The Opioid Epidemic and Infectious Diseases**
作者	Brianna L. Norton
年度	2020
出版社	Elsevier
DOI	https://doi.org/10.1016/C2018-0-04198-5
序号	101
标题	**Vaccines for Veterinarians**
作者	Ian R. Tizard
年度	2020
出版社	Elsevier
DOI	https://doi.org/10.1016/C2018-0-01755-7
序号	102
标题	**Waterborne Pathogens**
副标题	Detection and Treatment
作者	Majeti Narasimha Vara Prasad, Anna Grobelak
年度	2020
出版社	Butterworth-Heinemann
DOI	https://doi.org/10.1016/C2018-0-02156-8
序号	103
标题	**Waterborne Pathogens(Second Edition)**
副标题	Detection Methods and Applications
作者	Helen Bridle
年度	2020

续表

出版社	Academic Press
DOI	https://doi.org/10.1016/C2018-0-00309-6
序号	104
标题	**Bacteriology Methods for the Study of Infectious Diseases**
作者	Rowena Jenkins, Sarah Maddocks
年度	2019
出版社	Academic Press
DOI	https://doi.org/10.1016/C2017-0-02665-4
序号	105
标题	**Genomic and Precision Medicine (Third Edition)**
副标题	Infectious and Inflammatory Disease
作者	Geoffrey S. Ginsburg, Huntington F. Willard, Ephraim L. Tsalik, Christopher W. Woods
年度	2019
出版社	Academic Press
DOI	https://doi.org/10.1016/C2015-0-06902-7
序号	106
标题	**Human Papillomavirus**
副标题	Proving and Using a Viral Cause for Cancer
作者	David Jenkins, F. Xavier Bosch
年度	2019
出版社	Academic Press
DOI	https://doi.org/10.1016/C2016-0-02398-7
序号	107
标题	**Infectious Disease and Pharmacology**
副标题	Neonatology Questions and Controversies
作者	William E. Benitz, P. Brian Smith
年度	2019
出版社	Elsevier
DOI	https://doi.org/10.1016/C2016-0-00250-4
序号	108

标题	Modeling and Control of Infectious Diseases in the Host	
副标题	With MATLAB and R	
作者	Edgar Sánchez	
年度	2019	
出版社	Academic Press	
DOI	https://doi.org/10.1016/C2016-0-04398-X	
序号	109	
标题	Nontuberculous Mycobacteria(NTM)	
副标题	Microbiological, Clinical and Geographical Distribution	
作者	Ali Akbar Velayati, Parissa Farnia	
年度	2019	
出版社	Academic Press	
DOI	https://doi.org/10.1016/C2017-0-01938-9	
序号	110	
标题	Rhinovirus Infections	
副标题	Rethinking the Impact on Human Health and Disease	
作者	Nathan Bartlett, Peter Wark, Darryl Knight	
年度	2019	
出版社	Academic Press	
DOI	https://doi.org/10.1016/C2017-0-04472-5	
序号	111	
标题	Taxonomic Guide to Infectious Diseases(Second Edition)	
副标题	Understanding the Biologic Classes of Pathogenic Organisms	
作者	Jules J. Berman	
年度	2019	
出版社	Academic Press	
DOI	https://doi.org/10.1016/C2018-0-00339-4	
序号	112	
标题	Virus as Populations(Second Edition)	
副标题	Composition, Complexity, Quasispecies, Dynamics, and Biological Implications	

续表

作者	Esteban Domingo
年度	2019
出版社	Academic Press
DOI	https://doi.org/10.1016/C2017-0-04115-0
序号	113
标题	**Canine Parasites and Parasitic Diseases**
作者	Seppo Saari, Anu Näreaho, Sven Nikander
年度	2018
出版社	Academic Press
DOI	https://doi.org/10.1016/C2016-0-05286-5
序号	114
标题	**Chikungunya and Zika Viruses**
副标题	Global Emerging Health Threats
作者	Stephen Higgs, Dana L. Vanlandingham, Ann M. Powers
年度	2018
出版社	Academic Press
DOI	https://doi.org/10.1016/C2016-0-01089-6
序号	115
标题	**Diagnostic Pathology of Infectious Disease(Second Edition)**
作者	Richard L. Kradin
年度	2018
出版社	Elsevier
序号	116
标题	**Ebola's Curse**
副标题	2013—2016 Outbreak in West Africa
作者	Michael B.A. Oldstone, Madeleine Rose Oldstone
年度	2018
出版社	Academic Press
序号	117
标题	**Harnessing the Power of Viruses**
作者	Boriana Marintcheva

续表

年度	2018
出版社	Academic Press
DOI	https://doi.org/10.1016/C2015-0-05654-4
序号	118
标题	**HIV/AIDS**
副标题	Oxidative Stress and Dietary Antioxidants
作者	Victor R. Preedy, Ronald Ross Watson
年度	2018
出版社	Academic Press
DOI	https://doi.org/10.1016/C2014-0-02340-4
序号	119
标题	**Human Microbiota in Health and Disease**
副标题	From Pathogenesis to Therapy
作者	Bryan Tungland
年度	2018
出版社	Academic Press
DOI	https://doi.org/10.1016/C2017-0-01893-1
序号	120
标题	**New and Future Developments in Microbial Biotechnology and Bioengineering**
副标题	Actinobacteria: Diversity and Biotechnological Applications
作者	Bhim Pratap Singh, Vijai Kumar Gupta, Ajit Kumar Passari
年度	2018
出版社	Elsevier
DOI	https://doi.org/10.1016/C2016-0-03789-0
序号	121
标题	**Plotkin's Vaccines(Seventh Edition)**
作者	Stanley A. Plotkin, Walter A. Orenstein, Paul A. Offit, Kathryn M. Edwards
年度	2018
出版社	Elsevier

续表

DOI	https://doi.org/10.1016/C2013-0-18914-3
序号	122
标题	**Principles and Practice of Pediatric Infectious Diseases(Fifth Edition)**
作者	Sarah S. Long, Charles G. Prober, Marc Fischer
年度	2018
出版社	Elsevier
DOI	https://doi.org/10.1016/C2013-0-19020-4
序号	123
标题	**Retrovirus-Cell Interactions**
作者	Leslie J. Parent
年度	2018
出版社	Academic Press
DOI	https://doi.org/10.1016/C2014-0-03142-5
序号	124
标题	**Studies on Hepatitis Viruses**
副标题	Life Cycle, Structure, Functions, and Inhibition
作者	Satya P. Gupta
年度	2018
出版社	Academic Press
DOI	https://doi.org/10.1016/C2016-0-03430-7
序号	125
标题	**The Bifidobacteria and Related Organisms**
副标题	Biology, Taxonomy, Applications
作者	Paola Mattarelli, Bruno Biavati, Wilhelm H. Holzapfel, Brian J.B. Wood
年度	2018
出版社	Academic Press
DOI	https://doi.org/10.1016/C2015-0-02462-5
序号	126
标题	**Vaccines for Cancer Immunotherapy**
副标题	An Evidence-Based Review on Current Status and Future Perspectives

续表

作者	Nima Rezaei, Mahsa Keshavarz-Fathi
年度	2018
出版社	Academic Press
DOI	https://doi.org/10.1016/C2017-0-01055-8
序号	127
标题	**Viruses**
副标题	Molecular Biology, Host Interactions and Applications to Biotechnology
作者	Paula Tennant, Gustavo Fermin, Jerome E. Foster
年度	2018
出版社	Academic Press
DOI	https://doi.org/10.1016/C2015-0-05650-7
序号	128
标题	**Zika Virus Disease**
副标题	From Origin to Outbreak
作者	Adnan I. Qureshi
年度	2018
出版社	Academic Press
DOI	https://doi.org/10.1016/C2016-0-01326-8
序号	129
标题	**A Historical Introduction to Mathematical Modeling of Infectious Diseases**
副标题	Seminal Papers in Epidemiology
作者	Ivo M. Foppa
年度	2017
出版社	Academic Press
DOI	https://doi.org/10.1016/C2014-0-01347-0
序号	130
标题	**Arthropod Vector: Controller of Disease Transmission, Volume 2**
副标题	Vector Saliva-Host Pathogen Interactions
作者	Stephen K. Wikel, Serap Aksoy, George Dimopoulos
年度	2017

续表

出版社	Academic Press
序号	131
标题	**Atlas of Mycobacterium Tuberculosis**
作者	Ali Akbar Velayati and Parissa Farnia
年度	2017
出版社	Academic Press
DOI	https://doi.org/10.1016/C2015-0-00386-0
序号	132
标题	**Early Warning for Infectious Disease Outbreak**
副标题	Theory and Practice
作者	Weizhong Yang
年度	2017
出版社	Academic Press
DOI	https://doi.org/10.1016/C2015-0-01494-0
序号	133
标题	**Fundamentals of Biologicals Regulation**
副标题	Vaccines and Biotechnology Medicines
作者	Rebecca Sheets
年度	2017
出版社	Academic Press
DOI	https://doi.org/10.1016/C2015-0-02183-9
序号	134
标题	**Genetics and Evolution of Infectious Diseases (Second Edition)**
作者	Michel Tibayrenc
年度	2017
出版社	Elsevier
序号	135
标题	**Hepatitis C in Developing Countries**
副标题	Current and Future Challenges
作者	Sanaa M. Kamal

续表

年度	2017
出版社	Academic Press
DOI	https://doi.org/10.1016/C2014-0-03892-0
序号	136
标题	**Human Vaccines**
副标题	Emerging Technologies in Design and Development
作者	Kayvon Modjarrad, Wayne C. Koff
年度	2017
出版社	Academic Press
DOI	https://doi.org/10.1016/C2014-0-00813-1
序号	137
标题	**Immunopotentiators in Modern Vaccines(Second Edition)**
作者	Virgil E.J.C. Schijns, Derek T. O'Hagan
年度	2017
出版社	Academic Press
序号	138
标题	**Infectious Diseases(Fourth Edition)**
作者	Jonathan Cohen, William G. Powderly, Steven M. Opal
年度	2017
出版社	Elsevier
DOI	https://doi.org/10.1016/C2013-1-00044-3
序号	139
标题	**Micro- and Nanotechnology in Vaccine Development**
作者	Mariusz Skwarczynski, Istvan Toth
年度	2017
出版社	Elsevier
序号	140
标题	**Molecular Virology of Human Pathogenic Viruses**
作者	Wang-Shick Ryu
年度	2017

续表

出版社	Academic Press	
DOI	https://doi.org/10.1016/C2013-0-15172-0	
序号	141	
标题	**The Norovirus**	
副标题	Features, Detection, and Prevention of Foodborne Disease	
作者	Paul K.S. Chan	
年度	2017	
出版社	Academic Press	
序号	142	
标题	**Viruses**	
副标题	From Understanding to Investigation	
作者	Susan Payne	
年度	2017	
出版社	Academic Press	
DOI	https://doi.org/10.1016/C2014-0-03894-4	
序号	143	
标题	**Core Concepts in Clinical Infectious Diseases（CCCID）**	
作者	Carlos Franco-Paredes	
年度	2016	
出版社	Academic Press	
DOI	https://doi.org/10.1016/C2015-0-01653-7	
序号	144	
标题	**Diagnostic Pathology: Infectious Diseases**	
作者	Danny A. Milner, Jr., Nicole Pecora, Isaac Solomon, Thing Rinda Soong	
年度	2016	
出版社	Elsevier	
序号	145	
标题	**Ebola Virus Disease**	
副标题	From Origin to Outbreak	
作者	Adnan I Qureshi	

年度	2016
出版社	Academic Press
DOI	https://doi.org/10.1016/C2015-0-00100-9
序号	146
标题	**Genome Stability**
副标题	From Virus to Human Application
作者	Igor Kovalchuk, Olga Kovalchuk
年度	2016
出版社	Academic Press
DOI	https://doi.org/10.1016/C2014-0-03956-1
序号	147
标题	**Linked by Blood: Hemophilia and AIDS**
作者	David Green
年度	2016
出版社	Academic Press
DOI	https://doi.org/10.1016/C2015-0-04898-5
序号	148
标题	**Mims' Pathogenesis of Infectious Disease(Sixth Edition)**
作者	Anthony A. Nash, Robert G. Dalziel, J. Ross Fitzgerald
年度	2016
出版社	Academic Press
序号	149
标题	**The Vaccine Book(Second Edition)**
作者	Barry R. Bloom, Paul-Henri Lambert
年度	2016
出版社	Academic Press
DOI	https://doi.org/10.1016/C2014-0-00804-0
序号	150
标题	**Vascular Responses to Pathogens**
作者	Felicity N.E. Gavins, Karen Y. Stokes

续表

年度	2016
出版社	Academic Press
序号	151
标题	**Viral Gastroenteritis**
副标题	Molecular Epidemiology and Pathogenesis
作者	Lennart Svensson, Ulrich Desselberger, Harry B. Greenberg, Mary K. Estes
年度	2016
出版社	Academic Press
DOI	https://doi.org/10.1016/C2014-0-03000-6
序号	152
标题	**Viral Pathogenesis(Third Edition)**
副标题	From Basics to Systems Biology
作者	Michael G. Katze, Marcus J. Korth, G. Lynn Law, Neal Nathanson
年度	2016
出版社	Academic Press
DOI	https://doi.org/10.1016/C2013-0-18782-X
序号	153
标题	**Virus as Populations**
副标题	Composition, Complexity, Dynamics, and Biological Implications
作者	Esteban Domingo
年度	2016
出版社	Academic Press
DOI	https://doi.org/10.1016/C2013-0-19052-6
序号	154
标题	**Foodborne Parasites in the Food Supply Web**
副标题	Occurrence and Control
作者	Alvin A. Gajadhar
年度	2015
出版社	Woodhead Publishing
DOI	https://doi.org/10.1016/C2014-0-02593-2

续表

序号	155
标题	**Health of HIV Infected People**
副标题	Food, Nutrition and Lifestyle with Antiretroviral Drugs
作者	Ronald Ross Watson
年度	2015
出版社	Academic Press
DOI	https://doi.org/10.1016/C2013-0-15173-2
序号	156
标题	**Health of HIV Infected People**
副标题	Food, Nutrition and Lifestyle Without Antiretroviral Drugs
作者	Ronald Ross Watson
年度	2015
出版社	Academic Press
DOI	https://doi.org/10.1016/C2013-0-16024-2
序号	157
标题	**Imported Infectious Diseases**
副标题	The Impact in Developed Countries
作者	Fernando Cobo
年度	2015
出版社	Woodhead Publishing
DOI	https://doi.org/10.1016/C2013-0-18223-2
序号	158
标题	**Mandell, Douglas, and Bennett's Principles and Practice of Infectious Diseases(Eighth Edition)**
作者	John E. Bennett, Raphael Dolin, Martin J. Blaser
年度	2015
出版社	Saunders
DOI	https://doi.org/10.1016/C2012-1-00075-6
序号	159
标题	**Nanotechnology in Diagnosis, Treatment and Prophylaxis of Infectious Diseases**
作者	Mahendra Rai, Kateryna Kon

续表

年度	2015
出版社	Academic Press
DOI	https://doi.org/10.1016/C2013-0-19425-1
序号	160
标题	Novel Approaches and Strategies for Biologics, Vaccines and Cancer Therapies
作者	Manmohan Singh, Maya Salnikova
年度	2015
出版社	Academic Press
DOI	https://doi.org/10.1016/C2013-0-00324-6
序号	161
标题	Streptococcus Pneumoniae
副标题	Molecular Mechanisms of Host-Pathogen Interactions
作者	Jeremy Brown, Sven Hammerschmidt, Carlos Orihuela
年度	2015
出版社	Academic Press
DOI	https://doi.org/10.1016/C2012-0-00722-3
序号	162
标题	The Comprehensive Sourcebook of Bacterial Protein Toxins (Fourth Edition)
作者	Joseph Alouf, Daniel Ladant, Michel R. Popoff
年度	2015
出版社	Elsevier
DOI	https://doi.org/10.1016/C2013-0-14258-4
序号	163
标题	Zoonotic Viruses of Northern Eurasia
副标题	Taxonomy and Ecology
作者	Dimitry Konstantinovich Lvov, Mikhail Yurievich Shchelkanov, Sergey Vladimirovich Alkhovsky, Petr Grigorievich Deryabin
年度	2015
出版社	Academic Press
DOI	https://doi.org/10.1016/C2014-0-01020-9

续表

序号	164
标题	**Canine and Feline Infectious Diseases**
作者	Jane E. Sykes
年度	2014
出版社	Saunders
DOI	https://doi.org/10.1016/C2009-0-41370-9
序号	165
标题	**Emerging Infectious Diseases**
副标题	Clinical Case Studies
作者	Önder Ergönül, Füsun Can, Lawrence Madoff, Murat Akova
年度	2014
出版社	Academic Press
DOI	https://doi.org/10.1016/C2012-0-07077-9
序号	166
标题	**Human Herpesviruses HHV-6A, HHV-6B & HHV-7(Third Edition)**
副标题	Diagnosis and Clinical Management
作者	Louis Flamand, Irmeli Lautenschlager, Gerhard R.F. Krueger, Dharam V. Ablashi
年度	2014
出版社	Elsevier Science
DOI	https://doi.org/10.1016/C2011-0-08453-3
序号	167
标题	**Manson's Tropical Infectious Diseases(Twenty-third Edition)**
作者	Jeremy Farrar, Peter J. Hotez, Thomas Junghanss, Gagandeep Kang, David Lalloo, Nicholas J. White
年度	2014
出版社	Saunders Ltd
DOI	https://doi.org/10.1016/C2010-0-66223-7
序号	168
标题	**Natural Hosts of SIV**
副标题	Implication in AIDS

续表

作者	Aftab A. Ansari, Guido Silvestri
年度	2014
出版社	Elsevier
DOI	https://doi.org/10.1016/C2012-0-00104-4
序号	169
标题	**The Flagellar World**
副标题	Electron Microscopic Images of Bacterial Flagella and Related Surface Structures
作者	Shin-Ichi Aizawa
年度	2014
出版社	Academic Press
DOI	https://doi.org/10.1016/C2013-0-06810-7
序号	170
标题	**Ascaris: The Neglected Parasite**
作者	Celia Holland
年度	2013
出版社	Academic Press
DOI	https://doi.org/10.1016/C2011-0-06705-4
序号	171
标题	**Bacterial Cellular Metabolic Systems**
副标题	Metabolic Regulation of a Cell System with 13c-Metabolic Flux Analysis
作者	Kazuyuki Shimizu
年度	2013
出版社	Woodhead Publishing
序号	172
标题	**Computer-Aided Vaccine Design**
作者	Joo Chuan Tong, Shoba Ranganathan
年度	2013
出版社	Woodhead Publishing
序号	173

一、图书

续表

标题	**Escherichia Coli（Second Edition）**
副标题	Pathotypes and Principles of Pathogenesis
作者	Michael S. Donnenberg
年度	2013
出版社	Academic Press
DOI	https://doi.org/10.1016/C2011-0-07692-5
序号	174
标题	**Nonclinical Development of Novel Biologics, Biosimilars, Vaccines and Specialty Biologics**
作者	Lisa M. Plitnick, Danuta J. Herzyk
年度	2013
出版社	Academic Press
DOI	https://doi.org/10.1016/C2011-0-07530-0
序号	175
标题	**Sexually Transmitted Diseases（Second Edition）**
副标题	Vaccines, Prevention, and Control
作者	Lawrence R. Stanberry, Susan L. Rosenthal
年度	2013
出版社	Academic Press
DOI	https://doi.org/10.1016/C2010-0-65551-9
序号	176
标题	**Vaccines（Sixth Edition）**
作者	Stanley A. Plotkin, Walter A. Orenstein, Paul A. Offit
年度	2013
出版社	Saunders
DOI	https://doi.org/10.1016/C2009-0-49973-2
序号	177
标题	**Viruses in Food and Water**
副标题	Risks, Surveillance and Control
作者	Nigel Cook

续表

年度	2013
出版社	Woodhead Publishing
序号	178
标题	**Waterborne Pathogens**
副标题	Detection Methods and Applications
作者	Helen Bridle
年度	2013
出版社	Academic Press
DOI	https://doi.org/10.1016/C2011-0-08797-5
序号	179
标题	**Bacterial Biogeochemistry（Third Edition）**
作者	T. Fenchel, G.M. King, T.H. Blackburn
年度	2012
出版社	Academic Press
DOI	https://doi.org/10.1016/C2010-0-67238-5
序号	180
标题	**Hematology, Immunology and Infectious Disease: Neonatology Questions and Controversies（Second Edition）**
作者	Robin K. Ohls, Akhil Maheshwari
年度	2012
出版社	Saunders
DOI	https://doi.org/10.1016/C2009-0-63835-6
序号	181
标题	**Human Papillomavirus Infections**
副标题	From the Laboratory to Clinical Practice
作者	Fernando Cobo
年度	2012
出版社	Woodhead Publishing
序号	182
标题	**Hunter's Tropical Medicine and Emerging Infectious Disease（Ninth Edition）**
作者	Alan J. Magill, David R Hill, Tom Solomon, Edward T Ryan

年度	2012
出版社	Saunders
DOI	https://doi.org/10.1016/C2009-0-51934-4
序号	183
标题	**Infectious Disease in Aquaculture**
副标题	Prevention and Control
作者	Brian Austin
年度	2012
出版社	Woodhead Publishing
序号	184
标题	**Netter's Infectious Diseases**
作者	Elaine C. Jong, Dennis L. Stevens
年度	2012
出版社	Saunders
序号	185
标题	**Parasitoid Viruses**
副标题	Symbionts and Pathogens
作者	Nancy E. Beckage, Jean-Michel Drezen
年度	2012
出版社	Academic Press
DOI	https://doi.org/10.1016/C2009-0-64055-1
序号	186
标题	**Principles and Practice of Pediatric Infectious Diseases(Fourth Edition)**
作者	Sarah S. Long
年度	2012
出版社	Saunders
序号	187
标题	**Sande's HIV/AIDS Medicine**
作者	Paul A. Volberding, Warner C. Greene, Joep M.A. Lange, Joel E. Gallant, Nelson Sewankambo

续表

年度	2012
出版社	Saunders
DOI	https://doi.org/10.1016/C2012-0-00849-6
序号	188
标题	**Taxonomic Guide to Infectious Diseases**
作者	Jules J. Berman
年度	2012
出版社	Academic Press
DOI	https://doi.org/10.1016/C2011-0-04443-5
序号	189
标题	**Atlas of Sexually Transmitted Diseases and AIDS（Fourth Edition）**
作者	Stephen A. Morse, Ronald C. Ballard, King K. Holmes, Adele A. Moreland
年度	2011
出版社	Saunders
序号	190
标题	**Genetics and Evolution of Infectious Diseases**
作者	Michel Tibayrenc
年度	2011
出版社	Elsevier
DOI	https://doi.org/10.1016/C2010-0-65658-6
序号	191
标题	**Infectious Diseases of the Fetus and Newborn（Seventh Edition）**
作者	Jack S. Remington, Jerome O. Klein, Christopher B. Wilson, Victor Nizet, Yvonne A. Maldonado
年度	2011
出版社	Saunders
DOI	https://doi.org/10.1016/C2009-0-50442-4
序号	192
标题	**Models of Protection Against HIV/SIV**
副标题	Avoiding AIDS in Humans and Monkeys

续表

作者	Gianfranco Pancino, Guido Silvestri, Keith R. Fowke
年度	2011
出版社	Academic Press
DOI	https://doi.org/10.1016/C2010-0-66611-9
序号	193
标题	Molecular Tools and Infectious Disease Epidemiology
作者	Betsy Foxman
年度	2011
出版社	Academic Press
DOI	https://doi.org/10.1016/C2009-0-01643-2
序号	194
标题	Tracing Pathogens in the Food Chain
作者	Stanley Brul, Pina M. Fratamico, Tom A. McMeekin
年度	2011
出版社	Woodhead Publishing
序号	195
标题	Tropical Infectious Diseases(Third Edition)
作者	Richard L. Guerrant, David H. Walker, Peter F. Weller
年度	2011
出版社	Saunders
DOI	https://doi.org/10.1016/C2009-0-40410-0
序号	196
标题	Virus Taxonomy: Ninth Report of the International Committee on Taxonomy of Viruses
副标题	Ninth Report of the International Committee on Taxonomy of Viruses
作者	Andrew M.Q. King, Michael J. Adams, Eric B. Carstens, Elliot J. Lefkowitz
年度	2011
出版社	Elsevier
序号	197
标题	Diagnostic Pathology of Infectious Disease
作者	Richard L. Kradin

续表

年度	2010
出版社	Saunders
序号	198
标题	**Infectious Diseases（Third Edition）**
作者	Jonathan Cohen, Steven M. Opal, William G. Powderly
年度	2010
出版社	Mosby
序号	199

Wiley

标题	Coronavirus Disease 2019（COVID-19）: A Clinical Guide
作者	Ali Gholamrezanezhad, Michael P. Dube
年度	2023
DOI	10.1002/9781119789741
序号	1
标题	Herbal Drugs for the Management of Infectious Diseases
作者	Inderbir Singh, Rakesh K. Sindhu, Atul Shirkhedkar, Pharkphoom Panichayupakaranant
年度	2022
DOI	10.1002/9781119818779
序号	2
标题	Impacts of the COVID-19 Pandemic: International Laws, Policies, and Civil Liberties
作者	Nadav Morag
年度	2022
DOI	10.1002/9781119812203
序号	3
标题	The COVID-19 Crisis: From a Question of an Epidemic to a Societal Questioning, Volume 4
作者	Bruno Salgues, Jacques Barnouin
年度	2022
DOI	10.1002/9781394163755
序号	4
标题	Unravelling Long COVID
作者	Don Goldenberg, Marc Dichter
年度	2022
DOI	10.1002/9781119891338
序号	5
标题	Communicating Science in Times of Crisis: The COVID-19 Pandemic
作者	H. Dan O'Hair, Mary John O'Hair

续表

年度	2021
DOI	10.1002/9781119751809
序号	6
标题	Detection and Analysis of SARS Coronavirus: Advanced Biosensors for Pandemic Viruses and Related Pathogens
作者	Chaudhery Mustansar Hussain, Sudheesh K. Shukla
年度	2021
DOI	10.1002/9783527832521
序号	7
标题	Enabling Healthcare 4.0 for Pandemics: A Roadmap Using AI, Machine Learning, IoT and Cognitive Technologies
作者	Abhinav Juneja, Vikram Bali, Sapna Juneja, Vishal Jain, Prashant Tyagi
年度	2021
DOI	10.1002/9781119769088
序号	8
标题	New Drug Development for Known and Emerging Viruses
作者	Helga Rübsamen-Schaeff, Helmut Buschmann
年度	2021
DOI	10.1002/9783527810697
序号	9
标题	Studies in Viral Ecology, Second Edition
作者	Christon J. Hurst
年度	2021
DOI	10.1002/9781119608370
序号	10
标题	Tuberculosis and Nontuberculous Mycobacterial Infections, Sixth Edition
作者	David Schlossberg
年度	2021
DOI	10.1128/9781555817138
序号	11

续表

标题	Veterinary Vaccines: Principles and Applications
作者	Samia Metwally, Ahmed El Idrissi, Gerrit Viljoen
年度	2021
DOI	10.1002/9781119506287
序号	12
标题	Atlas of Clinical Dermatopathology: Infectious and Parasitic Dermatoses
作者	Günter Burg, Heinz Kutzner, Werner Kempf, Josef Feit, Omar Sangueza
年度	2020
DOI	10.1002/9781119647096
序号	13
标题	Clinical Dilemmas in Viral Liver Disease, Second Edition
作者	Graham R. Foster, K. Rajender Reddy
年度	2020
DOI	10.1002/9781119533481
序号	14
标题	Infections of the Central Nervous System: Pathology and Genetics
作者	Fabrice Chrétien, Kum Thong Wong, Leroy R. Sharer, Catherine (Katy) Keohane, Françoise Gray
年度	2020
DOI	10.1002/9781119467748
序号	15
标题	Structure and Function of the Bacterial Genome
作者	Charles J. Dorman
年度	2020
DOI	10.1002/9781119309697
序号	16
标题	Bacteria and Intracellularity
作者	Pascale Cossart, Craig R. Roy, Philippe Sansonetti
年度	2019
DOI	10.1128/9781683670261

续表

序号	17
标题	**Bacterial Resistance to Antibiotics—From Molecules to Man**
作者	Boyan B. Bonev, Nicholas M. Brown
年度	2019
DOI	10.1002/9781119593522
序号	18
标题	**Gram–Positive Pathogens, Third Edition**
作者	Vincent A. Fischetti, Richard P. Novick, Joseph J. Ferretti, Daniel A. Portnoy, Miriam Braunstein, Julian I. Rood
年度	2019
DOI	10.1128/9781683670131
序号	19
标题	**Protein Secretion in Bacteria**
作者	Maria Sandkvist, Eric Cascales, Peter J. Christie
年度	2019
DOI	10.1128/9781683670285
序号	20
标题	**Antimicrobial Resistance in Bacteria from Livestock and Companion Animals**
作者	Stefan Schwarz, Lina Maria Cavaco, Jianzhong Shen
年度	2018
DOI	10.1128/9781555819804
序号	21
标题	**Communicable Disease Control and Health Protection Handbook, Fourth Edition**
作者	Jeremy Hawker, Norman Begg, Ralf Reintjes, Karl Ekdahl, Obaghe Edeghere, Jim van Steenbergen
年度	2018
DOI	10.1002/9781119328070
序号	22
标题	**Diagnostics to Pathogenomics of Sexually Transmitted Infections**
作者	Sunit K. Singh

续表

年度	2018
DOI	10.1002/9781119380924
序号	23
标题	**Evidence – Based Infectious Diseases, Third Edition**
作者	Dominik Mertz, Fiona Smaill, Nick Daneman
年度	2018
DOI	10.1002/9781119260363
序号	24
标题	**Microneedles for Drug and Vaccine Delivery and Patient Monitoring**
作者	F Donnelly Ryan
年度	2018
DOI	10.1002/9781119305101
序号	25
标题	**Rapid Infectious Diseases and Tropical Medicine**
作者	Rachel Isba
年度	2018
DOI	10.1002/9781119548430
序号	26
标题	**Regulating with RNA in Bacteria and Archaea**
作者	Gisela Storz, Kai Papenfort
年度	2018
DOI	10.1128/9781683670247
序号	27
标题	**Zika Virus and Diseases: From Molecular Biology to Epidemiology**
作者	Suzane Ramos da Silva, Fan Cheng, Shou-Jiang Gao
年度	2018
DOI	10.1002/9781119408673
序号	28
标题	**Bats and Human Health: Ebola, SARS, Rabies and Beyond**
作者	Lisa A. Beltz

续表

年度	2017
DOI	10.1002/9781119150060
序号	29
标题	Control of Salmonella and Other Bacterial Pathogens in Low Moisture Foods
作者	Richard Podolak, Darryl G. Black
年度	2017
DOI	10.1002/9781119071051
序号	30
标题	Infectious Diseases: A Geographic Guide, Second Edition
作者	Eskild Petersen, Lin H. Chen, Patricia Schlagenhauf-Lawlor
年度	2017
DOI	10.1002/9781119085751
序号	31
标题	Moonlighting Proteins: Novel Virulence Factors in Bacterial Infections
作者	Brian Henderson
年度	2017
DOI	10.1002/9781118951149
序号	32
标题	Tuberculosis and Nontuberculous Mycobacterial Infections, Seventh Edition
作者	David Schlossberg
年度	2017
DOI	10.1128/9781555819866
序号	33
标题	Tuberculosis and the Tubercle Bacillus, 2nd Edition
作者	William R. Jacobs Jr., Helen McShane, Valerie Mizrahi, Ian M. Orme
年度	2017
DOI	10.1128/9781555819569
序号	34
标题	Animal Influenza, Second Edition
作者	David E Swayne

续表

年度	2016
DOI	10.1002/9781118924341
序号	35
标题	Cases in Clinical Infectious Disease Practice: Obtaining a Good History from the Patient Remains The Cornerstone of an Accurate Clinical Diagnosis: Lessons Learned in Many Years of Clinical Practice
作者	Okechukwu Ekenna
年度	2016
DOI	10.1002/9781119044246
序号	36
标题	Chronic Pain and HIV: A Practical Approach
作者	Jessica S. Merlin, Peter A. Selwyn, Glenn J. Treisman, Angela G. Giovanniello
年度	2016
DOI	10.1002/9781118777374
序号	37
标题	Comprehensive Analysis of Parasite Biology: From Metabolism to Drug Discovery
作者	Sylke Müller, Rachel Cerdan, Ovidiu Radulescu
年度	2016
DOI	10.1002/9783527694082
序号	38
标题	Drug Delivery Systems for Tuberculosis Prevention and Treatment
作者	Anthony J. Hickey, Amit Misra, P. Bernard Fourie
年度	2016
DOI	10.1002/9781118943182
序号	39
标题	Emerging Infections 10
作者	W. Michael Scheld, James M. Hughes, Richard J. Whitley
年度	2016
DOI	10.1128/9781555819453

续表

序号	40
标题	Foodborne Pathogens and Antibiotic Resistance
作者	Om V. Singh
年度	2016
DOI	10.1002/9781119139188
序号	41
标题	Host – Pathogen Interaction: Microbial Metabolism, Pathogenicity and Antiinfectives
作者	Gottfried Unden, Eckhard Thines, Anja Schüffler
年度	2016
DOI	10.1002/9783527682386
序号	42
标题	Infections of Leisure, 5th Edition
作者	David Schlossberg
年度	2016
DOI	10.1128/9781555819231
序号	43
标题	Stress and Environmental Regulation of Gene Expression and Adaptation in Bacteria, Ⅰ & Ⅱ
作者	Frans J. de Bruijn
年度	2016
DOI	10.1002/9781119004813
序号	44
标题	The Bacterial Spore: From Molecules to Systems
作者	Adam Driks, Patrick Eichenberger
年度	2016
DOI	10.1128/9781555819323
序号	45
标题	Virulence Mechanisms of Bacterial Pathogens, 5th Edition
作者	Indira T. Kudva, Nancy A. Cornick, Paul J. Plummer, Qijing Zhang, Tracy L. Nicholson, John P. Bannantine, Bryan H. Bellaire

一、图书

续表

年度	2016
DOI	10.1128/9781555819286
序号	46
标题	**Antibodies for Infectious Diseases**
作者	James E. Crowe Jr., Diana Boraschi, Rino Rappuoli
年度	2015
DOI	10.1128/9781555817411
序号	47
标题	**Bats and Viruses: A New Frontier of Emerging Infectious Diseases**
作者	Lin-fa Wang, Christopher Cowled
年度	2015
DOI	10.1002/9781118818824
序号	48
标题	**Bergey's Manual of Systematics of Archaea and Bacteria**
年度	2015
DOI	10.1002/9781118960608
序号	49
标题	**Human Emerging and Re-Emerging Infections: Viral and Parasitic Infections, Volume Ⅰ**
作者	Sunit Kumar Singh
年度	2015
DOI	10.1002/9781118644843
序号	50
标题	**Metabolism and Bacterial Pathogenesis**
作者	Tyrrell Conway, Paul Cohen
年度	2015
DOI	10.1128/9781555818883
序号	51
标题	**Modern Techniques for Pathogen Detection**
作者	Jürgen Popp, Michael Bauer

续表

年度	2015
DOI	10.1002/9783527687978
序号	52
标题	**Vaccines and Autoimmunity**
作者	Yehuda Shoenfeld, Nancy Agmon-Levin, Lucija Tomljenovic
年度	2015
DOI	10.1002/9781118663721
序号	53
标题	**Zoonoses: Infectious Diseases Transmissible Between Animals and Humans**
作者	Rolf Bauerfeind, Alexander von Graevenitz, Peter Kimmig, Hans Gerd Schiefer, Tino Schwarz, Werner Slenczka, Horst Zahner
年度	2015
DOI	10.1128/9781555819262
序号	54
标题	**Analyzing and Modeling Spatial and Temporal Dynamics of Infectious Diseases**
作者	Dongmei Chen, Bernard Moulin, Jianhong Wu
年度	2014
DOI	10.1002/9781118630013
序号	55
标题	**Autophagy, Infection, and the Immune Response**
作者	William T. Jackson, Michele S. Swanson
年度	2014
DOI	10.1002/9781118677551
序号	56
标题	**Concepts and Methods in Infectious Disease Surveillance**
作者	Nkuchia M. M'ikanatha, John K. Iskander
年度	2014
DOI	10.1002/9781118928646
序号	57

标题	DNA Methods in Food Safety: Molecular Typing of Foodborne and Waterborne Bacterial Pathogens
作者	Omar A. Oyarzabal, Sophia Kathariou
年度	2014
DOI	10.1002/9781118278666
序号	58
标题	HIV and Psychiatry
作者	John A. Joska, Dan J. Stein, Igor Grant
年度	2014
DOI	10.1002/9781118339503
序号	59
标题	Microsporidia: Pathogens of Opportunity, First Edition
作者	Louis M. Weiss, James J. Becnel
年度	2014
DOI	10.1002/9781118395264
序号	60
标题	Protein Aggregation in Bacteria: Functional and Structural Properties of Inclusion Bodies in Bacterial Cells
作者	Silvia Maria Doglia, Marina Lotti
年度	2014
DOI	10.1002/9781118845363
序号	61
标题	Vaccine Development and Manufacturing
作者	Emily P. Wen, Ronald Ellis, Narahari S. Pujar
年度	2014
DOI	10.1002/9781118870914
序号	62
标题	Zoonotic Tuberculosis: Mycobacterium Bovis and Other Pathogenic Mycobacteria, Third Edition
作者	Charles O. Thoen, James H. Steele, John B. Kaneene
年度	2014

续表

DOI	10.1002/9781118474310	
序号	63	
标题	Diagnostic Imaging of Infections and Inflammatory Diseases: A Multidisciplinary Approach	
作者	Alberto Signore, Ana María Quintero	
年度	2013	
DOI	10.1002/9781118484388	
序号	64	
标题	Evidence – Based Neonatal Infections	
作者	David Isaacs	
年度	2013	
DOI	10.1002/9781118636657	
序号	65	
标题	Guide to Foodborne Pathogens, Second Edition	
作者	Ronald G. Labbé, Santos García	
年度	2013	
DOI	10.1002/9781118684856	
序号	66	
标题	Identification of Pathogenic Fungi, Second Edition	
作者	Colin K. Campbell, Elizabeth M. Johnson, David W. Warnock	
年度	2013	
DOI	10.1002/9781118520055	
序号	67	
标题	Infectious Disease Surveillance, Second Edition	
作者	Nkuchia M. M'ikanatha, Ruth Lynfield, Chris A. Van Beneden, Henriette de Valk	
年度	2013	
DOI	10.1002/9781118543504	
序号	68	
标题	Pandemics and Emerging Infectious Diseases: The Sociological Agenda	
作者	Robert Dingwall, Lily M. Hoffman, Karen Staniland	

续表

年度	2013
DOI	10.1002/9781118553923
序号	69
标题	**Protein Phosphorylation in Parasites**
作者	Christian Doerig, Gerald Späth, Martin Wiese
年度	2013
DOI	10.1002/9783527675401
序号	70
标题	**Textbook of Influenza, 2nd Edition**
作者	Robert G. Webster, Arnold S. Monto, Thomas J. Braciale, Robert A. Lamb
年度	2013
DOI	10.1002/9781118636817
序号	71
标题	**To Catch a Virus**
作者	John Booss, Marilyn J. August
年度	2013
DOI	10.1128/9781555818586
序号	72
标题	**Viral Hepatitis, Fourth Edition**
作者	Howard C. Thomas, Anna S.F. Lok, Stephen A. Locarnini, Arie J. Zuckerman
年度	2013
DOI	10.1002/9781118637272
序号	73
标题	**Viral Infections and Global Change**
作者	Sunit K. Singh
年度	2013
DOI	10.1002/9781118297469
序号	74
标题	**A Concise Manual of Pathogenic Microbiology**
作者	Saroj K. Mishra, Dipti Agrawal

续表

年度	2012
DOI	10.1002/9781118301234
序号	75
标题	**Atlas of Human Infectious Diseases**
作者	Heiman F. L. Wertheim, Peter Horby, John P. Woodall
年度	2012
DOI	10.1002/9781444354690
序号	76
标题	**Communicable Disease Control and Health Protection Handbook, Third Edition**
作者	Jeremy Hawker, Norman Begg, Iain Blair, Ralf Reintjes, Julius Weinberg, Karl Ekdahl
年度	2012
DOI	10.1002/9781444346961
序号	77
标题	**Fungal Infection: Diagnosis and Management, Fourth Edition**
作者	Malcolm D. Richardson, David W. Warnock
年度	2012
DOI	10.1002/9781118321492
序号	78
标题	**Genome Plasticity and Infectious Diseases**
作者	Jörg Hacker, Ulrich Dobrindt, Reinhard Kurth President Emeritus
年度	2012
DOI	10.1128/9781555817213
序号	79
标题	**Immunity to Parasitic Infection**
作者	Tracey J. Lamb
年度	2012
DOI	10.1002/9781118393321
序号	80

续表

标题	Intracellular Pathogens Ⅰ: Chlamydiales
作者	Ming Tan, Patrik M. Bavoil
年度	2012
DOI	10.1128/9781555817329
序号	81
标题	Intracellular Pathogens Ⅱ: Rickettsiales
作者	Guy H. Palmer, Abdu F. Azad
年度	2012
DOI	10.1128/9781555817336
序号	82
标题	Non-Neoplastic Hematopathology and Infections
作者	Hernani D. Cualing, Parul Bhargava, Ramon L. Sandin
年度	2012
DOI	10.1002/9781118158562
序号	83
标题	Parasitic Helminths: Targets, Screens, Drugs and Vaccines
作者	Conor R. Caffrey
年度	2012
DOI	10.1002/9783527652969
序号	84
标题	Regulation of Bacterial Virulence
作者	Michael L. Vasil, Andrew J. Darwin
年度	2012
DOI	10.1128/9781555818524
序号	85
标题	Reverse Genetics of RNA Viruses: Applications and Perspectives
作者	Anne Bridgen
年度	2012
DOI	10.1002/9781118405338
序号	86

续表

标题	Advanced Therapy for Hepatitis C
作者	Geoffrey W. McCaughan, John G. McHutchison, Jean-Michel Pawlotsky
年度	2011
DOI	10.1002/9781444346343
序号	87
标题	Apicomplexan Parasites: Molecular Approaches Toward Targeted Drug Development
作者	Katja Becker
年度	2011
DOI	10.1002/9783527633883
序号	88
标题	Bacteria: The Benign, the Bad, and the Beautiful
作者	Trudy M. Wassenaar
年度	2011
DOI	10.1002/9781118143391
序号	89
标题	Development of Vaccines: From Discovery to Clinical Testing
作者	Manmohan Singh, Indresh K. Srivastava
年度	2011
DOI	10.1002/9781118023648
序号	90
标题	Flexible Viruses: Structural Disorder in Viral Proteins
作者	Vladimir N. Uversky, Sonia Longhi
年度	2011
DOI	10.1002/9781118135570
序号	91
标题	Germ Theory: Medical Pioneers in Infectious Diseases
作者	Robert P. Gaynes MD
年度	2011
DOI	10.1128/9781555817220

续表

序号	92
标题	HIV – 1 Integrase: Mechanism and Inhibitor Design
作者	Nouri Neamati
年度	2011
DOI	10.1002/9781118015377
序号	93
标题	Infectious Diseases: A Geographic Guide
作者	Eskild Petersen, Lin H. Chen, Patricia Schlagenhauf
年度	2011
DOI	10.1002/9781119971641
序号	94
标题	Molecular Techniques for the Study of Hospital – Acquired Infection
作者	Steven L. Foley, Anne Y. Chen, Shabbir Simjee, Marcus J. Zervos
年度	2011
DOI	10.1002/9781118063842
序号	95
标题	Population Genetics of Bacteria: A Tribute to Thomas S. Whittam
作者	Seth T. Walk, Peter C. H. Feng
年度	2011
DOI	10.1128/9781555817114
序号	96
标题	Rapid Detection, Characterization, and Enumeration of Foodborne Pathogens
作者	J. Hoorfar
年度	2011
DOI	10.1128/9781555817121
序号	97
标题	Salmon Lice: An Integrated Approach to Understanding Parasite Abundance and Distribution
作者	Simon Jones, Richard Beamish
年度	2011

续表

DOI	10.1002/9780470961568
序号	98
标题	**Studies in Viral Ecology: Animal Host Systems, Volume 2**
作者	Christon J. Hurst
年度	2011
DOI	10.1002/9781118025710
序号	99
标题	**Studies in Viral Ecology: Microbial and Botanical Host Systems, Volume 1**
作者	Christon J. Hurst
年度	2011
DOI	10.1002/9781118025666
序号	100
标题	**The AST Handbook of Transplant Infections**
作者	Deepali Kumar, Atul Humar
年度	2011
DOI	10.1002/9781444397949
序号	101
标题	**Veterinary Infection Prevention and Control**
作者	Linda Caveney, Barbara Jones, Kimberly Ellis
年度	2011
DOI	10.1002/9781119266037
序号	102
标题	**Bacillus Anthracis and Anthrax**
作者	Nicholas H. Bergman
年度	2010
DOI	10.1002/9780470891193
序号	103
标题	**Bacterial Population Genetics in Infectious Disease**
作者	D. Ashley Robinson, Daniel Falush, Edward J. Feil
年度	2010

续表

DOI	10.1002/9780470600122
序号	104
标题	**Bacterial Stress Responses, Second Edition**
作者	Gisela Storz, Regine Hengge
年度	2010
DOI	10.1128/9781555816841
序号	105
标题	**Bacterial Virulence: Basic Principles, Models and Global Approaches**
作者	Philippe Sansonetti
年度	2010
DOI	10.1002/9783527629664
序号	106
标题	**Bacteriophages in the Control of Food- and Waterborne Pathogens**
作者	Parviz M. Sabour, Mansel W. Griffiths
年度	2010
DOI	10.1128/9781555816629
序号	107
标题	**Biofilm Eradication and Prevention: A Pharmaceutical Approach to Medical Device Infections**
作者	Tamilvanan Shunmugaperumal
年度	2010
DOI	10.1002/9780470640463
序号	108
标题	**Clinical Dilemmas in Viral Liver Disease**
作者	Graham R. Foster, K. Rajender Reddy
年度	2010
DOI	10.1002/9781444319590
序号	109
标题	**Cryptococcus: From Human Pathogen to Model Yeast**
作者	Joseph Heitman, Thomas R. Kozel, Kyung J. Kwon-Chung, John R. Perfect, Arturo Casadevall

续表

年度	2010	
DOI	10.1128/9781555816858	
序号	110	
标题	**Emerging Infections 9**	
作者	W. Michael Scheld, M. Lindsay Grayson, James M. Hughes	
年度	2010	
DOI	10.1128/9781555816803	
序号	111	
标题	**Genomes of Foodborne and Waterborne Pathogens**	
作者	Pina Fratamico, Yanhong Liu, Sophia Kathariou	
年度	2010	
DOI	10.1128/9781555816902	
序号	112	
标题	**Infectious Causes of Cancer: A Guide for Nurses and Healthcare Professionals**	
作者	Kenneth Campbell	
年度	2010	
DOI	10.1002/9780470753651	
序号	113	
标题	**Nutrition and HIV**	
作者	Vivian Pribram	
年度	2010	
DOI	10.1002/9781118786529	
序号	114	
标题	**Pathogenesis of Bacterial Infections in Animals, Fourth Edition**	
作者	Carlton L. Gyles, John F. Prescott, J. Glenn Songer, Charles O. Thoen	
年度	2010	
DOI	10.1002/9780470958209	
序号	115	
标题	**The Fecal Bacteria**	
作者	Michael J. Sadowsky, Richard L. Whitman	

续表

年度	2010
DOI	10.1128/9781555816865
序号	116
标题	**The Immune Response to Infection**
作者	Stefan H. E. Kaufmann, Barry T. Rouse, David L. Sacks
年度	2010
DOI	10.1128/9781555816872
序号	117
标题	**The Lure of Bacterial Genetics: A Tribute to John Roth**
作者	Stanley Maloy, Kelly T. Hughes, Josep Casadesús
年度	2010
DOI	10.1128/9781555816810
序号	118
标题	**Topley & Wilson's Microbiology and Microbial Infections**
作者	Brian W. J. Mahy, Volker ter Meulen, S. Peter Borriello
年度	2010
DOI	10.1002/9780470688618
序号	119

Taylor Francis

标题	Case Studies in Infectious Disease
作者	Peter Lydyard, Michael Cole, John Holton, Will Irving, Nino Porakishvili, Pradhib Venkatesan, te Ward
年度	2023
出版社	CRC Press
DOI	https://doi.org/10.1201/9781003155447
序号	1
标题	Communicating Through a Pandemic
副标题	A Chronicle of Experiences, Lessons Learned, and a Vision for the Future
作者	Amelia Burke-Garcia
年度	2023
出版社	Productivity Press
DOI	https://doi.org/10.4324/9781003267522
序号	2
标题	COVID Conspiracy Theories in Global Perspective
作者	Michael Butter, Peter Knight
年度	2023
出版社	Routledge
DOI	https://doi.org/10.4324/9781003330769
序号	3
标题	COVID-19 in Brooklyn
副标题	Everyday Life During a Pandemic
作者	Jerome Krase, Judith DeSena
年度	2023
出版社	Routledge
DOI	https://doi.org/10.4324/9781003302124
序号	4
标题	COVID-19: Individual Rights and Community Responsibilities
作者	J. Michael Ryan

续表

年度	2023
出版社	Routledge
DOI	https://doi.org/10.4324/9781003302643
序号	5
标题	Democracy, State Capacity and the Governance of COVID-19 in Asia-Oceania
作者	Aurel Croissant, Olli Hellmann
年度	2023
出版社	Routledge
DOI	https://doi.org/10.4324/9781003362456
序号	6
标题	From Hippocrates to COVID-19
副标题	A Bibliographic History of Medicine
作者	Dale A. Stirling
年度	2023
出版社	Jenny Stanford Publishing
DOI	https://doi.org/10.1201/9781003282785
序号	7
标题	From the Pandemic to Utopia
副标题	The Future Begins Now
作者	Boaventura de Sousa Santos
年度	2023
出版社	Routledge
DOI	https://doi.org/10.4324/9781003327400
序号	8
标题	Mental Health and Psychosocial Support During the COVID-19 Response
副标题	An Overview
作者	Joseph O. Prewitt Diaz
年度	2023
出版社	Apple Academic Press

续表

DOI	https://doi.org/10.1201/9781003347620	
序号	9	
标题	**Opportunistic Premise Plumbing Pathogens**	
作者	Joseph O. Falkinham, Ⅲ	
年度	2023	
出版社	Jenny Stanford Publishing	
DOI	https://doi.org/10.1201/9781003321002	
序号	10	
标题	**Pandemic Communication**	
作者	Stephen M. Croucher, Audra Diers-Lawson	
年度	2023	
出版社	Routledge	
DOI	https://doi.org/10.4324/9781003214496	
序号	11	
标题	**Pandemic Pedagogies**	
副标题	Teaching and Learning During the COVID-19 Pandemic	
作者	J. Michael Ryan	
年度	2023	
出版社	Routledge	
DOI	https://doi.org/10.4324/9781003324096	
序号	12	
标题	**Policy Evaluation in the Era of COVID-19**	
作者	Pearl Eliadis, Indran A. Naidoo, Ray C. Rist	
年度	2023	
出版社	Routledge	
DOI	https://doi.org/10.4324/9781003376316	
序号	13	
标题	**Psychoanalysis, COVID and Mass Trauma**	
副标题	The Trauma of Reality	
作者	Tihamér Bakó, Katalin Zana	

续表

年度	2023
出版社	Routledge
DOI	https://doi.org/10.4324/9781003194064
序号	14
标题	Racial Equity, COVID-19, and Public Policy
副标题	The Triple Pandemic
作者	Elsie L. Harper-Anderson, Jay S. Albanese, Susan T. Gooden
年度	2023
出版社	Routledge
DOI	https://doi.org/10.4324/9781003286967
序号	15
标题	Rights at Stake and the COVID-19 Pandemic
副标题	Two Special Issues of the Journal of Human Rights
作者	Shareen Hertel, Catherine Buerger
年度	2023
出版社	Routledge
DOI	https://doi.org/10.4324/9781003270195
序号	16
标题	The Role of GIS in COVID-19 Management and Control
作者	Esra Ozdenerol
年度	2023
出版社	CRC Press
DOI	https://doi.org/10.1201/9781003227106
序号	17
标题	The Usage and Impact of ICTs During the COVID-19 Pandemic
作者	Shengnan Yang, Xiaohua Zhu, Pnina Fichman
年度	2023
出版社	Routledge
DOI	https://doi.org/10.4324/9781003231769
序号	18

续表

标题	Understanding the Behavioral and Medical Impact of Long COVID
副标题	An Empirical Guide to Assessment and Treatment of Post-Acute Sequelae of SARS CoV-2 Infection
作者	Leonard A. Jason, Charles Lapp
年度	2023
出版社	Routledge
DOI	https://doi.org/10.4324/9781003371090
序号	19
标题	**Virus Detection**
作者	Charles H. Wick
年度	2023
出版社	CRC Press
DOI	https://doi.org/10.1201/9781003106623
序号	20
标题	**Art-Based Research in the Context of a Global Pandemic**
作者	Usva Seregina, Astrid Van den Bossche
年度	2022
出版社	Routledge
DOI	https://doi.org/10.4324/9781003170518
序号	21
标题	**Artificial Intelligence Applications in a Pandemic COVID-19**
作者	Salah-ddine Krit, Vrijendra Singh, Mohamed Elhoseny, Yashbir Singh
年度	2022
出版社	CRC Press
DOI	https://doi.org/10.1201/9781003126218
序号	22
标题	**Bioprocessing of Viral Vaccines**
作者	Amine Kamen, Laura Cervera
年度	2022
出版社	CRC Press

DOI	https://doi.org/10.1201/9781003229797
序号	23
标题	**Capitalism, Coronavirus and War**
副标题	A Geopolitical Economy
作者	Radhika Desai
年度	2022
出版社	Routledge
DOI	https://doi.org/10.4324/9781003200000
序号	24
标题	**Cities Learning from a Pandemic**
副标题	Towards Preparedness
作者	Simonetta Armondi, Alessandro Balducci, Martina Bovo, Beatrice Galimberti
年度	2022
出版社	Routledge
DOI	https://doi.org/10.4324/9781003240983
序号	25
标题	**Community Colleges' Responses to COVID-19**
副标题	What Worked, What Did Not Work, and Lessons Learned
作者	Deborah L. Floyd, Christopher M. Mullin, Gianna Ramdin
年度	2022
出版社	Routledge
DOI	https://doi.org/10.4324/9781003297123
序号	26
标题	**Conspiracy Theories in the Time of COVID-19**
作者	Clare Birchall, Peter Knight
年度	2022
出版社	Routledge
DOI	https://doi.org/10.4324/9781003315438
序号	27
标题	**Contemporary States and the Pandemic**
作者	Jolanta Itrich-Drabarek

续表

年度	2022
出版社	Routledge India
DOI	https://doi.org/10.4324/9781003353805
序号	28
标题	**COVID Transmission Modeling**
副标题	An Insight into Infectious Diseases Mechanism
作者	DM Basavarajaiah, B Narasimha Murthy
年度	2022
出版社	Chapman and Hall/CRC
DOI	https://doi.org/10.1201/9781003204794
序号	29
标题	**COVID-19**
副标题	Confronting a New World Risk
作者	Jamie K. Wardman, Ragnar Löfstedt
年度	2022
出版社	Routledge
DOI	https://doi.org/10.4324/9781003316169
序号	30
标题	**COVID-19**
副标题	From Bench to Bedside
作者	Debmalya Barh, Kenneth Lundstrom
年度	2022
出版社	CRC Press
DOI	https://doi.org/10.1201/9781003190394
序号	31
标题	**COVID-19 and Atrocity Prevention in East Asia**
作者	Noel M. Morada, Mely Caballero-Anthony
年度	2022
出版社	Routledge
DOI	https://doi.org/10.4324/9781003307471

续表

序号	32
标题	**COVID-19 and Childhood Inequality**
作者	Nazneen Khan
年度	2022
出版社	Routledge
DOI	https://doi.org/10.4324/9781003250937
序号	33
标题	**COVID-19 and Education in Africa**
副标题	Challenges, Possibilities, and Opportunities
作者	Lydia Namatende-Sakwa, Sarah Lewinger, Catherine Langsford
年度	2022
出版社	Routledge
DOI	https://doi.org/10.4324/9781003269625
序号	34
标题	**COVID-19 and Foreign Aid**
副标题	Nationalism and Global Development in a New World Order
作者	Viktor Jakupec, Max Kelly, Michael de Percy
年度	2022
出版社	Routledge
DOI	https://doi.org/10.4324/9781003273844
序号	35
标题	**COVID-19 and India's Northeast**
副标题	Psychological and Social Imprints
作者	Indranee Phookan Borooah, Sabiha Alam Choudhury, Bidita Das
年度	2022
出版社	Routledge India
DOI	https://doi.org/10.4324/9781003289654
序号	36
标题	**COVID-19 and SARS-CoV-2**
副标题	The Science and Clinical Application of Conventional and Complementary Treatments

续表

作者	Srijan Goswami, Chiranjeeb Dey
年度	2022
出版社	CRC Press
DOI	https://doi.org/10.1201/9781003178514
序号	37
标题	COVID-19 and Social Change in Spain
作者	Carlos de Castro, Andrés Pedreño, Marta Latorre
年度	2022
出版社	Routledge
DOI	https://doi.org/10.4324/9781003281719
序号	38
标题	COVID-19 and Speech-Language Pathology
作者	Louise Cummings
年度	2022
出版社	Routledge
DOI	https://doi.org/10.4324/9781003257318
序号	39
标题	COVID-19 and the Global Political Economy
作者	Tim Di Muzio, Matt Dow
年度	2022
出版社	Routledge
DOI	https://doi.org/10.4324/9781003250432
序号	40
标题	COVID-19 and the Soccer World
作者	Kausik Bandyopadhyay
年度	2022
出版社	Routledge
DOI	https://doi.org/10.4324/9781003318811
序号	41
标题	COVID-19 and the Tourism Industry
副标题	Sustainability, Resilience and New Directions

作者	Anukrati Sharma, Azizul Hassan, Priyakrushna Mohanty
年度	2022
出版社	Routledge
DOI	https://doi.org/10.4324/9781003207467
序号	42
标题	**COVID-19 in India, Disease, Health and Culture**
副标题	Can Wellness Be Far Behind?
作者	Anindita Chatterjee, Nilanjana Chatterjee
年度	2022
出版社	Routledge
DOI	https://doi.org/10.4324/9781003300762
序号	43
标题	**COVID-19 in Indonesia**
副标题	Impacts on the Economy and Ways to Recovery
作者	Lili Yan Ing, M. Chatib Basri
年度	2022
出版社	Routledge
DOI	https://doi.org/10.4324/9781003243670
序号	44
标题	**COVID-19 in Italy**
副标题	Social Behavior and Governmental Policies
作者	Lucia Velotti, Gabriella Punziano, Felice Addeo
年度	2022
出版社	Routledge
DOI	https://doi.org/10.4324/9781003187752
序号	45
标题	**COVID-19 in South, West, and Southeast Asia**
副标题	Risk and Response in the Early Phase
作者	Mohd Mizan Aslam, Rohan Gunaratna
年度	2022

出版社	Routledge
DOI	https://doi.org/10.4324/9781003291909
序号	46
标题	COVID-19 in the Commonwealth
作者	Derek McDougall, Suan Ee Ong
年度	2022
出版社	Routledge
DOI	https://doi.org/10.4324/9781003341291
序号	47
标题	COVID-19 Pandemic
副标题	The Threat and Response
作者	Rohan Kumar Gunaratna, Mohd Aslam
年度	2022
出版社	Routledge
DOI	https://doi.org/10.4324/9781003197416
序号	48
标题	COVID-19 Pandemic, Public Policy, and Institutions in India
副标题	Issues of Labour, Income, and Human Development
作者	Indranil De, Soumyadip Chattopadhyay, Hippu Salk Kristle Nathan, Kingshuk Sarkar
年度	2022
出版社	Routledge
DOI	https://doi.org/10.4324/9781003226970
序号	49
标题	COVID-19 Responses of Local Communities Around the World
副标题	Exploring Trust in the Context of Risk and Fear
作者	Khun Eng Kuah, Gilles Guiheux, Francis K.G. Lim
年度	2022
出版社	Routledge
DOI	https://doi.org/10.4324/9781003291220

续表

序号	50
标题	COVID-19 Through the Lens of Mental Health in India
副标题	Present Status and Future Directions
作者	Tilottama Mukherjee
年度	2022
出版社	Routledge India
DOI	https://doi.org/10.4324/9781003348429
序号	51
标题	COVID-19, Older Adults and the Ageing Society
作者	Suhita Chopra Chatterjee, Debolina Chatterjee
年度	2022
出版社	Routledge
DOI	https://doi.org/10.4324/9781003286936
序号	52
标题	COVID-19, the LGBTQIA+ Community, and Public Policy
作者	Wallace Swan
年度	2022
出版社	Routledge
DOI	https://doi.org/10.4324/9781003270713
序号	53
标题	COVID-19: Cultural Change and Institutional Adaptations
作者	J. Michael Ryan
年度	2022
出版社	Routledge
DOI	https://doi.org/10.4324/9781003302612
序号	54
标题	COVID-19: Social Inequalities and Human Possibilities
作者	J. Michael Ryan, Serena Nanda
年度	2022
出版社	Routledge
DOI	https://doi.org/10.4324/9781003178019

续表

序号	55
标题	**COVID-19: Surviving a Pandemic**
作者	J. Michael Ryan
年度	2022
出版社	Routledge
DOI	https://doi.org/10.4324/9781003302698
序号	56
标题	**COVID-ology**
副标题	A Field Guide
作者	Michael T. Myers, Jr
年度	2022
出版社	CRC Press
DOI	https://doi.org/10.1201/9781003310525
序号	57
标题	**Creative Resilience and COVID-19**
副标题	Figuring the Everyday in a Pandemic
作者	Irene Gammel, Jason Wang
年度	2022
出版社	Routledge
DOI	https://doi.org/10.4324/9781003213536
序号	58
标题	**Crowdsourcing During COVID-19**
副标题	Case Studies in Health and Education
作者	Carmen Bueno Muñoz, Luis R Murillo Zamorano, José Ángel López Sánchez
年度	2022
出版社	Routledge
DOI	https://doi.org/10.4324/9781003290872
序号	59
标题	**Data Science for Infectious Disease Data Analytics**
副标题	An Introduction with R

作者	Lily Wang
年度	2022
出版社	Chapman and Hall/CRC
DOI	https://doi.org/10.1201/9781003256328
序号	60
标题	Designing Smart and Resilient Cities for a Post-Pandemic World
副标题	Metropandemic Revolution
作者	Anthony Larsson, Andreas Hatzigeorgiou
年度	2022
出版社	Routledge
DOI	https://doi.org/10.4324/9781003222583
序号	61
标题	Digital Innovation for Pandemics
副标题	Concepts, Challenges, Constraints, and Opportunities
作者	Jasleen Kaur, Navjot Sidhu
年度	2022
出版社	Auerbach Publications
DOI	https://doi.org/10.1201/9781003328438
序号	62
标题	Discourses, Modes, Media and Meaning in an Era of Pandemic
副标题	A Multimodal Discourse Analysis Approach
作者	Sabine Tan, Marissa K. L. E
年度	2022
出版社	Routledge
DOI	https://doi.org/10.4324/9781003168195
序号	63
标题	Early Childhood Education and Care in a Global Pandemic
副标题	How the Sector Responded, Spoke Back and Generated Knowledge
作者	Linda Henderson, Katherine Bussey, Hasina Banu Ebrahim
年度	2022

续表

出版社	Routledge
DOI	https://doi.org/10.4324/9781003257684
序号	64
标题	Embracing the Future: Creative Industries for Environment and Advanced Society 5.0 in a Post-Pandemic Era
副标题	Proceedings of the 8th Bandung Creative Movement International Conference on Creative Industries (8th BCM 2021), Bandung, Indonesia, 9 September 2021
作者	Rahmiati Aulia, Diani Apsari, Sri Maharani Budi Haswati, Hana Faza Surya Rusyda, Aisyi Syafikarani, Angelia Lionardi, Setiamurti Rahardjo, Ariesa Farida, Wibisono Tegar Guna Putra, Yelly Andriani Barlian
年度	2022
出版社	Routledge
DOI	https://doi.org/10.1201/9781003263135
序号	65
标题	Emerging Technologies for Combatting Pandemics
副标题	AI, IoMT, and Analytics
作者	M. Rubaiyat Hossain Mondal, Utku Kose, V. B. Surya Prasath, Prajoy Podder, Subrato Bharati, Joarder Kamruzzaman
年度	2022
出版社	Auerbach Publications
DOI	https://doi.org/10.1201/9781003324447
序号	66
标题	Existentialism in Pandemic Times
副标题	Implications for Psychotherapists, Coaches and Organisations
作者	Monica Hanaway
年度	2022
出版社	Routledge
DOI	https://doi.org/10.4324/9781003255765
序号	67
标题	Experiences of Health Workers in the COVID-19 Pandemic
副标题	In Their Own Words

续表

作者	Marie Bismark, Karen Willis, Sophie Lewis, Natasha Smallwood
年度	2022
出版社	Routledge
DOI	https://doi.org/10.4324/9781003228394
序号	68
标题	**Exploring the Consequences of the COVID-19 Pandemic**
副标题	Social, Cultural, Economic, and Psychological Insights and Perspectives
作者	Usha Rana, Jayanathan Govender
年度	2022
出版社	Apple Academic Press
DOI	https://doi.org/10.1201/9781003277286
序号	69
标题	**From the Great Recession to the COVID-19 Pandemic**
副标题	A Financial History of the United States 2010—2020
作者	Jerry W. Markham
年度	2022
出版社	Routledge
DOI	https://doi.org/10.4324/9781003247043
序号	70
标题	**Frontline Workers and Women as Warriors in the COVID-19 Pandemic**
作者	R. C. Sobti, Vipin Sobti
年度	2022
出版社	Routledge India
DOI	https://doi.org/10.4324/9781003324515
序号	71
标题	**Gender, Food and COVID-19**
副标题	Global Stories of Harm and Hope
作者	Paige Castellanos, Carolyn E. Sachs, Ann R. Tickamyer
年度	2022
出版社	Routledge

续表

DOI	https://doi.org/10.4324/9781003198277
序号	72
标题	**Global Feminist Autoethnographies During COVID-19**
副标题	Displacements and Disruptions
作者	Melanie Heath, Akosua Darkwah, Josephine Beoku-Betts, Bandana Purkayastha
年度	2022
出版社	Routledge
DOI	https://doi.org/10.4324/9781003223832
序号	73
标题	**Global Pandemics and Media Ethics**
副标题	Issues and Perspectives
作者	Tendai Chari, Martin N. Ndlela
年度	2022
出版社	Routledge India
DOI	https://doi.org/10.4324/9781003306603
序号	74
标题	**Governing Human Lives and Health in Pandemic Times**
副标题	Social Control Policies
作者	Matilda Hellman, Tom Kettunen, Saara Salmivaara, Janne Stoneham
年度	2022
出版社	Routledge
DOI	https://doi.org/10.4324/9781003241157
序号	75
标题	**Indigenous Health and Well-Being in the COVID-19 Pandemic**
作者	Nicholas D. Spence, Fatih Sekercioglu
年度	2022
出版社	Routledge
DOI	https://doi.org/10.4324/9781003220381
序号	76

续表

标题	International Case Studies on Tourism Destination Management and COVID-19
副标题	Impacts and Responses
作者	Simon Hudson
年度	2022
出版社	Routledge
DOI	https://doi.org/10.4324/9781003310624
序号	77
标题	Interpreting COVID-19 Through Turbulence Theory
副标题	Perspectives and Cases from Early Childhood and Special Education
作者	Susan H. Shapiro
年度	2022
出版社	Routledge
DOI	https://doi.org/10.4324/9781003214410
序号	78
标题	Leisure in the Time of Coronavirus
副标题	A Rapid Response
作者	Brett Lashua, Corey W. Johnson, Diana C. Parry
年度	2022
出版社	Routledge
DOI	https://doi.org/10.4324/9781003145301
序号	79
标题	Leveraging Technology as a Response to the COVID Pandemic
副标题	Adapting Diverse Technologies, Workflow, and Processes to Optimize Integrated Clinical Management
作者	Harry Pappas, Paul Frisch
年度	2022
出版社	Productivity Press
DOI	https://doi.org/10.4324/b23264
序号	80

续表

标题	Literary Representations of Pandemics, Epidemics and Pestilence
作者	Nishi Pulugurtha
年度	2022
出版社	Routledge India
DOI	https://doi.org/10.4324/9781003294436
序号	81
标题	Logistics, Transport and the COVID-19 Crisis
副标题	Managing and Operating Logistics Processes
作者	Jacek Woźniak, Wioletta Sylwia Wereda, Bogdan Nogalski
年度	2022
出版社	Routledge
DOI	https://doi.org/10.4324/9781003285731
序号	82
标题	Making Complex Decisions Toward Revamping Supply Chains Amid COVID-19 Outbreak
作者	Dinesh Kumar, Kanika Prasad
年度	2022
出版社	CRC Press
DOI	https://doi.org/10.1201/9781003150084
序号	83
标题	Management of Tourism Ecosystem Services in a Post Pandemic Context
副标题	Global Perspectives
作者	Vanessaa G. B. Gowreesunkar, Shem Wambugu Maingi, Felix Lamech Mogambi Ming'ate
年度	2022
出版社	Routledge
DOI	https://doi.org/10.4324/b23145
序号	84
标题	Managing Complexity and COVID-19
副标题	Life, Liberty, or the Pursuit of Happiness

续表

作者	Aurobindo Ghosh, Amit Haldar, Kalyan Bhaumik
年度	2022
出版社	Routledge
DOI	https://doi.org/10.4324/9781003218807
序号	85
标题	Managing the Digital Workplace in the Post-Pandemic
副标题	A Companion for Study and Practice
作者	Fahri Özsungur
年度	2022
出版社	Routledge
DOI	https://doi.org/10.4324/9781003283386
序号	86
标题	Marketing by Contingency in the Time of COVID-19
副标题	Overcoming Business Crises and Meeting Marketing Challenges
作者	Alicia de la Peña, Juan Bernardo Amezcua Nuñez
年度	2022
出版社	Apple Academic Press
DOI	https://doi.org/10.1201/9781003300694
序号	87
标题	Media, Migrants and the Pandemic in India
副标题	A Reader
作者	Bharat Bhushan
年度	2022
出版社	Routledge
DOI	https://doi.org/10.4324/9781003291527
序号	88
标题	Multi-Pronged Omics Technologies to Understand COVID-19
作者	Sanjeeva Srivastava
年度	2022
出版社	CRC Press
DOI	https://doi.org/10.1201/9781003220787

续表

序号	89
标题	**Nanomaterials in the Battle Against Pathogens and Disease Vectors**
作者	Kaushik Pal, Tean Zaheer
年度	2022
出版社	CRC Press
DOI	https://doi.org/10.1201/9781003126256
序号	90
标题	**Navigating Students' Mental Health in the Wake of COVID-19**
副标题	Using Public Health Crises to Inform Research and Practice
作者	James M. Kauffman, Jeanmarie Badar
年度	2022
出版社	Routledge
DOI	https://doi.org/10.4324/9781003264033
序号	91
标题	**Negotiating the Pandemic**
副标题	Cultural, National, and Individual Constructions of COVID-19
作者	Inayat Ali, Robbie Davis-Floyd
年度	2022
出版社	Routledge
DOI	https://doi.org/10.4324/9781003187462
序号	92
标题	**Organizational Management and the COVID-19 Crisis**
副标题	Security and Risk Management Dilemmas
作者	Wioletta Sylwia Wereda, Jacek Woźniak, Justyna Stochaj
年度	2022
出版社	Routledge
DOI	https://doi.org/10.4324/9781003285717
序号	93
标题	**Pandemic and Crisis of Democracy**
副标题	Biopolitics, Neoliberalism, and Necropolitics in Bolsonaro's Brazil

续表

作者	André Duarte
年度	2022
出版社	Routledge
DOI	https://doi.org/10.4324/9781003295525
序号	94
标题	**Pandemic Detection and Analysis Through Smart Computing Technologies**
作者	Ram Shringar Raw，Vishal Jain，Sanjoy Das，Meenakshi Sharma
年度	2022
出版社	Apple Academic Press
DOI	https://doi.org/10.1201/9781003281610
序号	95
标题	**Pandemic Governance**
副标题	Learning from COVID and Future Pathways
作者	Walter Amedzro St-Hilaire
年度	2022
出版社	Productivity Press
DOI	https://doi.org/10.4324/9781003270898
序号	96
标题	**Pandemic of Perspectives**
副标题	Creative Re-imaginings
作者	Rimple Mehta，Sandali Thakur，Debaroti Chakraborty
年度	2022
出版社	Routledge India
DOI	https://doi.org/10.4324/9781003320524
序号	97
标题	**Pandemics and Public Value Management**
作者	Usman W. Chohan
年度	2022
出版社	Routledge
DOI	https://doi.org/10.4324/9781003223139

续表

序号	98
标题	**Pandemics, Wars, Traumas and Literature**
副标题	Echoes from the Front Lines
作者	Françoise Davoine
年度	2022
出版社	Routledge
DOI	https://doi.org/10.4324/9781003257592
序号	99
标题	**Pathogen Removal in Aerobic Granular Sludge Treatment Systems**
作者	Mary Luz Barrios Hernàndez
年度	2022
出版社	CRC Press
DOI	https://doi.org/10.1201/9781003231622
序号	100
标题	**Pathogens Crossing Borders**
副标题	Global Animal Diseases and International Responses, 1860—1947
作者	Cornelia Knab
年度	2022
出版社	Routledge
DOI	https://doi.org/10.4324/9781003033998
序号	101
标题	**Philosophy, Sport and the Pandemic**
作者	Jeffrey P. Fry, Andrew Edgar
年度	2022
出版社	Routledge
DOI	https://doi.org/10.4324/9781003214243
序号	102
标题	**Playful Pedagogy in the Pandemic**
副标题	Pivoting to Game-Based Learning
作者	Emily K. Johnson, Anastasia Salter

年度	2022
出版社	Routledge
DOI	https://doi.org/10.4324/9781003281696
序号	103
标题	Policy Styles and Trust in the Age of Pandemics
副标题	Global Threat, National Responses
作者	Nikolaos Zahariadis, Evangelia Petridou, Theofanis Exadaktylos, Jörgen Sparf
年度	2022
出版社	Routledge
DOI	https://doi.org/10.4324/9781003137399
序号	104
标题	Populism, the Pandemic and the Media
副标题	Journalism in the Age of Covid, Trump, Brexit and Johnson
作者	John Mair, Tor Clark, Neil Fowler, Raymond Snoddy, Richard Tait
年度	2022
出版社	Routledge
DOI	https://doi.org/10.4324/9781003253822
序号	105
标题	Populists and the Pandemic
副标题	How Populists Around the World Responded to COVID-19
作者	Nils Ringe, Lucio Rennó
年度	2022
出版社	Routledge
DOI	https://doi.org/10.4324/9781003197614
序号	106
标题	Posthuman Pathogenesis
副标题	Contagion in Literature, Arts, and Media
作者	Başak Ağın, Şafak Horzum
年度	2022

续表

出版社	Routledge
DOI	https://doi.org/10.4324/9781003288244
序号	107
标题	Post-Pandemic Leadership
副标题	Exploring Solutions to a Crisis
作者	Morgen Witzel
年度	2022
出版社	Routledge
DOI	https://doi.org/10.4324/9781003171737
序号	108
标题	Psychological Impact of Behaviour Restrictions During the Pandemic
副标题	Lessons from COVID-19
作者	Barrie Gunter
年度	2022
出版社	Routledge
DOI	https://doi.org/10.4324/9781003274377
序号	109
标题	Psychological Insights on the Role and Impact of the Media During the Pandemic
副标题	Lessons from COVID-19
作者	Barrie Gunter
年度	2022
出版社	Routledge
DOI	https://doi.org/10.4324/9781003274629
序号	110
标题	Public Behavioural Responses to Policy Making During the Pandemic
副标题	Comparative Perspectives on Mask-Wearing Policies
作者	Noriko Suzuki, Xavier Mellet, Susumu Annaka, Masahisa Endo
年度	2022
出版社	Routledge

续表

DOI	https://doi.org/10.4324/9781003244127
序号	111
标题	**Public Policy and the Impact of COVID-19 in Europe**
副标题	Economic, Political and Social Dimensions
作者	Magdalena Tomala, Maryana Prokop, Aleksandra Kordonska
年度	2022
出版社	Routledge
序号	112
标题	**Racialized Health, COVID-19, and Religious Responses**
副标题	Black Atlantic Contexts and Perspectives
作者	R. Drew Smith, Stephanie C. Boddie, Bertis D. English
年度	2022
出版社	Routledge
DOI	https://doi.org/10.4324/9781003214281
序号	113
标题	**Reconstructing Care in Teacher Education After COVID-19**
副标题	Caring Enough to Change
作者	Melanie Shoffner, Angela W. Webb
年度	2022
出版社	Routledge
DOI	https://doi.org/10.4324/9781003244875
序号	114
标题	**Regional and International Cooperation in South America After COVID**
副标题	Challenges and Opportunities Post-Pandemic
作者	Melisa Deciancio, Cintia Quiliconi
年度	2022
出版社	Routledge
DOI	https://doi.org/10.4324/9781003230403
序号	115
标题	**Religion and the COVID-19 Pandemic in Southern Africa**
作者	Fortune Sibanda, Tenson Muyambo, Ezra Chitando

续表

年度	2022
出版社	Routledge
DOI	https://doi.org/10.4324/9781003241096
序号	116
标题	Role of Essential Oils in the Management of COVID-19
作者	Ahmed Al-Harrasi, Saurabh Bhatia, Tapan Behl, Deepak Kaushik, Md. Khalid Anwer, ohammed Muqtader Ahmed, Pritam Babu Sharma, Ajay Sharma, Md. Tanvir Kabir, Vineet ttal
年度	2022
出版社	CRC Press
DOI	https://doi.org/10.1201/9781003175933
序号	117
标题	Routledge Handbook of Law and the COVID-19 Pandemic
作者	Joelle Grogan, Alice Donald
年度	2022
出版社	Routledge
DOI	https://doi.org/10.4324/9781003211952
序号	118
标题	Social and Political Issues on Sustainable Development in the Post COVID-19 Crisis
副标题	Proceedings of the International Conference on Social and Political Issues on Sustainable Development in the Post COVID-19 Crisis（ICHSOS 2021）, Malang, Indonesia, 18-19 June 2021
作者	Oman Sukmana, Salahudin, Iqbal Robbie, Ali Roziqin, Shannaz Mutiara Deniar, Iradhad T. Sihidi, Dedik F. Suhermanto
年度	2022
出版社	Routledge
DOI	https://doi.org/10.1201/9781003263586
序号	119
标题	Social and Political Representations of the COVID-19 Crisis
作者	Daniel Feierstein, Douglas Andrew Town
年度	2022

续表

出版社	Routledge
DOI	https://doi.org/10.4324/9781003267614
序号	120
标题	Sounds of the Pandemic
副标题	Accounts, Experiences, Perspectives in Times of COVID-19
作者	Maurizio Agamennone, Daniele Palma, Giulia Sarno
年度	2022
出版社	Focal Press
DOI	https://doi.org/10.4324/9781003200369
序号	121
标题	Space, Structures and Design in a Post-Pandemic World
作者	Thomas Fisher
年度	2022
出版社	Routledge
DOI	https://doi.org/10.4324/9781003198192
序号	122
标题	Sport Mega-Events, Security and COVID-19
副标题	Securing the Football World
作者	Jan Andre Lee Ludvigsen
年度	2022
出版社	Routledge
DOI	https://doi.org/10.4324/9781003258445
序号	123
标题	Sustainable Development in Post-Pandemic Africa
副标题	Effective Strategies for Resource Mobilization
作者	Fred Olayele, Yiagadeesen Samy
年度	2022
出版社	Routledge
DOI	https://doi.org/10.4324/9781003185062
序号	124

续表

标题	Sweden's Pandemic Experiment
作者	Sigurd Bergmann, Martin Lindström
年度	2022
出版社	Routledge
DOI	https://doi.org/10.4324/9781003289364
序号	125
标题	System Innovation in a Post-Pandemic World
副标题	Proceedings of the IEEE 7th International Conference on Applied System Innovation(ICASI 2021), September 24–25, 2021, Alishan, Taiwan, China
作者	Artde Kin-Tak Lam, Stephen D Prior, Sheng-Joue Young, Siu-Tsen Shen, Liang-Wen Ji
年度	2022
出版社	CRC Press
DOI	https://doi.org/10.1201/9781003278474
序号	126
标题	Teacher Education and Teacher Professional Development in the COVID-19 Turn
副标题	Proceedings of the International Conference on Teacher Training and Education (ICTTE 2021), Surakarta, Indonesia, August 25–26, 2021
作者	Nur Arifah Drajati, Kristian Adi Putra
年度	2022
出版社	Routledge
DOI	https://doi.org/10.1201/9781003347798
序号	127
标题	Teachers' Work During the Pandemic
作者	Nina Bascia
年度	2022
出版社	Routledge
DOI	https://doi.org/10.4324/9781003196860
序号	128
标题	Technological Innovations for Effective Pandemic Response
作者	Harish Hirani

一、图书

续表

年度	2022
出版社	CRC Press
DOI	https://doi.org/10.1201/9781003331179
序号	129
标题	**The Color of COVID-19**
副标题	The Racial Inequality of Marginalized Communities
作者	Sharon A. Navarro, Samantha L. Hernandez
年度	2022
出版社	Routledge
DOI	https://doi.org/10.4324/9781003268710
序号	130
标题	**The COVID-19 Crisis in South Asia**
副标题	Coping with the Pandemic
作者	Sumit Ganguly, Dinsha Mistree
年度	2022
出版社	Routledge
DOI	https://doi.org/10.4324/9781003248149
序号	131
标题	**The COVID-19 Pandemic**
副标题	The Deadly Coronavirus Outbreak
作者	Tapas Kumar Koley, Monika Dhole
年度	2022
出版社	Routledge India
DOI	https://doi.org/10.4324/9781003345091
序号	132
标题	**The COVID-19 Pandemic**
副标题	A Multidisciplinary Review of Diagnosis, Prevention, and Treatment
作者	Hanadi Talal Ahmedah, Muhammad Riaz, Sagheer Ahmed, Marius Alexandru Moga
年度	2022

续表

出版社	Apple Academic Press
DOI	https://doi.org/10.1201/9781003283607
序号	133
标题	The COVID-19 Pandemic and Older Adults
副标题	Experiences, Impacts, and Innovations
作者	Edward Alan Miller
年度	2022
出版社	Routledge
DOI	https://doi.org/10.4324/9781003273462
序号	134
标题	The COVID-19 Pandemic and Risks in East Asia
副标题	Media, Social Reactions, and Theories
作者	Nobuto Yamamoto
年度	2022
出版社	Routledge
DOI	https://doi.org/10.4324/9781003286684
序号	135
标题	The COVID-19 Pandemic and the Future of Working Spaces
作者	Ilaria Mariotti, Mina Di Marino, Pavel Bednář
年度	2022
出版社	Routledge
DOI	https://doi.org/10.4324/9781003181163
序号	136
标题	The COVID-19 Pandemic as a Challenge for Media and Communication Studies
作者	Katarzyna Kopecka-Piech, Bartłomiej Łódzki
年度	2022
出版社	Routledge
DOI	https://doi.org/10.4324/9781003232049
序号	137

续表

标题	The COVID-19 Pandemic in the Middle East and North Africa
副标题	Public Policy Responses
作者	Anis Ben Brik
年度	2022
出版社	Routledge
DOI	https://doi.org/10.4324/9781003266259
序号	138
标题	The Cultural Politics of COVID-19
作者	John Nguyet Erni, Ted Striphas
年度	2022
出版社	Routledge
DOI	https://doi.org/10.4324/9781003310419
序号	139
标题	The Ethics of Pandemics
副标题	An Introduction
作者	Iwao Hirose
年度	2022
出版社	Routledge
DOI	https://doi.org/10.4324/9781003203759
序号	140
标题	The Impact of COVID-19 on Prison Conditions and Penal Policy
作者	Frieder Dünkel, Stefan Harrendorf, Dirk van Zyl Smit
年度	2022
出版社	Routledge
序号	141
标题	The Implications of COVID-19 for Children and Youth
副标题	Global Perspectives
作者	Grant Charles, Kiaras Gharabaghi, Shadan Hyder, Ashley Quinn
年度	2022
出版社	Routledge
DOI	https://doi.org/10.4324/9781003273981

续表

序号	142
标题	**The Languages of COVID-19**
副标题	Translational and Multilingual Perspectives on Global Healthcare
作者	Piotr Blumczynski, Steven Wilson
年度	2022
出版社	Routledge
DOI	https://doi.org/10.4324/9781003267843
序号	143
标题	**The MENA Region and COVID-19**
副标题	Impact, Implications and Prospects
作者	Zeina Hobaika, Lena-Maria Möller, Jan Claudius Völkel
年度	2022
出版社	Routledge
DOI	https://doi.org/10.4324/9781003240044
序号	144
标题	**The Nature of Pandemics**
作者	Dag K.J.E. von Lubitz, Candace J. Gibson
年度	2022
出版社	CRC Press
DOI	https://doi.org/10.4324/9781315170220
序号	145
标题	**The Pandemic in Central Europe**
副标题	A Case Study
作者	Jolanta Itrich-Drabarek
年度	2022
出版社	Routledge India
DOI	https://doi.org/10.4324/9781003353812
序号	146
标题	**The Political Economy of Covid-19**
副标题	Covid-19, Inequality and Government Responses

作者	Jonathan Michie, Maura Sheehan
年度	2022
出版社	Routledge
DOI	https://doi.org/10.4324/9781003307440
序号	147
标题	**The Remarkable Story of Vaccines**
副标题	Milkmaid to Genome
作者	Norman Begg
年度	2022
出版社	CRC Press
DOI	https://doi.org/10.1201/9781003303879
序号	148
标题	**The Routledge Handbook of Media Education Futures Post-Pandemic**
作者	Yonty Friesem, Usha Raman, Igor Kanižaj, Grace Y. Choi
年度	2022
出版社	Routledge
DOI	https://doi.org/10.4324/9781003283737
序号	149
标题	**Translation and Social Media Communication in the Age of the Pandemic**
作者	Tong King Lee, Dingkun Wang
年度	2022
出版社	Routledge
DOI	https://doi.org/10.4324/9781003183907
序号	150
标题	**Understanding Individual Experiences of COVID-19 to Inform Policy and Practice in Higher Education**
副标题	Helping Students, Staff, and Faculty to Thrive in Times of Crisis
作者	Amy Aldous Bergerson, Shawn R. Coon
年度	2022
出版社	Routledge

续表

DOI	https://doi.org/10.4324/9781003189855
序号	151
标题	Understanding the Politics of Pandemic Emergencies in the Time of COVID-19
副标题	An Introduction to Global Politosomatics
作者	Mika Aaltola
年度	2022
出版社	Routledge
DOI	https://doi.org/10.4324/9781003169147
序号	152
标题	Vaccine Efficacy Evaluation
副标题	The Gnotobiotic Pig Model
作者	Lijuan Yuan
年度	2022
出版社	CRC Press
DOI	https://doi.org/10.1201/b22816
序号	153
标题	Viruses and Society
作者	Patricia G. Melloy
年度	2022
出版社	CRC Press
DOI	https://doi.org/10.1201/9781003172260
序号	154
标题	Virus-Like Particles
副标题	A Comprehensive Guide
作者	Paul Pumpens, Peter Pushko
年度	2022
出版社	CRC Press
DOI	https://doi.org/10.1201/b22819
序号	155

续表

标题	Advances in Clinical Immunology, Medical Microbiology, COVID-19, and Big Data
作者	Raj Bawa
年度	2021
出版社	Jenny Stanford Publishing
DOI	https://doi.org/10.1201/9781003180432
序号	156
标题	Ageing and COVID-19
副标题	Making Sense of a Disrupted World
作者	Maria Łuszczyńska, Marvin Formosa
年度	2021
出版社	Routledge
DOI	https://doi.org/10.4324/b22774
序号	157
标题	Assessment of the Fate of Surrogates for Enteric Pathogens Resulting from the Surcharging of Combined Sewer Systems
作者	Iosif Marios Scoullos
年度	2021
出版社	CRC Press
DOI	https://doi.org/10.1201/9781003094739
序号	158
标题	Bayesian Analysis of Infectious Diseases
副标题	COVID-19 and Beyond
作者	Lyle D. Broemeling
年度	2021
出版社	Chapman and Hall/CRC
DOI	https://doi.org/10.1201/9781003125983
序号	159
标题	Building a Platform for Data-Driven Pandemic Prediction
副标题	From Data Modelling to Visualisation—The CovidLP Project
作者	Dani Gamerman, Marcos O. Prates, Thais Paiva, Vinicius D. Mayrink

续表

年度	2021
出版社	Chapman and Hall/CRC
DOI	https://doi.org/10.1201/9781003148883
序号	160
标题	**Christianity and COVID-19**
副标题	Pathways for Faith
作者	Chammah J. Kaunda, Atola Longkumer, Kenneth R. Ross, Esther Mombo
年度	2021
出版社	Routledge
DOI	https://doi.org/10.4324/9781003244080
序号	161
标题	**Comparative Federalism and Covid-19**
副标题	Combating the Pandemic
作者	Nico Steytler
年度	2021
出版社	Routledge
DOI	https://doi.org/10.4324/9781003166771
序号	162
标题	**Computational Modeling and Data Analysis in COVID-19 Research**
作者	Chhabi Rani Panigrahi, Bibudhendu Pati, Mamata Rath, Rajkumar Buyya
年度	2021
出版社	CRC Press
DOI	https://doi.org/10.1201/9781003137481
序号	163
标题	**Computational Modelling and Imaging for SARS-CoV-2 and COVID-19**
作者	S. Prabha, P. Karthikeyan, K. Kamalanand, N. Selvaganesan
年度	2021
出版社	CRC Press
DOI	https://doi.org/10.1201/9781003142584
序号	164

续表

标题	**Conflict Resolution After the Pandemic**
副标题	Building Peace, Pursuing Justice
作者	Richard E. Rubenstein, Solon Simmons
年度	2021
出版社	Routledge
DOI	https://doi.org/10.4324/9781003153832
序号	165
标题	**Coronavirus, Psychoanalysis, and Philosophy**
副标题	Conversations on Pandemics, Politics and Society
作者	Fernando Castrillón, Thomas Marchevsky
年度	2021
出版社	Routledge
DOI	https://doi.org/10.4324/9781003150497
序号	166
标题	**COVID-19**
副标题	Origin, Detection and Impact Analysis Using Artificial Intelligence Computational Techniques
作者	Parag Verma, Ankur Dumka, Alaknanda Ashok, Anuj Bhardwaj, Amit Dumka
年度	2021
出版社	CRC Press
DOI	https://doi.org/10.1201/9781003131410
序号	167
标题	**COVID-19**
副标题	Two Volume Set
作者	J. Michael Ryan
年度	2021
出版社	Routledge
DOI	https://doi.org/10.4324/9781003155911
序号	168

续表

标题	**COVID-19 and Entrepreneurship**
副标题	Challenges and Opportunities for Small Business
作者	Vanessa Ratten
年度	2021
出版社	Routledge
DOI	https://doi.org/10.4324/9781003149248
序号	169
标题	**COVID-19 and Governance**
副标题	Crisis Reveals
作者	Jan Nederveen Pieterse, Haeran Lim, Habibul Khondker
年度	2021
出版社	Routledge
DOI	https://doi.org/10.4324/9781003154037
序号	170
标题	**COVID-19 and Human Rights**
作者	Morten Kjaerum, Martha F. Davis, Amanda Lyons
年度	2021
出版社	Routledge
DOI	https://doi.org/10.4324/9781003139140
序号	171
标题	**COVID-19 and Islamic Social Finance**
作者	M. Kabir Hassan, Aishath Muneeza, Adel M. Sarea
年度	2021
出版社	Routledge
DOI	https://doi.org/10.4324/9781003121718
序号	172
标题	**COVID-19 and Psychology in Malaysia**
副标题	Psychosocial Effects, Coping, and Resilience
作者	D. Gerard Joseph Louis, Surinderpal Kaur, Huey Fen Cheong
年度	2021

续表

出版社	Routledge
DOI	https://doi.org/10.4324/9781003178576
序号	173
标题	**COVID-19 Assemblages**
副标题	Queer and Feminist Ethnographies from South Asia
作者	Niharika Banerjea, Jasbir K Puar, Paul Boyce, Rohit K. Dasgupta
年度	2021
出版社	Routledge India
DOI	https://doi.org/10.4324/9781003262251
序号	174
标题	**COVID-19 in International Media**
副标题	Global Pandemic Perspectives
作者	John C. Pollock, Douglas A. Vakoch
年度	2021
出版社	Routledge
DOI	https://doi.org/10.4324/9781003181705
序号	175
标题	**COVID-19 Pandemic, Geospatial Information, and Community Resilience**
副标题	Global Applications and Lessons
作者	Abbas Rajabifard, Daniel Paez, Greg Foliente
年度	2021
出版社	CRC Press
DOI	https://doi.org/10.1201/9781003181590
序号	176
标题	**COVID-19 Public Health Measures**
副标题	An Augmented Reality Perspective
作者	Nuzhat F. Shaikh, Ajinkya Kunjir, Juveriya Shaikh, Parikshit Narendra Mahalle
年度	2021
出版社	CRC Press

续表

DOI	https://doi.org/10.1201/9781003173878
序号	177
标题	**COVID-19, Business, and Economy in Malaysia**
副标题	Retrospective and Prospective Perspectives
作者	Weng Marc Lim, Surinderpal Kaur, Huey Fen Cheong
年度	2021
出版社	Routledge
DOI	https://doi.org/10.4324/9781003182740
序号	178
标题	**COVID-19, Education, and Literacy in Malaysia**
副标题	Social Contexts of Teaching and Learning
作者	Ambigapathy Pandian, Surinderpal Kaur, Huey Fen Cheong
年度	2021
出版社	Routledge
DOI	https://doi.org/10.4324/9781003182733
序号	179
标题	**COVID-19, Familism, and South Korean Governance**
作者	Jai Chang Park
年度	2021
出版社	Routledge
DOI	https://doi.org/10.4324/9781003240709
序号	180
标题	**COVID-19: The Global Environmental Health Experience**
作者	Chris Day
年度	2021
出版社	Routledge
DOI	https://doi.org/10.1201/9781003157229
序号	181
标题	**Cultural Industries and the COVID-19 Pandemic**
副标题	A European Focus

续表

作者	Elisa Salvador, Trilce Navarrete, Andrej Srakar
年度	2021
出版社	Routledge
DOI	https://doi.org/10.4324/9781003128274
序号	182
标题	**Cybersecurity in the COVID-19 Pandemic**
作者	Kenneth Okereafor
年度	2021
出版社	CRC Press
DOI	https://doi.org/10.1201/9781003104124
序号	183
标题	**Cybersecurity Lessons from COVID-19**
作者	Robert Slade
年度	2021
出版社	CRC Press
DOI	https://doi.org/10.1201/9781003136675
序号	184
标题	**Death, Grief and Loss in the Context of COVID-19**
作者	Panagiotis Pentaris
年度	2021
出版社	Routledge
DOI	https://doi.org/10.4324/9781003125990
序号	185
标题	**Digital Transformation in a Post-Covid World**
副标题	Sustainable Innovation, Disruption, and Change
作者	Adrian T. H. Kuah, Roberto Dillon
年度	2021
出版社	CRC Press
DOI	https://doi.org/10.1201/9781003148715
序号	186

续表

标题	**Economic Policy and the Covid-19 Crisis**
副标题	The Macroeconomic Response in the US, Europe and East Asia
作者	Bernadette Andreosso-O'Callaghan, Woosik Moon, Wook Sohn
年度	2021
出版社	Routledge
DOI	https://doi.org/10.4324/9781003153603
序号	187
标题	**Emerging Pathogens at the Poles**
副标题	Disease and International Trade Law
作者	Alexandra L. Carleton
年度	2021
出版社	Routledge
DOI	https://doi.org/10.4324/9780367808341
序号	188
标题	**Federalism and the Response to COVID-19**
副标题	A Comparative Analysis
作者	Rupak Chattopadhyay, John Light, Felix Knüpling, Diana Chebenova, Liam Whittington, Phillip Gonzalez
年度	2021
出版社	Routledge India
DOI	https://doi.org/10.4324/9781003251217
序号	189
标题	**Gerontological Social Work and COVID-19**
副标题	Calls for Change in Education, Practice, and Policy from International Voices
作者	Michelle Putnam, Huei-Wern Shen
年度	2021
出版社	Routledge
DOI	https://doi.org/10.4324/9781003138280
序号	190
标题	**Global Pandemic, Security and Human Rights**
副标题	Comparative Explorations of COVID-19 and the Law

作者	Ben Stanford, Steve Foster, Carlos Espaliu Berdud
年度	2021
出版社	Routledge
DOI	https://doi.org/10.4324/9781003176824
序号	191
标题	**Global Pandemic, Technology and Business**
副标题	Comparative Explorations of COVID-19 and the Law
作者	Luo Li, Carlos Espaliu Berdud, Steve Foster, Ben Stanford
年度	2021
出版社	Routledge
DOI	https://doi.org/10.4324/9781003176848
序号	192
标题	**Global Pandemics and Epistemic Crises in Psychology**
副标题	A Socio-Philosophical Approach
作者	Martin Dege, Irene Strasser
年度	2021
出版社	Routledge
DOI	https://doi.org/10.4324/9781003145417
序号	193
标题	**Global Tourism and COVID-19**
副标题	Implications for Theory and Practice
作者	Alan A. Lew, Joseph M. Cheer, Patrick Brouder, Mary Mostafanezhad
年度	2021
出版社	Routledge
DOI	https://doi.org/10.4324/9781003223252
序号	194
标题	**Health Informatics and Technological Solutions for Coronavirus（COVID-19）**
作者	Suman Lata Tripathi, Kanav Dhir, Deepika Ghai, Shashikant Patil
年度	2021

出版社	CRC Press
DOI	https://doi.org/10.1201/9781003161066
序号	195
标题	Immunity Boosting Functional Foods to Combat COVID-19
作者	Apurba Giri
年度	2021
出版社	CRC Press
DOI	https://doi.org/10.1201/9781003242604
序号	196
标题	Impacts of COVID-19 on International Students and the Future of Student Mobility
副标题	International Perspectives and Experiences
作者	Krishna Bista, Ryan M. Allen, Roy Y. Chan
年度	2021
出版社	Routledge
DOI	https://doi.org/10.4324/9781003138402
序号	197
标题	India's Migrant Workers and the Pandemic
作者	Ritajyoti Bandyopadhyay, Paula Banerjee, Ranabir Samaddar
年度	2021
出版社	Routledge
DOI	https://doi.org/10.4324/9781003246121
序号	198
标题	Inequality in a Context of Climate Crisis After COVID
副标题	A Complex Realist Approach
作者	David Byrne
年度	2021
出版社	Routledge
DOI	https://doi.org/10.4324/9781003028970
序号	199

续表

标题	**Infectious Inequalities**
副标题	Epidemics, Trust, and Social Vulnerabilities in Cinema
作者	Qijun Han, Daniel R. Curtis
年度	2021
出版社	Routledge
DOI	https://doi.org/10.4324/9781003261667
序号	200
标题	**Intelligent Computing Applications for COVID-19**
副标题	Predictions, Diagnosis, and Prevention
作者	Tanzila Saba, Amjad Rehman Khan
年度	2021
出版社	CRC Press
DOI	https://doi.org/10.1201/9781003141105
序号	201
标题	**Islamic Economics and COVID-19**
副标题	The Economic, Social and Scientific Consequences of a Global Pandemic
作者	Masudul Alam Choudhury
年度	2021
出版社	Routledge
DOI	https://doi.org/10.4324/9781003160229
序号	202
标题	**Legacy, Pathogenic and Emerging Contaminants in the Environment**
作者	Manish Kumar, Meththika Vithanage, Sanjeeb Mohapatra, Kishor Acharya
年度	2021
出版社	CRC Press
DOI	https://doi.org/10.1201/9781003157465
序号	203
标题	**Lessons from the Transition to Pandemic Education in the US**
副标题	Analyses of Parent, Student, and Educator Experiences
作者	Marni Fisher, Kimiya Maghzi, Charlotte Achieng-Evensen, Meredith Dorner, Holly Pearson, Mina Chun

续表

年度	2021
出版社	Routledge
DOI	https://doi.org/10.4324/9781003183785
序号	204
标题	**Living with COVID-19**
副标题	Economics, Ethics, and Environmental Issues
作者	Chaudhery Mustansar Hussain, Gustavo Marques da Costa
年度	2021
出版社	Jenny Stanford Publishing
DOI	https://doi.org/10.1201/9781003168287
序号	205
标题	**Mathematical Modeling in the Age of the Pandemic**
作者	William P. Fox
年度	2021
出版社	Chapman and Hall/CRC
DOI	https://doi.org/10.1201/9781003145639
序号	206
标题	**Medical Physics During the COVID-19 Pandemic**
副标题	Global Perspectives in Clinical Practice, Education and Research
作者	Kwan Hoong Ng, Magdalena S. Stoeva
年度	2021
出版社	CRC Press
DOI	https://doi.org/10.1201/9781003144380
序号	207
标题	**Medicinal Plants in the Asia Pacific for Zoonotic Pandemics, Volume 1**
副标题	Family Amborellaceae to Vitaceae
作者	Christophe Wiart
年度	2021
出版社	CRC Press
DOI	https://doi.org/10.1201/9781351059077

序号	208
标题	**Medicinal Plants in the Asia Pacific for Zoonotic Pandemics, Volume 2**
副标题	Family Zygophyllaceae to Salvadoraceae
作者	Christophe Wiart
年度	2021
出版社	CRC Press
DOI	https://doi.org/10.1201/9781003176398
序号	209
标题	**Medicinal Plants in the Asia Pacific for Zoonotic Pandemics, Volume 3**
副标题	Family Bixaceae to Portulacaceae
作者	Christophe Wiart
年度	2021
出版社	CRC Press
DOI	https://doi.org/10.1201/9781003180371
序号	210
标题	**Numerical Modeling of COVID-19 Neurological Effects**
副标题	ODE/PDE Analysis in R
作者	William Schiesser
年度	2021
出版社	CRC Press
DOI	https://doi.org/10.1201/9781003243052
序号	211
标题	**Older Adults and COVID-19**
副标题	Implications for Aging Policy and Practice
作者	Edward Alan Miller
年度	2021
出版社	Routledge
DOI	https://doi.org/10.4324/9781003118695
序号	212
标题	**Online Teaching and Learning in Higher Education During COVID-19**
副标题	International Perspectives and Experiences

续表

作者	Roy Chan, Krishna Bista, Ryan Allen
年度	2021
出版社	Routledge
DOI	https://doi.org/10.4324/9781003125921
序号	213
标题	**Outsmarting the Next Pandemic**
副标题	What COVID-19 Can Teach Us
作者	Elizabeth Anne Kirley, Deborah Porter
年度	2021
出版社	Routledge
DOI	https://doi.org/10.4324/9781003215769
序号	214
标题	**Pandemic Economics**
作者	Thomas R. Sadler
年度	2021
出版社	Routledge
DOI	https://doi.org/10.4324/9781003133629
序号	215
标题	**Pandemic Performance**
副标题	Resilience, Liveness, and Protest in Quarantine Times
作者	Kendra Capece, Patrick Scorese
年度	2021
出版社	Routledge
DOI	https://doi.org/10.4324/9781003205876
序号	216
标题	**Pandemic, Governance and Communication**
副标题	The Curious Case of COVID-19
作者	Dipankar Sinha
年度	2021
出版社	Routledge India

续表

DOI	https://doi.org/10.4324/9781003247388
序号	217
标题	**Pandemics, Authoritarian Populism, and Science Fiction**
副标题	Medicine, Military, and Morality in American Film
作者	Jeremiah Morelock
年度	2021
出版社	Routledge
DOI	https://doi.org/10.4324/9781003003779
序号	218
标题	**Pandemics: The Basics**
作者	Elisa Pieri
年度	2021
出版社	Routledge
DOI	https://doi.org/10.4324/9781003102892
序号	219
标题	**Performance in a Pandemic**
作者	Laura Bissell, Lucy Weir
年度	2021
出版社	Routledge
DOI	https://doi.org/10.4324/9781003165644
序号	220
标题	**Pesticides, Organic Contaminants, and Pathogens in Air**
副标题	Chemodynamics, Health Effects, Sampling, and Analysis
作者	James N. Seiber, Thomas M. Cahill
年度	2021
出版社	CRC Press
DOI	https://doi.org/10.1201/9781003217602
序号	221
标题	**Political Communication and COVID-19**
副标题	Governance and Rhetoric in Times of Crisis

续表

作者	Darren Lilleker, Ioana A. Coman, Miloš Gregor, Edoardo Novelli
年度	2021
出版社	Routledge
DOI	https://doi.org/10.4324/9781003120254
序号	222
标题	**Political Communication in the Time of Coronavirus**
作者	Peter Van Aelst, Jay G. Blumler
年度	2021
出版社	Routledge
DOI	https://doi.org/10.4324/9781003170051
序号	223
标题	**Post Pandemic L2 Pedagogy**
副标题	Proceedings of the Language Teacher and Training Education Virtual International Conference (LTTE 2020), 22-25 September, 2020
作者	Kristian Adi Putra, Nur Drajati
年度	2021
出版社	Routledge
DOI	https://doi.org/10.1201/9781003199267
序号	224
标题	**Post-AIDS Discourse in Health Communication**
副标题	Sociocultural Interpretations
作者	Ambar Basu, Andrew R. Spieldenner, Patrick J. Dillon
年度	2021
出版社	Routledge
DOI	https://doi.org/10.4324/9781003000945
序号	225
标题	**Post-Pandemic Sustainable Tourism Management**
副标题	The New Reality of Managing Ethical and Responsible Tourism
作者	Marko Koščak, Tony O'Rourke
年度	2021

出版社	Routledge
DOI	https://doi.org/10.4324/9781003153108
序号	226
标题	**Power, Media and the Covid-19 Pandemic**
副标题	Framing Public Discourse
作者	Stuart Price, Ben Harbisher
年度	2021
出版社	Routledge
DOI	https://doi.org/10.4324/9781003147299
序号	227
标题	**Psychoanalytic Diaries of the COVID-19 Pandemic**
作者	Pietro Roberto Goisis, Angelo Antonio Moroni
年度	2021
出版社	Routledge
DOI	https://doi.org/10.4324/9781003198734
序号	228
标题	**Race and Ethnicity in Pandemic Times**
作者	John Solomos
年度	2021
出版社	Routledge
DOI	https://doi.org/10.4324/9781003206521
序号	229
标题	**Remote Learning in Times of Pandemic**
副标题	Issues, Implications and Best Practice
作者	Linda Daniela, Anna Visvizi
年度	2021
出版社	Routledge
DOI	https://doi.org/10.4324/9781003167594
序号	230
标题	**Robotics for Pandemics**
作者	Hooman Samani

续表

年度	2021
出版社	Chapman and Hall/CRC
DOI	https://doi.org/10.1201/9781003195061
序号	231
标题	**Strategic Management During a Pandemic**
作者	Vikas Kumar, Gaurav Gupta
年度	2021
出版社	Routledge
DOI	https://doi.org/10.4324/9781003125648
序号	232
标题	**Sustainable Lifestyles After COVID-19**
作者	Fabián Echegaray, Valerie Brachya, Philip J. Vergragt, Lei Zhang
年度	2021
出版社	Routledge
DOI	https://doi.org/10.4324/9781003162391
序号	233
标题	**Synthetic Peptide Vaccine Models**
副标题	Design, Synthesis, Purification and Characterization
作者	Mesut Karahan
年度	2021
出版社	CRC Press
DOI	https://doi.org/10.1201/9781003144533
序号	234
标题	**The COVID-19 Crisis**
副标题	Social Perspectives
作者	Deborah Lupton, Karen Willis
年度	2021
出版社	Routledge
DOI	https://doi.org/10.4324/9781003111344
序号	235

续表

标题	The COVID-19 Pandemic, India and the World
副标题	Economic and Social Policy Perspectives
作者	Rajib Bhattacharyya, Ananya Ghosh Dastidar, Soumyen Sikdar
年度	2021
出版社	Routledge India
DOI	https://doi.org/10.4324/9781003220145
序号	236
标题	The Future of Diplomacy After COVID-19
副标题	Multilateralism and the Global Pandemic
作者	Hana Alhashimi, Andres Fiallo, Toni-Shae Freckleton, Mona Ali Khalil, Vahd Mulachela, Jonathan Viera
年度	2021
出版社	Routledge
DOI	https://doi.org/10.4324/9781003166801
序号	237
标题	The Global Impact of the COVID-19 Pandemic on Institutional and Community Corrections
作者	James M. Byrne, Don Hummer, Sabrina S. Rapisarda
年度	2021
出版社	Routledge
DOI	https://doi.org/10.4324/9781003189572
序号	238
标题	The Pandemic Crisis and the European Union
副标题	COVID-19 and Crisis Management
作者	Paulo Vila Maior, Isabel Camisão
年度	2021
出版社	Routledge
DOI	https://doi.org/10.4324/9781003153900
序号	239
标题	The Socioeconomic Impact of COVID-19 on Eastern European Countries
作者	Rafał Wisła, Paweł Dykas

续表

年度	2021
出版社	Routledge
DOI	https://doi.org/10.4324/9781003211891
序号	240
标题	**Tourism, Safety and COVID-19**
副标题	Security, Digitization and Tourist Behaviour
作者	Salvatore Monaco
年度	2021
出版社	Routledge
DOI	https://doi.org/10.4324/9781003195177
序号	241
标题	**Traditional Ecological Knowledge and Global Pandemics**
副标题	Biodiversity and Planetary Health Beyond Covid-19
作者	Ngozi Finette Unuigbe
年度	2021
出版社	Routledge
DOI	https://doi.org/10.4324/9781003141280
序号	242
标题	**Use of AI, Robotics and Modelling Tools to Fight Covid-19**
作者	Arpit Jain, Abhinav Sharma, Jianwu Wang, Mangey Ram
年度	2021
出版社	River Publishers
DOI	https://doi.org/10.1201/9781003339960
序号	243
标题	**Viral Sovereignty and the Political Economy of Pandemics**
副标题	What Explains How Countries Handle Outbreaks?
作者	Sophal Ear
年度	2021
出版社	Routledge
DOI	https://doi.org/10.4324/9781003228974

续表

序号	244
标题	**Virus Bioinformatics**
作者	Dmitrij Frishman，Manja Marz
年度	2021
出版社	Chapman and Hall/CRC
DOI	https://doi.org/10.1201/9781003097679
序号	245
标题	**"Ending AIDS" in the Age of Biopharmaceuticals**
副标题	The Individual，the State and the Politics of Prevention
作者	Tony Sandset
年度	2020
出版社	Routledge
DOI	https://doi.org/10.4324/9780429197000
序号	246
标题	**AI-Powered IoT for COVID-19**
作者	Fadi Al-Turjman
年度	2020
出版社	CRC Press
DOI	https://doi.org/10.1201/9781003098881
序号	247
标题	**Bacterial Genetics and Genomics**
作者	Lori Snyder
年度	2020
出版社	Garland Science
DOI	https://doi.org/10.1201/9780429293016
序号	248
标题	**Clinical Tuberculosis**
作者	Lloyd N. Friedman，Martin Dedicoat，Peter D. O. Davies
年度	2020
出版社	CRC Press

续表

DOI	https://doi.org/10.1201/9781351249980
序号	249
标题	Comparing and Contrasting the Impact of the COVID-19 Pandemic in the European Union
作者	Linda Hantrais, Marie-Thérèse Letablier
年度	2020
出版社	Routledge
DOI	https://doi.org/10.4324/9781003140719
序号	250
标题	**Coronavirus News, Markets and AI**
副标题	The COVID-19 Diaries
作者	Pankaj Sharma
年度	2020
出版社	Routledge India
DOI	https://doi.org/10.4324/9781003138976
序号	251
标题	**COVID-19**
副标题	Volume Ⅰ: Global Pandemic, Societal Responses, Ideological Solutions
作者	J. Michael Ryan
年度	2020
出版社	Routledge
DOI	https://doi.org/10.4324/9781003142089
序号	252
标题	**COVID-19**
副标题	Volume Ⅱ: Social Consequences and Cultural Adaptations
作者	J. Michael Ryan
年度	2020
出版社	Routledge
DOI	https://doi.org/10.4324/9781003142065
序号	253

续表

标题	COVID-19 and Emerging Environmental Trends
副标题	A Way Forward
作者	Joystu Dutta, Srijan Goswami, Abhijit Mitra
年度	2020
出版社	CRC Press
DOI	https://doi.org/10.1201/9781003108887
序号	254
标题	COVID-19 and International Business
副标题	Change of Era
作者	Marin Marinov, Svetla Marinova
年度	2020
出版社	Routledge
DOI	https://doi.org/10.4324/9781003108924
序号	255
标题	COVID-19 and Public Policy in the Digital Age
作者	Andrea Monti, Raymond Wacks
年度	2020
出版社	Routledge India
DOI	https://doi.org/10.4324/9781003096122
序号	256
标题	Data Analytics for Pandemics
副标题	A COVID-19 Case Study
作者	Gitanjali Rahul Shinde, Asmita Balasaheb Kalamkar, Parikshit N. Mahalle, Nilanjan Dey
年度	2020
出版社	CRC Press
DOI	https://doi.org/10.1201/9781003095415
序号	257
标题	Democracy and Public Policy in the Post-COVID-19 World
副标题	Choices and Outcomes

续表

作者	Rumki Basu
年度	2020
出版社	Routledge India
DOI	https://doi.org/10.4324/9781003142003
序号	258
标题	**HIV in the UK**
副标题	Voices from the Epidemic
作者	Jose Catalan, Barbara Hedge, Damien Ridge
年度	2020
出版社	Routledge
DOI	https://doi.org/10.4324/9780429401107
序号	259
标题	**Infectious Diseases and Antimicrobial Stewardship in Critical Care Medicine**
作者	Cheston B. Cunha, Burke A. Cunha
年度	2020
出版社	CRC Press
DOI	https://doi.org/10.1201/9781315099538
序号	260
标题	**Infectious Diseases and Pathology of Reptiles**
副标题	Color Atlas and Text, Diseases and Pathology of Reptiles Volume 1
作者	Elliott R. Jacobson, Michael M. Garner
年度	2020
出版社	CRC Press
DOI	https://doi.org/10.1201/9780429155567
序号	261
标题	**Pandemic Education and Viral Politics**
作者	Michael A. Peters, Tina Besley
年度	2020
出版社	Routledge

续表

DOI	https://doi.org/10.4324/9781003119579
序号	262
标题	Pandemic, Ecology and Theology
副标题	Perspectives on COVID-19
作者	Alexander Hampton
年度	2020
出版社	Routledge
DOI	https://doi.org/10.4324/9781003105602
序号	263
标题	Practical Clinical Microbiology and Infectious Diseases
副标题	A Hands-On Guide
作者	Firza Alexander Gronthoud
年度	2020
出版社	CRC Press
DOI	https://doi.org/10.1201/9781315194080
序号	264
标题	Preventing HIV Among Young People in Southern and Eastern Africa
副标题	Emerging Evidence and Intervention Strategies
作者	Kaymarlin Govender, Nana Poku
年度	2020
出版社	Routledge
DOI	https://doi.org/10.4324/9780429462818
序号	265
标题	Psychological Insights for Understanding COVID-19 and Families, Parents, and Children
作者	Marc H. Bornstein
年度	2020
出版社	Routledge
DOI	https://doi.org/10.4324/9781003136811
序号	266

续表

标题	Psychological Insights for Understanding COVID-19 and Media and Technology
作者	Ciarán Mc Mahon
年度	2020
出版社	Routledge
DOI	https://doi.org/10.4324/9781003121756
序号	267
标题	Psychological Insights for Understanding COVID-19 and Society
作者	S. Alexander Haslam
年度	2020
出版社	Routledge
DOI	https://doi.org/10.4324/9781003126126
序号	268
标题	Psychological Insights for Understanding COVID-19 and Work
作者	Cary L. Cooper
年度	2020
出版社	Routledge
DOI	https://doi.org/10.4324/9781003119951
序号	269
标题	Psychological Perspectives in HIV Care
副标题	An Inter-Professional Approach
作者	Michelle Croston, Sarah Rutter
年度	2020
出版社	Routledge
DOI	https://doi.org/10.4324/9781315211404
序号	270
标题	Public Policy Lessons from the AIDS Response in Africa
作者	Fred Eboko
年度	2020
出版社	Routledge

续表

DOI	https://doi.org/10.4324/9781003002130
序号	271
标题	**Social Analysis and the COVID-19 Crisis**
副标题	A Collective Journal
作者	Suman Gupta, Richard Allen, Maitrayee Basu, Fabio Akcelrud Durão, Ayan-Yue Gupta, lena Katsarska, Sebastian Schuller, John Seed, Peter H. Tu
年度	2020
出版社	Routledge India
DOI	https://doi.org/10.4324/9781003120155
序号	272
标题	**Sport and the Pandemic**
副标题	Perspectives on Covid-19's Impact on the Sport Industry
作者	Paul M. Pedersen, Brody J. Ruihley, Bo Li
年度	2020
出版社	Routledge
DOI	https://doi.org/10.4324/9781003105916
序号	273
标题	**The Business of Pandemics**
副标题	The COVID-19 Story
作者	Jay Liebowitz
年度	2020
出版社	Auerbach Publications
DOI	https://doi.org/10.1201/9781003094937
序号	274
标题	**The COVID-19 Pandemic**
副标题	The Deadly Coronavirus Outbreak
作者	Tapas Kumar Koley, Monika Dhole
年度	2020
出版社	Routledge India
DOI	https://doi.org/10.4324/9781003095590

续表

序号	275
标题	**The Covid-19 Reader**
副标题	The Science and What It Says About the Social
作者	William Cockerham, Geoffrey Cockerham
年度	2020
出版社	Routledge
DOI	https://doi.org/10.4324/9781003141402
序号	276
标题	**Viral Pandemics**
副标题	From Smallpox to COVID-19
作者	Rae-Ellen Kavey, Allison Kavey
年度	2020
出版社	Routledge
DOI	https://doi.org/10.4324/9781003006800
序号	277
标题	**Handbook of Infectious Disease Data Analysis**
作者	Leonhard Held, Niel Hens, Philip O'Neill, Jacco Wallinga
年度	2019
出版社	Chapman and Hall/CRC
DOI	https://doi.org/10.1201/9781315222912
序号	278
标题	**Human Extinction and the Pandemic Imaginary**
作者	Christos Lynteris
年度	2019
出版社	Routledge
DOI	https://doi.org/10.4324/9780429322051
序号	279
标题	**Living in the Shadows of China's HIV/AIDS Epidemics**
副标题	Sex, Drugs and Bad Blood
作者	Shelley Torcetti

一、图书

续表

年度	2019
出版社	Routledge
DOI	https://doi.org/10.4324/9780429265488
序号	280
标题	**Molecular and Cellular Biology of Viruses**
作者	Phoebe Lostroh
年度	2019
出版社	Garland Science
DOI	https://doi.org/10.1201/9780429021725
序号	281
标题	**Pocket Guide to Bacterial Infections**
作者	K Balamurugan, Prithika Udayakumar
年度	2019
出版社	CRC Press
DOI	https://doi.org/10.1201/b22196
序号	282
标题	**The Normalization of the HIV and AIDS Epidemic in South Africa**
作者	Katinka de Wet
年度	2019
出版社	Routledge
DOI	https://doi.org/10.4324/9780429201868
序号	283
标题	**Tuberculosis—The Singapore Experience, 1867—2018**
副标题	Disease, Society and the State
作者	Kah Seng Loh, Li Yang Hsu
年度	2019
出版社	Routledge
DOI	https://doi.org/10.4324/9780429331442
序号	284
标题	**Understanding Tuberculosis and Its Control**
副标题	Anthropological and Ethnographic Approaches

续表

作者	Helen Macdonald, Ian Harper
年度	2019
出版社	Routledge
DOI	https://doi.org/10.4324/9780429457104
序号	285
标题	**A Visual History of HIV/AIDS**
副标题	Exploring the Face of AIDS Film Archive
作者	Elisabet Björklund, Mariah Larsson
年度	2018
出版社	Routledge
DOI	https://doi.org/10.4324/9781315145310
序号	286
标题	**Chlamydiae and Chlamydial Infections**
作者	Svetoslav P. Martinov
年度	2018
出版社	River Publishers
序号	287
标题	**Geographies of Plague Pandemics**
副标题	The Spatial-Temporal Behavior of Plague to the Modern Day
作者	Mark Welford
年度	2018
出版社	Routledge
DOI	https://doi.org/10.4324/9781315307435
序号	288
标题	**Nutrition and HIV**
副标题	Epidemiological Evidence to Public Health
作者	Saurabh Mehta, Julia Finkelstein
年度	2018
出版社	CRC Press
DOI	https://doi.org/10.1201/9781351058193

续表

序号	289
标题	**Phylogeny and Evolution of Bacteria and Mitochondria**
作者	Mauro Degli Esposti
年度	2018
出版社	CRC Press
DOI	https://doi.org/10.1201/b22399
序号	290
标题	**Rethinking MSM, Trans* and Other Categories in HIV Prevention**
作者	Amaya G. Perez-Brumer, Richard Parker, Peter Aggleton
年度	2018
出版社	Routledge
DOI	https://doi.org/10.4324/9781315151120
序号	291
标题	**The Political Economy of HIV in Africa**
作者	Deborah Johnston, Kevin Deane, Matteo Rizzo
年度	2018
出版社	Routledge
DOI	https://doi.org/10.4324/9781315182629
序号	292
标题	**Tuberculosis in the Americas, 1870—1945**
副标题	Beneath the Anguish in Philadelphia and Buenos Aires
作者	Vera Blinn Reber
年度	2018
出版社	Routledge
DOI	https://doi.org/10.4324/9780429433702
序号	293
标题	**A Guide to AIDS**
作者	Omar Bagasra, Donald Gene Pace
年度	2017
出版社	CRC Press

续表

DOI	https://doi.org/10.1201/b21840
序号	294
标题	**Ebola**
副标题	Clinical Patterns, Public Health Concerns
作者	Joseph R. Masci, Elizabeth Bass
年度	2017
出版社	CRC Press
DOI	https://doi.org/10.1201/9781315119854
序号	295
标题	**Governing HIV in China**
副标题	Commercial Sex, Homosexuality and Rural-to-Urban Migration
作者	Elaine Jeffreys, Gang Su
年度	2017
出版社	Routledge
DOI	https://doi.org/10.4324/9781315175546
序号	296
标题	**HIV/AIDS in India**
副标题	Voices from the Margins
作者	Sunita Manian
年度	2017
出版社	Routledge
DOI	https://doi.org/10.4324/9781315209388
序号	297
标题	**Holistic Approaches to Infectious Diseases**
作者	Ann George, Joshy K. S., Mathew Sebastian, Oluwatobi Samuel Oluwafemi, Sabu Thomas
年度	2017
出版社	Apple Academic Press
DOI	https://doi.org/10.1201/b19944
序号	298

续表

标题	Modern Infectious Disease Epidemiology
作者	Johan Giesecke
年度	2017
出版社	CRC Press
DOI	https://doi.org/10.1201/9781315222714
序号	299
标题	**Quantitative Methods for HIV/AIDS Research**
作者	Cliburn Chan, Michael G. Hudgens, Shein-Chung Chow
年度	2017
出版社	Chapman and Hall/CRC
DOI	https://doi.org/10.1201/9781315120805
序号	300
标题	**The International Politics of Ebola**
作者	Anne Roemer-Mahler, Simon Rushton
年度	2017
出版社	Routledge
序号	301
标题	**Children and AIDS**
副标题	Sub-Saharan Africa
作者	Margaret Lombe, Alex Ochumbo
年度	2016
出版社	Routledge
DOI	https://doi.org/10.4324/9781315563015
序号	302
标题	**Civil Society Organizations and the Global Response to HIV/AIDS**
作者	Julia Smith
年度	2016
出版社	Routledge
DOI	https://doi.org/10.4324/9781315412771
序号	303

续表

标题	**Foodborne Viral Pathogens**
作者	Peter A. White, Natalie E. Netzler, Grant S. Hansman
年度	2016
出版社	CRC Press
DOI	https://doi.org/10.1201/9781315392301
序号	304
标题	**Mainstream AIDS Theatre, the Media, and Gay Civil Rights**
副标题	Making the Radical Palatable
作者	Jacob Juntunen
年度	2016
出版社	Routledge
DOI	https://doi.org/10.4324/9781315673554
序号	305
标题	**Molecular Detection of Animal Viral Pathogens**
作者	Dongyou Liu
年度	2016
出版社	CRC Press
DOI	https://doi.org/10.1201/b19719
序号	306
标题	**Risk Communication and Infectious Diseases in an Age of Digital Media**
作者	Anat Gesser-Edelsburg, Yaffa Shir-Raz
年度	2016
出版社	Routledge
DOI	https://doi.org/10.4324/9781315644073
序号	307
标题	**Silver Nanoparticles for Antibacterial Devices**
副标题	Biocompatibility and Toxicity
作者	Huiliang Cao
年度	2016
出版社	CRC Press

DOI	https://doi.org/10.1201/9781315370569
序号	308
标题	**The Cognitive Early Warning Predictive System Using the Smart Vaccine**
副标题	The New Digital Immunity Paradigm for Smart Cities and Critical Infrastructure
作者	Rocky Termanini
年度	2016
出版社	Auerbach Publications
DOI	https://doi.org/10.1201/b19155
序号	309
标题	**Therapeutic Applications of Adenoviruses**
作者	Philip Ng, Nicola Brunetti-Pierri
年度	2016
出版社	CRC Press
DOI	https://doi.org/10.1201/9781315368832
序号	310
标题	**Anthropology of Infectious Disease**
作者	Merrill Singer
年度	2015
出版社	Routledge
DOI	https://doi.org/10.4324/9781315434735
序号	311
标题	**Biology of Foodborne Parasites**
作者	Lihua Xiao, Una Ryan, Yaoyu Feng
年度	2015
出版社	CRC Press
DOI	https://doi.org/10.1201/b18317
序号	312
标题	**Childhood Sexuality and AIDS Education**
副标题	The Price of Innocence

续表

作者	Deevia Bhana
年度	2015
出版社	Routledge
DOI	https://doi.org/10.4324/9781315723051
序号	313
标题	**Clinical Tuberculosis**
副标题	A Practical Handbook
作者	Peter D. O. Davies
年度	2015
出版社	CRC Press
DOI	https://doi.org/10.1201/b20755
序号	314
标题	**Foodborne Pathogens and Food Safety**
作者	Md. Latiful Bari, Dike O. Ukuku
年度	2015
出版社	CRC Press
DOI	https://doi.org/10.1201/b19851
序号	315
标题	**Modeling to Inform Infectious Disease Control**
作者	Niels G. Becker
年度	2015
出版社	Chapman and Hall/CRC
DOI	https://doi.org/10.1201/b18377
序号	316
标题	**Nanoparticulate Vaccine Delivery Systems**
作者	Martin J. D'Souza
年度	2015
出版社	Jenny Stanford Publishing
DOI	https://doi.org/10.1201/b18096
序号	317

续表

标题	Post-Genomic Approaches in Drug and Vaccine Development
作者	Kishore R. Sakharkar, Meena K. Sakharkar, Ramesh Chandra
年度	2015
出版社	River Publishers
DOI	https://doi.org/10.1201/9781003339090
序号	318
标题	Prescribing HIV Prevention
副标题	Bringing Culture into Global Health Communication
作者	Nicola Bulled
年度	2015
出版社	Routledge
DOI	https://doi.org/10.4324/9781315421971
序号	319
标题	Religious Responses to HIV and AIDS
作者	Miguel Munoz-Laboy, Jonathan Garcia, Joyce Moon-Howard, Patrick Wilson, Richard Parker
年度	2015
出版社	Routledge
DOI	https://doi.org/10.4324/9781315760957
序号	320
标题	Sanitation, Latrines and Intestinal Parasites in Past Populations
作者	Piers D. Mitchell
年度	2015
出版社	Routledge
DOI	https://doi.org/10.4324/9781315607603
序号	321
标题	Values and Vaccine Refusal
副标题	Hard Questions in Ethics, Epistemology, and Health Care
作者	Mark Navin
年度	2015

续表

出版社	Routledge
DOI	https://doi.org/10.4324/9781315764078
序号	322
标题	**Bacteria in Britain, 1880—1939**
作者	Rosemary Wall
年度	2014
出版社	Routledge
DOI	https://doi.org/10.4324/9781315654478
序号	323
标题	**Cancer-Causing Viruses and Their Inhibitors**
作者	Satya Prakash Gupta
年度	2014
出版社	CRC Press
DOI	https://doi.org/10.1201/b16780
序号	324
标题	**Clinical Tuberculosis**
作者	Peter D. O. Davies, Stephen B Gordon, Geriant Davies
年度	2014
出版社	CRC Press
DOI	https://doi.org/10.1201/b16604
序号	325
标题	**Comprehensive Care for HIV/AIDS**
副标题	Community-Based Strategies
作者	Teresa L. Scheid
年度	2014
出版社	Routledge
DOI	https://doi.org/10.4324/9781315762579
序号	326
标题	**Drug Delivery and Development of Anti-HIV Microbicides**
作者	Jose das Neves, Bruno Sarmento

年度	2014
出版社	Jenny Stanford Publishing
DOI	https://doi.org/10.1201/b17559
序号	327
标题	**HIV/AIDS and the Social Consequences of Untamed Biomedicine**
副标题	Anthropological Complicities
作者	Graham Fordham
年度	2014
出版社	Routledge
DOI	https://doi.org/10.4324/9781315757292
序号	328
标题	**HIV/AIDS and the South African State**
副标题	Sovereignty and the Responsibility to Respond
作者	Annamarie Bindenagel Šehović
年度	2014
出版社	Routledge
DOI	https://doi.org/10.4324/9781315586946
序号	329
标题	**Integrated Virus Detection**
作者	Charles H. Wick
年度	2014
出版社	CRC Press
DOI	https://doi.org/10.1201/b17652
序号	330
标题	**Religion and AIDS Treatment in Africa**
副标题	Saving Souls, Prolonging Lives
作者	Rijk van Dijk, Hansjörg Dilger, Thera Rasing
年度	2014
出版社	Routledge
DOI	https://doi.org/10.4324/9781315604718

续表

序号	331
标题	**Representations of HIV/AIDS in Contemporary Hispano-American and Caribbean Culture**
副标题	Cuerpos suiSIDAs
作者	Gustavo Subero
年度	2014
出版社	Routledge
DOI	https://doi.org/10.4324/9781315605449
序号	332
标题	**Thinking Politically About HIV**
作者	Kent Buse, Dennis Altman
年度	2014
出版社	Routledge
DOI	https://doi.org/10.4324/9781315540474
序号	333
标题	**Understanding HIV and STI Prevention for College Students**
作者	Leo Wilton, Robert T. Palmer, Dina C. Maramba
年度	2014
出版社	Routledge
DOI	https://doi.org/10.4324/9781315884387
序号	334
标题	**Bacterial Integrative Mobile Genetic Elements**
作者	Adam P. Roberts, Peter Mullany
年度	2013
出版社	CRC Press
DOI	https://doi.org/10.1201/9780367813925
序号	335
标题	**Cutaneous Manifestations of HIV Disease**
作者	Clay Cockerell, Antoanella Calame
年度	2013

续表

出版社	CRC Press
DOI	https://doi.org/10.1201/b15910
序号	336
标题	**Economics and HIV**
副标题	The Sickness of Economics
作者	Deborah Johnston
年度	2013
出版社	Routledge
DOI	https://doi.org/10.4324/9780203768709
序号	337
标题	**Food Associated Pathogens**
作者	Wilhelm Tham, Marie Louise Danielsson-Tham
年度	2013
出版社	CRC Press
DOI	https://doi.org/10.1201/b15475
序号	338
标题	**HIV and East Africa**
副标题	Thirty Years in the Shadow of an Epidemic
作者	Janet Seeley
年度	2013
出版社	Routledge
DOI	https://doi.org/10.4324/9780203589977
序号	339
标题	**HIV in World Cultures**
副标题	Three Decades of Representations
作者	Gustavo Subero
年度	2013
出版社	Routledge
DOI	https://doi.org/10.4324/9781315586939
序号	340

续表

标题	Living with HIV and Dying with AIDS
副标题	Diversity, Inequality and Human Rights in the Global Pandemic
作者	Lesley Doyal
年度	2013
出版社	Routledge
DOI	https://doi.org/10.4324/9781315592817
序号	341
标题	The Politics of HIV/AIDS in Russia
作者	Ulla Pape
年度	2013
出版社	Routledge
DOI	https://doi.org/10.4324/9781315886756
序号	342
标题	AIDS Literature and Gay Identity
副标题	The Literature of Loss
作者	Monica Pearl
年度	2012
出版社	Routledge
DOI	https://doi.org/10.4324/9780203098615
序号	343
标题	Ethics and Security Aspects of Infectious Disease Control
副标题	Interdisciplinary Perspectives
作者	Michael J. Selgelid, Christian Enemark
年度	2012
出版社	Routledge
DOI	https://doi.org/10.4324/9781315580357
序号	344
标题	Microbiology and Infectious Diseases on the Move
作者	Thomas Locke, Sally Keat, Andrew Walker, Rory Mackinnon
年度	2012

续表

出版社	CRC Press
DOI	https://doi.org/10.1201/b13514
序号	345
标题	**Pandemic Planning**
作者	J. Eric Dietz, David R. Black
年度	2012
出版社	CRC Press
DOI	https://doi.org/10.1201/b11779
序号	346
标题	**AIDS, Behavior, and Culture**
副标题	Understanding Evidence-Based Prevention
作者	Edward C Green, Allison Herling Ruark
年度	2011
出版社	Routledge
DOI	https://doi.org/10.4324/9781315435176
序号	347
标题	**Cancer Vaccines**
副标题	From Research to Clinical Practice
作者	Adrian Bot, Mihail Obrocea, Francesco M. Marincola
年度	2011
出版社	CRC Press
DOI	https://doi.org/10.3109/9781841848303
序号	348
标题	**Feline Infectious Diseases**
副标题	Self-Assessment Color Review
作者	Katrin Hartmann, Julie Levy
年度	2011
出版社	CRC Press
DOI	https://doi.org/10.1201/b15189
序号	349

续表

标题	HIV/AIDS, Health and the Media in China
作者	Johanna Hood
年度	2011
出版社	Routledge
DOI	https://doi.org/10.4324/9780203832813
序号	350
标题	HIV/AIDS in China—The Economic and Social Determinants
作者	Dylan Sutherland, Jennifer Y.J. Hsu
年度	2011
出版社	Routledge
DOI	https://doi.org/10.4324/9780203253861
序号	351
标题	Molecular Detection of Human Bacterial Pathogens
作者	Dongyou Liu
年度	2011
出版社	CRC Press
DOI	https://doi.org/10.1201/b10848
序号	352
标题	Molecular Detection of Human Fungal Pathogens
作者	Dongyou Liu
年度	2011
出版社	CRC Press
DOI	https://doi.org/10.1201/b11375
序号	353
标题	Outpatient Management of HIV Infection(Fourth Edition)
作者	Joseph Masci
年度	2011
出版社	CRC Press
DOI	https://doi.org/10.3109/9781420087369
序号	354

续表

标题	The Politics of AIDS Denialism
副标题	South Africa's Failure to Respond
作者	Pieter Fourie, Melissa Meyer
年度	2011
出版社	Routledge
DOI	https://doi.org/10.4324/9781315554419
序号	355
标题	Understanding the Politics of Pandemic Scares
副标题	An Introduction to Global Politosomatics
作者	Mika Aaltola
年度	2011
出版社	Routledge
DOI	https://doi.org/10.4324/9780203805732
序号	356
标题	Viruses
副标题	Biology, Applications, and Control
作者	David Harper
年度	2011
出版社	Garland Science
DOI	https://doi.org/10.1201/9780429258466
序号	357
标题	A Color Atlas of Comparative Pathology of Pulmonary Tuberculosis
作者	Franz Joel Leong, Veronique Dartois, Thomas Dick
年度	2010
出版社	CRC Press
DOI	https://doi.org/10.1201/EBK1439835272
序号	358
标题	AIDS and Rural Livelihoods
副标题	Dynamics and Diversity in Sub-Saharan Africa
作者	Anke Niehof, Gabriel Rugalema

年度	2010
出版社	Routledge
DOI	https://doi.org/10.4324/9781849775779
序号	359
标题	**Avian Influenza**
副标题	Science, Policy and Politics
作者	Ian Scoones
年度	2010
出版社	Routledge
DOI	https://doi.org/10.4324/9781849775045
序号	360
标题	**Case Studies in Infectious Disease**
作者	Peter Lydyard, Michael Cole, John Holton, Will Irving, Nino Porakishvili, Pradhib Venkatesan, te Ward
年度	2010
出版社	Garland Science
DOI	https://doi.org/10.4324/9780203856871
序号	361
标题	**Case Studies in Infectious Disease: Aspergillus Fumigatus**
作者	Peter Lydyard, Michael Cole, John Holton, Will Irving, Nino Porakishvili, Pradhib Venkatesan, te Ward
年度	2010
出版社	Garland Science
DOI	https://doi.org/10.4324/9780203853733
序号	362
标题	**Influenza and Public Health**
副标题	Learning from Past Pandemics
作者	Jennifer Gunn, Tamara Giles-Vernick, Susan Craddock
年度	2010
出版社	Routledge
DOI	https://doi.org/10.4324/9781849776448

续表

序号	363
标题	**Molecular Detection of Human Viral Pathogens**
作者	Dongyou Liu
年度	2010
出版社	CRC Press
DOI	https://doi.org/10.1201/b13590
序号	364
标题	**New Generation Vaccines（Fourth Edition）**
作者	Myrone M. Levine, Myron M. Levine, Gordon Dougan, Michael F. Good, Gary J. Nabel, James P. Nataro, Rino Rappuoli
年度	2010
出版社	CRC Press
DOI	https://doi.org/10.3109/9781420060744
序号	365
标题	**Practical Atlas for Bacterial Identification（Second Edition）**
作者	D. Roy Cullimore
年度	2010
出版社	CRC Press
DOI	https://doi.org/10.1201/9781420087987
序号	366
标题	**The World Bank and HIV/AIDS**
副标题	Setting a Global Agenda
作者	Sophie Harman
年度	2010
出版社	Routledge
DOI	https://doi.org/10.4324/9780203849910
序号	367
标题	**Tuberculosis**
副标题	The Essentials, Fourth Edition
作者	Mario C. Raviglione

续表

年度	2010
出版社	CRC Press
DOI	https://doi.org/10.3109/9781420090239
序号	368

Harvard

标题	**Political Disappointment: A Cultural History from Reconstruction to the AIDS Crisis**
作者	Sara Marcus
年度	2023
ISBN	9780674248656
序号	1
标题	**Outbreak Culture: The Ebola Crisis and the Next Epidemic, with a New Preface and Epilogue**
作者	Pardis Sabeti, Lara Salahi
年度	2021
ISBN	9780674260474
序号	2
标题	**Superbugs: An Arms Race Against Bacteria**
作者	William Hall, Anthony McDonnell, Jim O'Neill
年度	2018
ISBN	9780674975989
序号	3
标题	**Viruses: Agents of Evolutionary Invention**
作者	Michael G. Cordingley
年度	2017
ISBN	9780674972087
序号	4
标题	**Long Shot: Vaccines for National Defense**
作者	Kendall Hoyt
年度	2012
ISBN	9780674061583
序号	5

Mitpress

标题	**Paris and the Parasite**	
副标题	Noise, Health, and Politics in the Media City	
作者	Macs Smith	
年度	2021	
ISBN	9780262045544	
序号	1	
标题	**Vaccination Ethics and Policy**	
副标题	An Introduction with Readings	
作者	Jason L. Schwartz, Arthur L. Caplan	
年度	2021	
ISBN	9780262544122	
序号	2	
标题	**Viruses, Pandemics, and Immunity**	
作者	Arup K. Chakraborty, Andrey S. Shaw	
年度	2021	
ISBN	9780262542388	
序号	3	
标题	**Economics in the Age of COVID-19**	
作者	Joshua Gans	
年度	2020	
ISBN	9780262362795	
序号	4	
标题	**The Pandemic Information Gap**	
副标题	The Brutal Economics of COVID-19	
作者	Joshua Gans	
年度	2020	
ISBN	9780262539128	
序号	5	

续表

标题	**Ebola's Message**
副标题	Public Health and Medicine in the Twenty-First Century
作者	Nicholas G. Evans, Tara C. Smith, Maimuna S. Majumder
年度	2016
ISBN	9780262035071
序号	6
标题	**Trace Metals and Infectious Diseases**
作者	Jerome O. Nriagu, Eric P. Skaar
年度	2015
ISBN	9780262029193
序号	7
标题	**Infectious Behavior**
副标题	Brain-Immune Connections in Autism, Schizophrenia, and Depression
作者	Paul H. Patterson
年度	2013
ISBN	9780262525343
序号	8
标题	**Parasites, Pathogens, and Progress**
副标题	Diseases and Economic Development
作者	Robert A. McGuire, Philip R. P. Coelho
年度	2011
ISBN	9780262015660
序号	9

Oxford

标题	**COVID-19, Law & Regulation**
副标题	Rights, Freedoms, and Obligations in a Pandemic
作者	Belinda Bennett, Ian Freckelton AO KC, Gabrielle Wolf
年度	2023
ISBN	9780192896742
序号	1
标题	**Infectious Disease: A Very Short Introduction**
版本	Second Edition
作者	Marta Wayne, Benjamin Bolker
年度	2023
ISBN	9780192858511
序号	2
标题	**Reading Novels During the Covid-19 Pandemic**
作者	Ben Davies, Christina Lupton, Johanne Gormsen Schmidt
年度	2023
ISBN	9780192857682
序号	3
标题	**Viruses: A Very Short Introduction**
版本	Third Edition
作者	Dorothy H. Crawford
年度	2023
ISBN	9780192865069
序号	4
标题	**A Multidisciplinary Approach to Pandemics**
副标题	COVID-19 and Beyond
作者	Philippe Bourbeau, Jean-Michel Marcoux, Brooke A. Ackerly
年度	2022
ISBN	9780192897855

续表

序号	5
标题	**Bacteria: A Very Short Introduction**
版本	Second Edition
作者	Sebastian G. B. Amyes
年度	2022
ISBN	9780192895240
序号	6
标题	**Covid and Custom in Rural South Africa**
副标题	Culture, Healthcare and the State
作者	Leslie Bank, Nelly Sharpley
年度	2022
ISBN	9780197659618
序号	7
标题	**Eco-Anxiety and Pandemic Distress**
副标题	Psychological Perspectives on Resilience and Interconnectedness
作者	Douglas Vakoch, Sam Mickey
年度	2022
ISBN	9780197622674
序号	8
标题	**Infectious Disease Ecology and Conservation**
作者	Johannes Foufopoulos, Gary A. Wobeser, Hamish McCallum
年度	2022
ISBN	9780199583515
序号	9
标题	**Mayo Clinic Infectious Disease Case Review**
副标题	With Board-Style Questions and Answers
作者	Larry M. Baddour, John C. O'Horo, Mark J. Enzler, Rahul Kashyap
年度	2022
ISBN	9780190052973
序号	10

续表

标题	**Microbiology of Infectious Disease**
副标题	Integrating Genomics with Natural History
作者	Sandy R. Primrose
年度	2022
ISBN	9780192863850
序号	11
标题	**Pandemic India**
副标题	From Cholera to Covid-19
作者	David Arnold
年度	2022
ISBN	9780197659625
序号	12
标题	**Pandemic Re-Awakenings**
副标题	The Forgotten and Unforgotten "Spanish" Flu of 1918—1919
作者	Guy Beiner
年度	2022
ISBN	9780192843739
序号	13
标题	**Reframing Globalization After COVID-19**
副标题	Pandemic Diplomacy Amid the Failure of Multilateral Cooperation
作者	Pablo Baisotti, Pierfrancesco Moscuzza
年度	2022
ISBN	9781789761764
序号	14
标题	**Schlossberg's Clinical Infectious Disease**
版本	Third Edition
作者	Cheston B. Cunha
年度	2022
ISBN	9780190888367
序号	15

续表

标题	Viruses
副标题	The Invisible Enemy
版本	Second Edition
作者	Dorothy H. Crawford
年度	2022
ISBN	9780192845030
序号	16
标题	COVID's Impact on Health and Healthcare Workers
作者	Don Goldenberg
年度	2021
ISBN	9780197575390
序号	17
标题	Fundamentals of HIV Medicine 2021
副标题	CME Edition
作者	W. David Hardy, The American Academy of HIV Medicine
年度	2021
ISBN	9780197576632
序号	18
标题	The Covid Consensus
副标题	The New Politics of Global Inequality
作者	Toby Green
年度	2021
ISBN	9781787385221
序号	19
标题	The Fight for Climate After COVID-19
作者	Alice C. Hill
年度	2021
ISBN	9780197549704
序号	20

续表

标题	The Queer Biopic in the AIDS Era
作者	Laura Stamm
年度	2021
ISBN	9780197604038
序号	21
标题	COVID-19 in Asia
副标题	Law and Policy Contexts
作者	Victor V. Ramraj
年度	2020
ISBN	9780197553831
序号	22
标题	HIV
作者	Gregory Huhn
年度	2020
ISBN	9780190088316
序号	23
标题	Motivational Interviewing in HIV Care
作者	Antoine Douaihy, K. Rivet Amico
年度	2020
ISBN	9780190619954
序号	24
标题	Oxford Case Histories in Infectious Diseases and Microbiology
版本	Third Edition
作者	Hilary Humphreys, William L. Irving, Bridget L. Atkins, Andrew Woodhouse
年度	2020
ISBN	9780198846482
序号	25
标题	Pandemics, Publics, and Narrative
作者	Mark Davis, Davina Lohm

续表

年度	2020
ISBN	9780190683764
序号	26
标题	**Viruses, Plagues, and History**
副标题	Past, Present, and Future
版本	Second Edition
作者	Michael B. A. Oldstone
年度	2020
ISBN	9780190056780
序号	27
标题	**Bartlett's Medical Management of HIV Infection**
版本	Seventeenth Edition
作者	John G. Bartlett, Robert R. Redfield, Paul A. Pham
年度	2019
ISBN	9780190924775
序号	28
标题	**Human Infectious Disease and Public Health**
作者	William Fullick
年度	2019
ISBN	9780198814382
序号	29
标题	**Oxford Handbook of Genitourinary Medicine, HIV, and Sexual Health**
版本	Third Edition
作者	Laura Mitchell, Bridie Howe, D. Ashley Price, Babiker E lawad, K. Nathan Sankar
年度	2019
ISBN	9780198783497
序号	30
标题	**Ecology and Evolution of Infectious Disease**
副标题	Pathogen Control and Public Health Management in Low-Income Countries

作者	Benjamin Roche, Helene Broutin, Frederic Simard
年度	2018
ISBN	9780198789833
序号	31
标题	**Enteric Hepatitis Viruses**
作者	Stanley M. Lemon, Christopher M. Walker
年度	2018
ISBN	9781621821625
序号	32
标题	**Immune Memory and Vaccines: Great Debates**
作者	Shane Crotty, Rafi Ahmed
年度	2018
ISBN	9781621821540
序号	33
标题	**Structural Interventions for HIV Prevention**
副标题	Optimizing Strategies for Reducing New Infections and Improving Care
作者	Richard A. Crosby, Ralph J. DiClemente
年度	2018
ISBN	9780190675486
序号	34
标题	**The New Hepatitis C**
副标题	Effective Clinical Management in the Age of All-Oral Therapy
版本	Second Edition
作者	Nancy Reau, Donald M. Jensen
年度	2018
ISBN	9780190238285
序号	35
标题	**Comprehensive Textbook of AIDS Psychiatry**
副标题	A Paradigm for Integrated Care

续表

版本	Second Edition
作者	Mary Ann Cohen, Jack M. Gorman, Scott L. Letendre, Jeffrey M. Jacobson, Paul Volberding
年度	2017
ISBN	9780199392742
序号	36
标题	**Ebola**
副标题	Profile of a Killer Virus
作者	Dorothy H. Crawford
年度	2017
ISBN	9780198759997
序号	37
标题	**HIV & AIDS: A Very Short Introduction**
版本	Second Edition
作者	Alan Whiteside
年度	2017
ISBN	9780198727491
序号	38
标题	**Handbook of Child and Adolescent Tuberculosis**
作者	Jeffrey R. Starke, Peter R. Donald
年度	2017
ISBN	9780190695316
序号	39
标题	**Oxford Handbook of Infectious Diseases and Microbiology**
版本	Second Edition
作者	Estée Török, Ed Moran, Fiona Cooke
年度	2017
ISBN	9780199671328
序号	40

续表

标题	**The Vaccine Handbook**
副标题	A Practitioner's Guide to Maximizing Use and Efficacy Across the Lifespan
作者	Tina Q. Tan, John P. Flaherty, Melvin V. Gerbie
年度	2017
ISBN	9780190604776
序号	41
标题	**Vaccines**
副标题	What Everyone Needs to Know®
作者	Kristen A. Feemster
年度	2017
ISBN	9780190277901
序号	42
标题	**From Herodotus to HIV**
副标题	A History of Haematology
作者	Shaun R. McCann
年度	2016
ISBN	9780198717607
序号	43
标题	**Global Management of Infectious Disease After Ebola**
作者	Sam F. Halabi, Lawrence O. Gostin, Jeffrey S. Crowley
年度	2016
ISBN	9780190604882
序号	44
标题	**Infectious Disease Epidemiology**
作者	Ibrahim Abubakar, Helen R. Stagg, Thed Cohen, Laura C. Rodrigues
年度	2016
ISBN	9780198719830
序号	45
标题	**Infectious Diseases Emergencies**
作者	Arjun S. Chanmugam, Richard Rothman, Sanjay Desai, Shannon Putman

续表

年度	2016
ISBN	9780199976805
序号	46
标题	**The Economics of the Global Response to HIV/AIDS**
作者	Markus Haacker
年度	2016
ISBN	9780198718048
序号	47
标题	**Pandemics: A Very Short Introduction**
作者	Christian W. McMillen
年度	2016
ISBN	9780199340071
序号	48
标题	**Infectious Disease: A Very Short Introduction**
作者	Benjamin Bolker, Marta Wayne
年度	2015
ISBN	9780199688937
序号	49
标题	**Virus Hunt**
副标题	The Search for the Origin of HIV/AIDs
作者	Dorothy H. Crawford
年度	2015
ISBN	9780198743873
序号	50
标题	**Cancer Virus**
副标题	The Discovery of the Epstein-Barr Virus
作者	Dorothy H. Crawford, Ingolfur Johannessen, Alan B. Rickinson
年度	2014
ISBN	9780199653119

续表

序号	51
标题	**Challenging Concepts in Infectious Diseases and Clinical Microbiology**
作者	Amber Arnold, George Griffin
年度	2014
ISBN	9780199665754
序号	52
标题	**The AIDS Generation**
副标题	Stories of Survival and Resilience
作者	Perry Halkitis
年度	2014
ISBN	9780190234331
序号	53
标题	**The Infectious Microbe**
作者	William Firshein
年度	2014
ISBN	9780199329618
序号	54
标题	**Before HIV**
副标题	Sexuality, Fertility and Mortality in East Africa, 1900—1980
作者	Shane Doyle
年度	2013
ISBN	9780197265338
序号	55
标题	**Handbook of HIV Medicine**
版本	Third Edition
作者	Douglas Wilson, Mark Cotton, Linda-Gail Bekker, Tammy Meyers, Francois Venter, Gary Maartens
年度	2013
ISBN	9780199053667
序号	56

续表

标题	Oxford Textbook of Infectious Disease Control Online
作者	Andrew Cliff, Matthew Smallman-Raynor
年度	2013
ISBN	9780199596614
序号	57
标题	**Pandemics**
副标题	What Everyone Needs to Know®
作者	Peter C. Doherty
年度	2013
ISBN	9780199898107
序号	58
标题	**Social Work with HIV and AIDS**
副标题	A Case-Based Guide
作者	Diana Rowan
年度	2013
ISBN	9780190616380
序号	59
标题	**The AIDS Generation**
副标题	Stories of Survival and Resilience
作者	Perry N. Halkitis
年度	2013
ISBN	9780199944972
序号	60
标题	**American Pandemic**
副标题	The Lost Worlds of the 1918 Influenza Epidemic
作者	Nancy K. Bristow
年度	2012
ISBN	9780199811342
序号	61

续表

标题	**Consultations in Infectious Disease**
副标题	A Case Based Approach to Diagnosis and Management
作者	Daniel Caplivski, W. Michael Scheld
年度	2012
ISBN	9780199735006
序号	62
标题	**Host Manipulation by Parasites**
作者	David P. Hughes, Jacques Brodeur, Frederic Thomas
年度	2012
ISBN	9780199642243
序号	63
标题	**Hepatitis C**
作者	Donald Jensen, Nancy Reau
年度	2012
ISBN	9780199844296
序号	64
标题	**HIV Prevention with Latinos**
副标题	Theory, Research, and Practice
作者	Kurt C. Organista
年度	2012
ISBN	9780199764303
序号	65
标题	**Host Manipulation by Parasites**
作者	David P. Hughes, Jacques Brodeur, Frederic Thomas
年度	2012
ISBN	9780199642236
序号	66
标题	**Protecting Childhood in the AIDS Pandemic**
副标题	Finding Solutions that Work
作者	Jody Heymann, Lorraine Sherr, Rachel Kidman

年度	2012	
ISBN	9780199765126	
序号	67	
标题	**Religion and AIDS in Africa**	
作者	Jenny Trinitapoli, Alexander Weinreb	
年度	2012	
ISBN	9780195335941	
序号	68	
标题	**Aging with HIV**	
副标题	A Gay Man's Guide	
作者	James Masten, James Schmidtberger	
年度	2011	
ISBN	9780199740581	
序号	69	
标题	**Oxford American Handbook of Infectious Diseases**	
作者	Aimee Zaas, Deverick J. Anderson, Kimberly E. Hanson, Elizabeth S. Dodds Ashley, Estee Torok, Ed Moran, Fiona J. Cooke	
年度	2011	
ISBN	9780195380132	
序号	70	
标题	**The Culture of AIDS in Africa**	
副标题	Hope and Healing Through Music and the Arts	
作者	Gregory Barz and Judah M. Cohen	
年度	2011	
ISBN	9780199744473	
序号	71	
标题	**The Neurology of AIDS**	
作者	Howard E. Gendelman, Igor Grant, Ian Paul Everall, Howard S. Fox, Harris A. Gelbard, Stuart A. Lipton, Susan Swindells	
年度	2011	

续表

ISBN	9780195399349
序号	72
标题	Vaccines for the Prevention of Cervical Cancer
作者	Peter Stern, Henry Kitchener
年度	2011
ISBN	9780199588633
序号	73
标题	Mayo Clinic Infectious Diseases Board Review
作者	Zelalem Temesgen
年度	2011
ISBN	9780199827626
序号	74
标题	Handbook of AIDS Psychiatry
作者	Mary Ann Cohen, Harold Goforth, Joseph Lux, Sharon Batista, Sami Khalife, Kelly Cozza, Jocelyn Soffer
年度	2010
ISBN	9780195372571
序号	75
标题	HIV and Cardiovascular Risk
作者	Marshall Glesby
年度	2010
ISBN	9780199737307
序号	76
标题	HPV and Other Infectious Agents in Cancer
副标题	Opportunities for Prevention and Public Health
作者	Hans Krueger, Gavin Stuart, Richard Gallagher, Dan Williams
年度	2010
ISBN	9780199732913
序号	77

标题	**The Biogeography of Host-Parasite Interactions**
副标题	Serge Morand, Boris R. Krasnov
年度	2010
ISBN	9780199561346
序号	78
标题	**An Introduction to Infectious Disease Modelling**
作者	Emilia Vynnycky, Richard White
年度	2010
ISBN	9780198565765
序号	79

Cambridge

标题	**Vaccines as Technology**
作者	Ana Santos Rutschman
年度	2022
ISBN	9781009125765
序号	1
标题	**After the Virus**
作者	Hilary Cooper, Simon Szreter
年度	2021
ISBN	9781009005203
序号	2
标题	**Understanding Coronavirus**
作者	Raul Rabadan
年度	2021
ISBN	9781009088572
序号	3
标题	**Democracy in Times of Pandemic**
副标题	Different Futures Imagined
作者	Miguel Poiares Maduro, Paul W. Kahn
年度	2020
ISBN	9781108845366
序号	4

中文图书

标题	致命地图：席卷全球的重大传染病及流行病
作者	［英］桑德拉·亨佩尔 (Sandra Hempel) 著；吴勐译
年度	2023
出版社	北京联合出版公司
ISBN	9787559665225
序号	1
标题	贝勒和斯科特诊断微生物学
作者	［美］帕特里夏·M. 蒂尔（Patricia M. Tille）主编；胡必杰，潘珏，高晓东主译
年度	2023
出版社	上海科学技术出版社
ISBN	9787547858851
序号	2
标题	国家病原微生物资源库目录——第三类病原微生物目录（2020年版）
作者	刘剑君，魏强
年度	2023
出版社	清华大学出版社
ISBN	9787302622475
序号	3
标题	基因、病毒与呼吸：从肺的进化起源到呼吸的治愈力量
作者	［美］迈克尔·J. 史蒂芬（Michael J. Stephen）著；杨泓译
年度	2023
出版社	中国科学技术出版社
ISBN	9787504698797
序号	4
标题	高级动物传染病学
作者	罗满林，单虎，朱战波
年度	2022
出版社	科学出版社

续表

ISBN	9787030733306
序号	5
标题	新发呼吸感染病学
作者	龙云铸，谭英征，李丹
年度	2022
出版社	中南大学出版社
ISBN	9787548750888
序号	6
标题	实用医学细菌分类与临床应用手册
作者	陈茶，屈平华
年度	2022
出版社	科学出版社
ISBN	9787030710673
序号	7
标题	病原与感染性疾病（第2版）
作者	李兰娟，唐红，程彦斌
年度	2022
出版社	人民卫生出版社
ISBN	9787117324816
序号	8
标题	进退两难：疫苗流言从何而起又为何驱之不散
作者	［英］海蒂·J.拉森（Heidi J. Larson）著；高峥荣，崔樱子主译
年度	2022
出版社	中国科学技术出版社
ISBN	9787504694652
序号	9
标题	历史、当下及未来的大流行病
作者	［德］海纳·房格劳（Heiner, Fangerau），［德］阿冯斯·腊碧士（Alfons Labisch）著；李雪涛，等译
年度	2022
出版社	东方出版社

续表

ISBN	9787520713795
序号	10
标题	吞噬危机Ⅰ：细菌、病毒与人类命运
作者	王哲
年度	2022
出版社	陕西人民出版社
ISBN	9787224144765
序号	11
标题	吞噬危机Ⅱ：人类对决天花、鼠疫、黄热病
作者	王哲
年度	2022
出版社	陕西人民出版社
ISBN	9787224144772
序号	12
标题	吞噬危机Ⅲ：人类对抗疟疾、流感、艾滋病
作者	王哲
年度	2022
出版社	陕西人民出版社
ISBN	9787224144789
序号	13
标题	改变人类的疫苗
作者	［英］斯图亚特·布鲁姆（Stuart Blume）著；谢芸，等译
年度	2022
出版社	湖南科学技术出版社
ISBN	9787571010942
序号	14
标题	中华感染病学
作者	李兰娟
年度	2022
出版社	人民卫生出版社

续表

ISBN	9787117322164
序号	15
标题	**懂病、懂微生物、懂药：感染性疾病的理念（第二版）**
作者	宁永忠，李祥
年度	2022
出版社	化学工业出版社
ISBN	9787122406477
序号	16
标题	**现代结核病学（第2版）**
作者	刘剑君，王黎霞
年度	2022
出版社	人民卫生出版社
ISBN	9787117322522
序号	17
标题	**细菌战**
作者	谢忠厚，谢丽丽
年度	2022
出版社	知识产权出版社
ISBN	9787513071086
序号	18
标题	**隐匿的暴行：细菌战、东京审判和美日交易**
作者	［美］珍妮·吉耶曼（Jeanne Guillemin）著；谭阳译
年度	2022
出版社	格致出版社
ISBN	9787543232723
序号	19
标题	**进击的病毒**
作者	史钧
年度	2021
出版社	世界图书出版公司

ISBN	9787519289614	
序号	20	
标题	恐慌帝国：传染病与统治焦虑	
作者	［英］白锦文（Robert Peckham）编；何文忠，蔡思慧，郑文慧译	
年度	2021	
出版社	浙江大学出版社	
ISBN	9787308218627	
序号	21	
标题	流行病的故事：从霍乱到埃博拉	
作者	［美］索尼娅·沙阿（Sonia Shah）著；苗小迪译	
年度	2021	
出版社	译林出版社	
ISBN	9787544787802	
序号	22	
标题	全球肿瘤疫苗创新力发展报告	
作者	池慧，欧阳昭连	
年度	2021	
出版社	科学出版社	
ISBN	9787030704696	
序号	23	
标题	Ferri临床诊疗指南——感染性疾病诊疗速查手册	
作者	［美］弗雷德·费里（Fred F. Ferri）著；张骅，徐国纲译	
年度	2021	
出版社	北京大学医学出版社	
ISBN	9787565925085	
序号	24	
标题	病毒、大流行及免疫力：探寻新冠后时代我们如何战胜传染病	
作者	［美］阿勒普·查克拉博蒂（Arup K. Chakraborty），［美］安德烈·肖(Andrey S. Shaw)著；张潞，等译	
年度	2021	

续表

出版社	人民卫生出版社
ISBN	9787117314596
序号	25
标题	病毒性肝炎（第3版）
作者	陈紫榕
年度	2021
出版社	人民卫生出版社
ISBN	9787117295475
序号	26
标题	分子疫苗
作者	［德］马蒂亚斯·吉斯（Matthias Giese）著；马维民，何继军，吴国华译
年度	2021
出版社	中国农业科学技术出版社
ISBN	9787511654526
序号	27
标题	牛津科普系列：疫苗
作者	［美］克里斯滕·A.菲姆斯特（Kristen A. Feemster）著；张波，叶寒青译
年度	2021
出版社	华中科技大学出版社
ISBN	9787568071543
序号	28
标题	柏林病人：艾滋病医疗史的转折
作者	［美］娜塔莉亚·霍尔特（Nathalia Holt）著；王年恺，王羿婷，杨雨樵译
年度	2021
出版社	社会科学文献出版社
ISBN	9787520183994
序号	29
标题	人兽共患病毒病
作者	严延生，张拥军，陈爱平
年度	2021

续表

出版社	福建科学技术出版社
ISBN	9787533564568
序号	30
标题	医学细菌名称及分类鉴定
作者	赵乃昕，苑广盈，边锋芝
年度	2021
出版社	山东大学出版社
ISBN	9787560771465
序号	31
标题	看不见的敌人：病毒的自然史
作者	［英］多萝西·克劳福德（Dorothy Crawford）著；章菁菁译
年度	2021
出版社	译林出版社
ISBN	9787544787000
序号	32
标题	细说幽门螺杆菌
作者	保志军
年度	2021
出版社	世界图书出版公司
ISBN	9787519287092
序号	33
标题	疫苗简史
作者	张文宏，王新宇
年度	2021
出版社	上海教育出版社
ISBN	9787572010705
序号	34
标题	我们身边的生物安全——新冠肺炎疫情下的关注
作者	国泰，郭舒杨，于晴川，等
年度	2021

续表

出版社	中国计划出版社
ISBN	9787518212064
序号	35
标题	媒介生物学
作者	国家自然科学基金委员会，中国科学院
年度	2021
出版社	科学出版社
ISBN	9787030658678
序号	36
标题	病毒的进化：从流感到埃博拉病毒
作者	［英］弗兰克·瑞安（Frank Ryan）著；牟文婷译
年度	2021
出版社	人民日报出版社
ISBN	9787511569394
序号	37
标题	苍白的骑士：西班牙流感如何改变了世界
作者	［英］劳拉·斯宾尼（Laura Spinney）著；祁长保译
年度	2021
出版社	社会科学文献出版社
ISBN	9787520181013
序号	38
标题	侵华日军1855细菌部队研究
作者	柳毅，陈致远
年度	2021
出版社	中国社会科学出版社
ISBN	9787520378536
序号	39
标题	疫苗是什么
作者	孙晓冬
年度	2021

一、图书

续表

出版社	上海科学技术出版社
ISBN	9787547853078
序号	40
标题	**病毒、传染病与人类**
作者	陈安,陈樱花
年度	2021
出版社	上海科学技术出版社
ISBN	9787547851807
序号	41
标题	**病原生物学(上册,第3版)**
作者	郭晓奎,潘卫
年度	2021
出版社	科学出版社
ISBN	9787030679413
序号	42
标题	**病原生物学(下册,第3版)**
作者	郭晓奎,潘卫
年度	2021
出版社	科学出版社
ISBN	9787030679420
序号	43
标题	**流感大历史:一部瘟疫启示录**
作者	[英]马克·霍尼斯鲍姆(Mark Honigsbaum)著;马百亮译
年度	2021
出版社	格致出版社
ISBN	9787543231986
序号	44
标题	**时不我待:追踪致命病毒的精彩人生**
作者	[比]彼得.皮奥特(Peter Piot)著;王奇慧,宋豪主译
年度	2021

续表

出版社	中国科学技术出版社
ISBN	9787504687197
序号	45
标题	中国病媒生物名录与地理分布
作者	徐保海
年度	2021
出版社	福建科学技术出版社
ISBN	9787533559892
序号	46
标题	医学病毒学原理
作者	刘文军，李晶
年度	2020
出版社	化学工业出版社
ISBN	9787122381613
序号	47
标题	战疫，让世界更了解中国
作者	刘元春
年度	2020
出版社	外文出版社
ISBN	9787119124759
序号	48
标题	后疫情时代：大重构
作者	［德］克劳斯·施瓦布（Klaus Schwab），［法］蒂埃里·马勒雷（Thierry Malleret）著；世界经济论坛北京代表处译
年度	2020
出版社	中信出版社
ISBN	9787521723137
序号	49
标题	疫苗：医学史上最伟大的救星及其争议
作者	［美］阿瑟·艾伦（Arthur Allen）著；徐宵寒，邹梦廉译

续表

年度	2020
出版社	生活·读书·新知三联书店
ISBN	9787108071781
序号	50
标题	疫苗工程学（第3版）
作者	窦骏
年度	2020
出版社	东南大学出版社
ISBN	9787564190736
序号	51
标题	全球"搏疫"与中国策
作者	迟福林
年度	2020
出版社	中国社会科学出版社
ISBN	9787520366687
序号	52
标题	疫苗竞赛：人类对抗疾病的代价
作者	［美］梅雷迪丝·瓦德曼（Meredith Wadman）著；罗爽译
年度	2020
出版社	译林出版社
ISBN	9787544781961
序号	53
标题	疫苗与免疫
作者	傅传喜，孙彩军，郑徽
年度	2020
出版社	人民卫生出版社
ISBN	9787117303682
序号	54
标题	张文宏说传染
作者	张文宏

续表

年度	2020
出版社	中信出版社
ISBN	9787521720433
序号	55
标题	病原生物学（第六版）
作者	罗恩杰
年度	2020
出版社	科学出版社
ISBN	9787030653277
序号	56
标题	史之疫：病毒、动物与人类
作者	张森森
年度	2020
出版社	中国工人出版社
ISBN	9787500873990
序号	57
标题	疫苗上市后临床研究与评价
作者	崔富强，杨焕
年度	2020
出版社	北京大学医学出版社
ISBN	9787565921896
序号	58
标题	致命接触：追踪全球大型传染病
作者	［美］大卫·奎曼（David Quammen）著；刘颖译
年度	2020
出版社	中信出版集团股份有限公司
ISBN	9787521717099
序号	59
标题	比较传染病学——病毒性疾病
作者	薛婧

续表

年度	2020
出版社	科学出版社
ISBN	9787030634924
序号	60
标题	人类大瘟疫
作者	［英］马克·霍尼斯鲍姆（Mark Honigsbaum）著；谷晓阳，李瞳译
年度	2020
出版社	中信出版社
ISBN	9787521716269
序号	61
标题	RNA疫苗：方法与操作
作者	［德］托马斯·克拉姆斯（Thomas Kramps），［德］纳特·埃尔斯（Knut Elbers）著；王升启主译
年度	2020
出版社	科学出版社
ISBN	9787030645890
序号	62
标题	死亡征战：中国援助非洲抗击"埃博拉"纪实
作者	何建明
年度	2020
出版社	漓江出版社
ISBN	9787540787882
序号	63
标题	新冠肺炎疫情的行业影响及对策分析
作者	陈方若
年度	2020
出版社	上海交通大学出版社
ISBN	9787313229380
序号	64
标题	1918年之疫：被流感改变的世界
作者	［英］凯瑟琳·阿诺德（Catharine Arnold）著；田奥译

续表

年度	2020
出版社	上海教育出版社
ISBN	978-7-5444-9769-5
序号	65
标题	传染性疾病与精准预防
作者	阚飙，等
年度	2020
出版社	上海交通大学出版社
ISBN	9787313204820
序号	66
标题	治疗性疫苗（第2版）
作者	闻玉梅
年度	2020
出版社	科学出版社
ISBN	9787030643056
序号	67
标题	致命流感：百年治疗史
作者	［美］杰里米·布朗（Dr. Jeremy Brown）著；王晨瑜译
年度	2020
出版社	社会科学文献出版社
ISBN	9787520159982
序号	68
标题	中国疫苗百年纪实（上下卷）
作者	江永红
年度	2020
出版社	人民出版社
ISBN	9787010216768
序号	69
标题	画说新冠：来自多学科专家的解读
作者	宋刚，唐芹

一、图书

续表

年度	2020
出版社	科学出版社
ISBN	9787030644503
序号	70
标题	中国抗疫简史
作者	张剑光
年度	2020
出版社	新华出版社
ISBN	9787516650646
序号	71
标题	病原真菌鉴定
作者	［英］柯林，K.坎贝尔（Colin K. Campbell），等著；邹先彪，桑红主译
年度	2020
出版社	上海科学技术出版社
ISBN	9787547845530
序号	72
标题	中国动物鼠疫监测
作者	丛显斌，张贵军，邵奎东
年度	2020
出版社	人民卫生出版社
ISBN	9787117293105
序号	73
标题	中国鼠疫自然疫源地（1950—2014）
作者	丛显斌，刘振才，李群
年度	2020
出版社	人民卫生出版社
ISBN	9787117286879
序号	74
标题	病原微生物保藏管理与技术手册
作者	刘剑君，魏强

续表

年度	2019
出版社	北京大学医学出版社
ISBN	9787565920646
序号	75
标题	感染病学名词
作者	医学名词审定委员会，感染病学名词审定分委员会
年度	2019
出版社	科学出版社
ISBN	9787030636799
序号	76
标题	疫苗遗传学
作者	褚嘉祐
年度	2019
出版社	上海科学技术出版社
ISBN	9787547845653
序号	77
标题	病毒学原理和应用（第2版）
作者	［英］约翰·B.卡特（John B. Carter），［英］威尼斯·A.桑德斯（Venetia A. Saunders）主编；杜瑞坤，荣立军主译
年度	2019
出版社	山东科学技术出版社
ISBN	9787533199692
序号	78
标题	当代新疫苗（第二版）
作者	杨晓明
年度	2019
出版社	高等教育出版社
ISBN	9787040529111
序号	79
标题	兽用疫苗学（第二版）
作者	宁宜宝

年度	2019
出版社	中国农业出版社
ISBN	9787109244535
序号	80
标题	细菌耐药危机下的挑战与对策——专家视角
作者	夏照帆，沈建忠
年度	2019
出版社	人民卫生出版社
ISBN	9787117286367
序号	81
标题	重点感染性疾病的防治（第2版）
作者	张文宏，卢洪洲，张永信
年度	2019
出版社	科学出版社
ISBN	9787030620507
序号	82
标题	常见病媒生物分类鉴定手册
作者	周明浩，褚宏亮
年度	2019
出版社	苏州大学出版社
ISBN	9787567228092
序号	83
标题	重大传染病规模化现场流行病学和干预研究：标准操作规程
作者	李兰娟，阮冰
年度	2019
出版社	浙江大学出版社
ISBN	9787308191265
序号	84
标题	寨卡病毒与寨卡病毒病
作者	高福

续表

年度	2019
出版社	人民卫生出版社
ISBN	9787117274289
序号	85
标题	鼠疫与近代中国：卫生的制度化和社会变迁
作者	[日]饭岛涉著；朴彦，余新忠，姜滨译
年度	2019
出版社	社会科学文献出版社
ISBN	9787520138581
序号	86
标题	疫苗的史诗
作者	[法]让·弗朗索瓦·萨吕佐（Jean-François Saluzzo）著；宋碧珺译
年度	2019
出版社	中国社会科学出版社
ISBN	9787520337151
序号	87
标题	流感病毒——躲也躲不过的敌人
作者	高福，刘欢
年度	2018
出版社	科学普及出版社
ISBN	9787110098974
序号	88
标题	医学寄生虫学（第5版）
作者	殷国荣，王中全
年度	2018
出版社	科学出版社
ISBN	9787030577726
序号	89
标题	病原耐药性（第1卷）：耐药机制（第2版）
作者	[美]道格拉斯·迈耶（Douglas L. Mayers）等编著；郑福英，陈启伟，宫晓炜，等译

年度	2018
出版社	中国农业科学技术出版社
ISBN	9787511634405
序号	90
标题	**侵华日军第9420部队及云南细菌战研究**
作者	张华
年度	2018
出版社	中国社会科学出版社
ISBN	9787520324199
序号	91
标题	**侵华日军广州8604细菌部队研究**
作者	曹卫平
年度	2018
出版社	中国社会科学出版社
ISBN	9787520323765
序号	92
标题	**731：石井四郎及细菌战部队揭秘**
作者	［日］青木富贵子著；凌凌译
年度	2018
出版社	哈尔滨出版社
ISBN	9787548441519
序号	93
标题	**病毒进化：研究现状和未来方向**
作者	［美］斯科特·C.韦弗（Scott C. Weaver）等著；顾大勇主译
年度	2018
出版社	暨南大学出版社
ISBN	9787566824301
序号	94
标题	**传染病学（第9版）**
作者	李兰娟，任红

续表

年度	2018
出版社	人民卫生出版社
ISBN	9787117266666
序号	95
标题	**侵华日军第七三一部队旧址：细菌实验室及特设监狱遗址考古发掘报告**
作者	李陈奇
年度	2018
出版社	科学出版社
ISBN	9787030582201
序号	96
标题	**人体寄生虫学（第9版）**
作者	诸欣平，苏川
年度	2018
出版社	人民卫生出版社
ISBN	9787117266604
序号	97
标题	**中国艾滋病感染者去污名化研究**
作者	王小平
年度	2018
出版社	华中科技大学出版社
ISBN	9787568032483
序号	98
标题	**中国境外重要病媒生物**
作者	郭天宇，许荣满
年度	2018
出版社	天津科学技术出版社
ISBN	9787557640224
序号	99
标题	**中国人间鼠疫**
作者	丛显斌，鞠成

续表

年度	2018
出版社	人民卫生出版社
ISBN	9787117270335
序号	100
标题	大流感：最致命瘟疫的史诗
作者	［美］约翰·M·巴里（John M. Barry）著；钟扬，赵佳媛，刘念译
年度	2018
出版社	上海科技教育出版社
ISBN	9787542867438
序号	101
标题	人体寄生虫学彩色图谱
作者	徐国成，韩秋生，王继春，等
年度	2018
出版社	湖北科学技术出版社
ISBN	9787570601844
序号	102
标题	医学微生物学（第9版）
作者	李凡，徐志凯
年度	2018
出版社	人民卫生出版社
ISBN	9787117266031
序号	103
标题	中国医院感染细菌
作者	房海，陈翠珍
年度	2018
出版社	科学出版社
ISBN	9787030571779
序号	104
标题	艾滋病危险性性行为干预面临的伦理难题及对策
作者	朱海林

续表

年度	2018
出版社	中国社会科学出版社
ISBN	9787520309103
序号	105
标题	科学与新闻之争：十年疫苗事件中的媒体与传播
作者	李希光，苏婧
年度	2018
出版社	清华大学出版社
ISBN	9787302498377
序号	106
标题	动物病毒图谱
作者	邹啸环，夏志平
年度	2018
出版社	科学出版社
ISBN	9787030373106
序号	107
标题	病原微生物实验室生物安全词汇
作者	武桂珍，魏强
年度	2018
出版社	人民卫生出版社
ISBN	9787117247221
序号	108
标题	哈里森感染性疾病（第3版·英文版）
作者	［美］Dennis L. Kasper，Anthony S. Fauci 等主编
年度	2018
出版社	北京联合出版公司
ISBN	9787559611055
序号	109
标题	巨人的对决
作者	［法］阿尼克·佩罗，［法］马克西姆·施瓦兹著；时利和译

续表

年度	2018
出版社	海天出版社
ISBN	9787550721609
序号	110
标题	中国丙型肝炎感染现状及防治对策研究报告
作者	庄辉，魏来，杨希忠
年度	2017
出版社	人民卫生出版社
ISBN	9787117258906
序号	111
标题	细菌外排耐药机制
作者	［加］Xian-Zhi Li,［美］Christopher A.Elkins,［美］Helen I.Zgurskaya 编著；郑福英，宫晓炜，陈启伟，等译
年度	2017
出版社	中国农业科学技术出版社
ISBN	9787511632876
序号	112
标题	人类病原生物学图传：发现、形态及其致病性
作者	程明亮，江滟
年度	2017
出版社	科学出版社
ISBN	9787030522795
序号	113
标题	疫苗（第6版·全2册）
作者	［美］普洛特金·斯坦利（Stanley A. Plotking），等主编；罗凤基，杨晓明，王军志，等主译
年度	2017
出版社	人民卫生出版社
ISBN	9787117236157
序号	114

续表

标题	实用传染病学（第4版）
作者	王宇明，李梦东
年度	2017
出版社	人民卫生出版社
ISBN	9787117219426
序号	115
标题	微生物定量风险评估
作者	［美］查尔斯·N.哈斯（Charles N. Haas），［美］琼·B.罗斯（John B. Rose），［美］查尔斯·P.格伯（Charles P. Gerba）著；滕婧杰译
年度	2017
出版社	中国环境出版社
ISBN	9787511129246
序号	116
标题	莱姆病：基础与临床
作者	宝福凯，柳爱华
年度	2017
出版社	科学出版社
ISBN	9787030515018
序号	117
标题	伯力审判档案：日军细菌战罪行披露
作者	张树军，李忠杰
年度	2016
出版社	中共党史出版社
ISBN	9787509837245
序号	118
标题	动物病毒分子生物学
作者	［德］托马斯·麦莱特（Thomas C.Mettenleiter），［西］弗朗西斯科·索利诺（Francisco Sobrino）编著；张杰，刘永生译
年度	2016
出版社	中国农业科学技术出版社

续表

ISBN	9787511628503
序号	119
标题	慢性乙型肝炎病毒感染预防、关怀和治疗指南
作者	贾继东
年度	2016
出版社	人民卫生出版社
ISBN	9787117229692
序号	120
标题	细菌分子遗传学（第三版）
作者	［美］拉瑞·斯尼德（Larry Snyder），温蒂·查姆普尼斯（Wendy Champness）编；杨勇译
年度	2016
出版社	中国轻工业出版社
ISBN	9787518405534
序号	121
标题	现代肝炎病毒分子免疫学（第2版）
作者	成军
年度	2016
出版社	科学出版社
ISBN	9787030496904
序号	122
标题	消失的微生物：滥用抗生素引发的健康危机
作者	［美］马丁·布莱泽（Martin J. Blaser）著；傅贺译
年度	2016
出版社	湖南科学技术出版社
ISBN	9787535785855
序号	123
标题	中国公共卫生：艾滋病防治实践
作者	吴尊友
年度	2016

续表

出版社	人民卫生出版社
ISBN	9787117228640
序号	124
标题	病原微生物实验活动风险评估报告实例
作者	蒋健敏，张双凤，周晓红，等
年度	2016
出版社	浙江大学出版社
ISBN	9787308157421
序号	125
标题	结核病现场流行病学
作者	成诗明，王黎霞，陈伟
年度	2016
出版社	人民卫生出版社
ISBN	9787117224208
序号	126
标题	病毒感染与人类肿瘤——从基础科学到临床预防
作者	［美］张美惠，等编著；卢建红，等编译
年度	2016
出版社	科学出版社
ISBN	9787030479426
序号	127
标题	病原生物学（供基础、预防、临床、口腔医学类专业用 第5版）
作者	罗恩杰
年度	2016
出版社	科学出版社
ISBN	9787030470287
序号	128
标题	黏膜免疫及其疫苗设计
作者	杨倩
年度	2016

续表

出版社	科学出版社
ISBN	9787030470768
序号	129
标题	猪流感
作者	童光志，李泽君
年度	2015
出版社	中国农业出版社
ISBN	9787109206410
序号	130
标题	人兽共患病医学：人兽共患感染性疾病、毒物及其他共有健康风险的临床应对
作者	［美］拉比诺维茨（Peter M. Rabinowitz），［美］康迪（Lisa A. Conti）主编；刘明远主译
年度	2015
出版社	中国农业出版社
ISBN	9787109164055
序号	131
标题	兽医病毒学（第4版）
作者	［美］马克拉克伦（N. James MacLachlan），［美］杜波维（Edward J. Dubovi）主编；孔宪刚，刘胜旺主译
年度	2015
出版社	中国农业出版社
ISBN	9787109199378
序号	132
标题	埃博拉病毒病
作者	李兰娟
年度	2015
出版社	浙江大学出版社
ISBN	9787308145930
序号	133

续表

标题	非典非自然起源和人制人新种病毒基因武器
作者	徐德忠，李峰
年度	2015
出版社	军事医学科学出版社
ISBN	9787516305874
序号	134
标题	纪实：侵华日军常德细菌战
作者	陈致远
年度	2015
出版社	中国社会科学出版社
ISBN	9787516168400
序号	135
标题	感染病学（第3版）
作者	李兰娟，王宇明
年度	2015
出版社	人民卫生出版社
ISBN	9787117208222
序号	136
标题	SIFIC医院感染预防与控制操作图解
作者	胡必杰，等
年度	2015
出版社	上海科学技术出版社
ISBN	9787547826515
序号	137
标题	侵华日军731部队细菌战资料选编
作者	中国社会科学院近代史研究所近代史资料编译室
年度	2015
出版社	社会科学文献出版社
ISBN	9787509770849
序号	138

续表

标题	幽门螺杆菌感染（第三版）
作者	陶可胜，吕丽娜，孙士海，等
年度	2015
出版社	科学技术文献出版社
ISBN	9787518901005
序号	139
标题	非结核分枝杆菌与临床感染
作者	李仲兴
年度	2015
出版社	科学出版社
ISBN	9787030436948
序号	140
标题	再造团结：中国艾滋病防治法律制度研究
作者	张剑源
年度	2015
出版社	法律出版社
ISBN	9787511876577
序号	141
标题	病原微生物实验室生物安全培训指南
作者	高福，王子军
年度	2015
出版社	人民卫生出版社
ISBN	9787117198912
序号	142
标题	病毒学原理（Ⅰ）——分子生物学
作者	[美]S. J. 弗林特（S. J. Flint），等著；刘文军，许崇凤主译
年度	2015
出版社	化学工业出版社
ISBN	9787122195340
序号	143

续表

标题	病毒学原理（Ⅱ）——致病机理与控制
作者	［美］S.J.弗林特（S.J.Flint），等著；刘文军，许崇凤主译
年度	2015
出版社	化学工业出版社
ISBN	9787122195357
序号	144
标题	实用疫苗学
作者	刁连东，孙晓冬
年度	2015
出版社	上海科学技术出版社
ISBN	9787547822708
序号	145
标题	现代瘟疫：埃博拉病毒病
作者	杨瑞馥，刘超，夏晓东
年度	2015
出版社	科学出版社
ISBN	9787030428141
序号	146
标题	现代动物病毒学
作者	扈荣良
年度	2014
出版社	中国农业出版社
ISBN	9787109197435
序号	147
标题	战争与恶疫：日军对华细菌战
作者	解学诗，等著
年度	2014
出版社	人民出版社
ISBN	9787010134772
序号	148

续表

标题	动物病毒反向遗传学（第2版）
作者	刘光清
年度	2014
出版社	科学出版社
ISBN	9787030420718
序号	149
标题	细菌致病机制：分子与细胞水平研究
作者	［法］罗切特（Camille Locht），［法］西莫内（Michel Simonet）主编；刘永生译
年度	2014
出版社	中国农业科学技术出版社
ISBN	9787511623553
序号	150
标题	耐药结核病学
作者	唐神结，许绍发，李亮
年度	2014
出版社	人民卫生出版社
ISBN	9787117194211
序号	151
标题	微战争：对决细菌病毒
作者	王哲
年度	2014
出版社	陕西人民出版社
ISBN	9787224110043
序号	152
标题	艾滋病疫苗研究与评价
作者	王佑春
年度	2014
出版社	科学出版社
ISBN	9787030396105

续表

序号	153
标题	正义绞索：挫败美帝细菌战阴谋
作者	周广双
年度	2014
出版社	蓝天出版社
ISBN	9787509410950
序号	154
标题	疫苗的质量控制与评价
作者	王军志
年度	2013
出版社	人民卫生出版社
ISBN	9787117168335
序号	155
标题	抗病毒药物及其研究方法（第2版）
作者	陈鸿珊，张兴权
年度	2013
出版社	化学工业出版社
ISBN	9787122155887
序号	156
标题	腺病毒感染
作者	谢立，刘社兰，丁华，等
年度	2013
出版社	科学出版社
ISBN	9787030371850
序号	157
标题	中国防痨史
作者	戴志澄，肖东楼，万利亚
年度	2013
出版社	人民卫生出版社
ISBN	9787117162050

一、图书

续表

序号	158
标题	**人兽共患细菌病**
作者	房海，秋梅，陈翠珍，等
年度	2012
出版社	中国农业科学技术出版社
ISBN	9787511608796
序号	159
标题	**病毒学方法**
作者	李德新，舒跃龙
年度	2012
出版社	科学出版社
ISBN	9787030358844
序号	160
标题	**衣原体**
作者	吴移谋，李忠玉，陈丽丽，等
年度	2012
出版社	人民卫生出版社
ISBN	9787117165365
序号	161
标题	**ABX指南：感染性疾病的诊断与治疗（第二版）**
作者	［美］巴特利特（Bartlett J. G.），奥威特（Auwaete P. G.），范（Pham P. A.）著；马小军，徐英春，刘正印主译
年度	2012
出版社	科学技术文献出版社
ISBN	978-7-5023-7332-0
序号	162
标题	**实用病毒名称**
作者	邵一鸣
年度	2012
出版社	人民卫生出版社

续表

ISBN	9787117148702
序号	163
标题	医学寄生虫图鉴
作者	李朝品，高兴政
年度	2012
出版社	人民卫生出版社
ISBN	9787117154383
序号	164
标题	细菌名称双解及分类词典
作者	杨瑞馥，等
年度	2011
出版社	化学工业出版社
ISBN	9787122091390
序号	165
标题	疫苗学（第5版）
作者	［美］普洛特金（Stanley A. Plotkin, Walter A.），等著；梁晓峰，罗凤基，封多佳主译
年度	2011
出版社	人民卫生出版社
ISBN	9787117142182
序号	166
标题	生命伦理学维度：艾滋病防控难题与对策
作者	韩跃红，等
年度	2011
出版社	人民出版社
ISBN	9787010098494
序号	167
标题	中国西北地区病媒生物物种名录
作者	刘增加
年度	2011

出版社	军事医学科学出版社
ISBN	9787802456815
序号	168
标题	牛津传染病学（第4版）
作者	［英］瓦瑞尔（David A. Warrell），等主编；李宁主译
年度	2011
出版社	人民卫生出版社
ISBN	9787117136020
序号	169
标题	感染性腹泻病（第2版）
作者	聂青和
年度	2011
出版社	人民卫生出版社
ISBN	9787117139427
序号	170
标题	艾滋病防治研究与调查
作者	李聪
年度	2011
出版社	科学出版社
ISBN	9787030300621
序号	171
标题	现场细菌学
作者	徐建国，等
年度	2011
出版社	科学出版社
ISBN	9787030301260
序号	172
标题	人类病毒性疾病（第2版）
作者	刘克洲，陈智
年度	2010

续表

出版社	人民卫生出版社
ISBN	9787117121897
序号	173
标题	现代鼠疫概论
作者	贺雄，王虎
年度	2010
出版社	科学出版社
ISBN	9787030264695
序号	174

二、期刊

SCI 期刊文献

标题	Adaptive Immunity to SARS-CoV-2 and COVID-19
作者	Sette A, Crotty S
期刊/页码	Cell, 184（4）: 861-880
年度	2021
DOI	10.1016/j.cell.2021.01.007
被引次数	788
序号	1
标题	SARS-CoV-2 Variants, Spike Mutations and Immune Escape
作者	Harvey W T, Carabelli A M, Jackson B, et al
期刊/页码	Nature Reviews Microbiology, 19（7）: 409-424
年度	2021
DOI	10.1038/s41579-021-00573-0
被引次数	1406
序号	2
标题	Yersinia Pestis: The Natural History of Plague
作者	Barbieri R, Signoli M, Chevé D, et al
期刊/页码	Clinical Microbiology Reviews, 34（1）: e00044-19
年度	2021
DOI	10.1128/CMR.00044-19
被引次数	36
序号	3
标题	Characteristics of SARS-CoV-2 and COVID-19
作者	Hu B, Guo H, Zhou P, et al
期刊/页码	Nature Reviews Microbiology, 19（3）: 141-154
年度	2020
DOI	10.1038/s41579-020-00459-7
被引次数	2053
序号	4

续表

标题	Ebola
作者	Feldmann H, Sprecher A, Geisbert T W
期刊/页码	New England Journal of Medicine, 382（19）：1832-1842
年度	2020
DOI	10.1056/NEJMra1901594
被引次数	75
序号	5
标题	Pathophysiology, Transmission, Diagnosis, and Treatment of Coronavirus Disease 2019（COVID-19）: A Review
作者	Wiersinga W J, Rhodes A, Cheng A C, et al
期刊/页码	Jama-Journal of The American Medical Association, 324（8）：782-793
年度	2020
DOI	10.1001/jama.2020.12839
被引次数	2607
序号	6
标题	Physical Distancing, Face Masks, and Eye Protection to Prevent Person-to-Person Transmission of SARS-CoV-2 and COVID-19: A Systematic Review and Meta-Analysis
作者	Chu D K, Akl E A, Stephanie D, et al
期刊/页码	Lancet, 395（10242）：1973-1987
年度	2020
DOI	10.1016/S0140-6736（20）31142-9
被引次数	2168
序号	7
标题	Smallpox in the Post-Eradication Era
作者	Meyer H, Ehmann R, Smith G L
期刊/页码	Viruses-basel, 12（2）：138
年度	2020
DOI	10.3390/v12020138
被引次数	48
序号	8

续表

标题	**The Trinity of COVID-19: Immunity, Inflammation and Intervention**	
作者	Tay M Z, Poh C M, Rénia L, et al	
期刊/页码	Nature Reviews Immunology, 20（6）：363-374	
年度	2020	
DOI	10.1038/s41577-020-0311-8	
被引次数	2568	
序号	9	
标题	**Ebola Virus Disease**	
作者	Malvy D, McElroy A K, Clerk H D	
期刊/页码	Lancet, 393（10174）：936-948	
年度	2019	
DOI	10.1016/S0140-6736（18）33132-5	
被引次数	199	
序号	10	
标题	**Origin and Evolution of Pathogenic Coronaviruses**	
作者	Cui J, Li F, Shi Z L	
期刊/页码	Nature Reviews Microbiology, 17（3）：181-192	
年度	2019	
DOI	10.1038/s41579-018-0118-9	
被引次数	2886	
序号	11	
标题	**Yersinia Pestis and Plague: An Updated View on Evolution, Virulence Determinants, Immune Subversion, Vaccination, and Diagnostics**	
作者	Demeure C E, Dussurget O, Fiol G M, et al	
期刊/页码	Genes and Immunity, 20（5）：357-370	
年度	2019	
DOI	10.1038/s41435-019-0065-0	
被引次数	84	
序号	12	
标题	**mRNA Vaccines—A New Era in Vaccinology**	
作者	Pardi N, Hogan M J, Porter F W, et al	

续表

期刊/页码	Nature Reviews Drug Discovery, 17（4）：261-279
年度	2018
DOI	10.1038/nrd.2017.243
被引次数	1789
序号	13
标题	**Towards Personalized, Tumour-Specific, Therapeutic Vaccines for Cancer**
作者	Hu Z, Ott P A, Wu C J
期刊/页码	Nature Reviews Immunology, 18（3）：168-182
年度	2018
DOI	10.1038/nri.2017.131
被引次数	543
序号	14
标题	**Immunogenic Cell Death in Cancer and Infectious Disease**
作者	Galluzzi L, Buque A, Kepp O, et al
期刊/页码	Nature Reviews Immunology, 17（2）：97-111
年度	2017
DOI	10.1038/nri.2016.107
被引次数	1550
序号	15
标题	**Mycoplasma Pneumoniae from the Respiratory Tract and Beyond**
作者	Waites K B, Xiao L, Liu Y, et al
期刊/页码	Clinical Microbiology Reviews, 30（3）：747-809
年度	2017
DOI	10.1128/CMR.00114-16
被引次数	324
序号	16
标题	**Chlamydia Cell Biology and Pathogenesis**
作者	Elwell C, Mirrashidi K, Engel J
期刊/页码	Nature Reviews Microbiology, 14（6）：385-400
年度	2016

续表

DOI	10.1038/nrmicro.2016.30
被引次数	337
序号	17
标题	Pneumonic Plague: The Darker Side of Yersinia pestis
作者	Pechous R D, Sivaraman V, Stasuli N M, et al
期刊/页码	Trends in Microbiology, 24（3）：190-197
年度	2016
DOI	10.1016/j.tim.2015.11.008
被引次数	86
序号	18
标题	SARS and MERS: Recent Insights Into Emerging Coronaviruses
作者	de Wit E, van Doremalen N, Falzarano D, et al
期刊/页码	Nature Reviews Microbiology, 14（8）：523-534
年度	2016
DOI	10.1038/nrmicro.2016.81
被引次数	2037
序号	19
标题	The Evolution of Ebola Virus: Insights from the 2013—2016 Epidemic
作者	Holmes E C, Dudas G, Rambaut A, et al
期刊/页码	Nature, 538（7624）：193-200
年度	2016
DOI	10.1038/nature19790
被引次数	184
序号	20
标题	Anthrax Pathogenesis
作者	Moayeri M, Leppla S H, Vrentas C, et al
期刊/页码	Annual Review of Microbiology, 69：185-208
年度	2015
DOI	10.1146/annurev-micro-091014-104523
被引次数	162

续表

序号	21
标题	Molecular Biology of Hepatitis B Virus Infection
作者	Seeger C，Mason W S
期刊/页码	Virology，479：672-686
年度	2015
DOI	10.1016/j.virol.2015.02.031
被引次数	551
序号	22
标题	Genotyping, Evolution and Epidemiological Findings of Rickettsia Species
作者	Merhej V，Angelakis E，Socolovschi C，et al
期刊/页码	Infection Genetics and Evolution，25：122-137
年度	2014
DOI	10.1016/j.meegid.2014.03.014
被引次数	100
序号	23
标题	Innate Immunity to Influenza Virus Infection
作者	Iwasaki A，Pillai P S
期刊/页码	Nature Reviews Immunology，14（5）：315-328
年度	2014
DOI	10.1038/nri3665
被引次数	676
序号	24
标题	Pandemic Preparedness and Response—Lessons from the H1N1 Influenza of 2009
作者	Fineberg H V
期刊/页码	New England Journal of Medicine，370（14）：1335-1342
年度	2014
DOI	10.1056/NEJMra1208802
被引次数	340
序号	25

续表

标题	Uniting the Classification of Cultured and Uncultured Bacteria and Archaea Using 16S rRNA Gene Sequences
作者	Yarza P, Yilmaz P, Pruesse E, et al
期刊/页码	Nature Reviews Microbiology, 12（9）: 635-645
年度	2014
DOI	10.1038/nrmicro3330
被引次数	1397
序号	26
标题	A Decade After SARS: Strategies for Controlling Emerging Coronaviruses
作者	Graham R L, Donaldson E F, Baric R S
期刊/页码	Nature Reviews Microbiology, 11（12）: 836-848
年度	2013
DOI	10.1038/nrmicro3143
被引次数	467
序号	27
标题	Tuberculosis
作者	Zumla A, Raviglione M, Hafner R, et al
期刊/页码	New England Journal of Medicine, 368（8）: 745-755
年度	2013
DOI	10.1056/NEJMra1200894
被引次数	579
序号	28
标题	The End of AIDS: HIV Infection as a Chronic Disease
作者	Deeks S G, Lewin S R, Havlir D V
期刊/页码	Lancet, 382（9903）: 1525-1533
年度	2013
DOI	10.1016/S0140-6736（13）61809-7
被引次数	1159
序号	29
标题	Vaccine Hesitancy an Overview
作者	Dube E, Laberge C, Guay M, et al

续表

期刊/页码	Human Vaccines & Immunotherapeutics, 9（8）: 1763-1773
年度	2013
DOI	10.4161/hv.24657
被引次数	961
序号	30
标题	Worldwide Burden of HIV in Transgender Women: A Systematic Review and Meta-Analysis
作者	Baral S D, Poteat T, Strömdahl S, et al
期刊/页码	Lancet Infectious Diseases, 13（3）: 214-222
年度	2013
DOI	10.1016/S1473-3099（12）70315-8
被引次数	896
序号	31
标题	The Keystone-Pathogen Hypothesis
作者	Hajishengallis G, Darveau R P, Curtis M A
期刊/页码	Nature Reviews Microbiology, 10（10）: 717-725
年度	2012
DOI	10.1038/nrmicro2873
被引次数	979
序号	32
标题	HIV Infection, Inflammation, Immunosenescence, and Aging
作者	Deeks S G
期刊/页码	Annual Review of Medicine, 62: 141-155
年度	2011
DOI	10.1146/annurev-med-042909-093756
被引次数	938
序号	33
标题	The Challenge of New Drug Discovery for Tuberculosis
作者	Koul A, Arnoult E, Lounis N, et al
期刊/页码	Nature, 469（7331）: 483-490

年度	2011
DOI	10.1038/nature09657
被引次数	848
序号	34
标题	CRISPR/Cas, the Immune System of Bacteria and Archaea
作者	Horvath P, Barrangou R
期刊/页码	Science, 327（5962）：167-170
年度	2010
DOI	10.1126/science.1179555
被引次数	1825
序号	35
标题	Hospital-Acquired Infections Due to Gram-Negative Bacteria
作者	Peleg A Y, Hooper D C
期刊/页码	New England Journal of Medicine, 362（19）：1804-1813
年度	2010
DOI	10.1056/NEJMra0904124
被引次数	991
序号	36
标题	Evolution of New Variants of Vibrio Cholerae O1
作者	Safa A, Nair G B, Kong R Y C
期刊/页码	Trends in Microbiology, 18（1）：46-54
年度	2010
DOI	10.1016/j.tim.2009.10.003
被引次数	232
序号	37
标题	Genomic Evolution of Vibrio Cholerae
作者	Cho Y J, Yi H, Lee J H, et al
期刊/页码	Current Opinion in Microbiology, 13（5）：646-651
年度	2010

续表

DOI	10.1016/j.mib.2010.08.007	
被引次数	42	
序号	38	
标题	How Antibiotics Kill Bacteria: From Targets to Networks	
作者	Kohanski M A, Dwyer D J, Collins J J	
期刊/页码	Nature Reviews Microbiology, 8（6）: 423-435	
年度	2010	
DOI	10.1038/nrmicro2333	
被引次数	1324	
序号	39	
标题	Impacts of Biodiversity on the Emergence and Transmission of Infectious Diseases	
作者	Keesing F, Belden L K, Daszak P, et al	
期刊/页码	Nature, 468（7324）: 647-652	
年度	2010	
DOI	10.1038/nature09575	
被引次数	1116	
序号	40	
标题	Vaccine Adjuvants: Putting Innate Immunity to Work	
作者	Coffman R L, Sher A, Seder R A	
期刊/页码	Immunity, 33（4）: 492-503	
年度	2010	
DOI	10.1016/j.immuni.2010.10.002	
被引次数	1272	
序号	41	
标题	Vaccine Delivery: A Matter of Size, Geometry, Kinetics and Molecular Patterns	
作者	Bachmann M F, Jennings G T	
期刊/页码	Nature Reviews Immunology, 10（11）: 787-796	
年度	2010	

DOI	10.1038/nri2868	
被引次数	1357	
序号	42	
标题	**Antibiotics for Emerging Pathogens**	
作者	Fischbach M A, Walsh C T	
期刊/页码	Science, 325（5944）：1089-1093	
年度	2009	
DOI	10.1126/science.1176667	
被引次数	1353	
序号	43	
标题	**Emergence and Pandemic Potential of Swine-Origin H1N1 Influenza Virus**	
作者	Neumann G, Noda T, Kawaoka Y	
期刊/页码	Nature, 459（7249）：931-939	
年度	2009	
DOI	10.1038/nature08157	
被引次数	1256	
序号	44	
标题	**Regulatory RNAs in Bacteria**	
作者	Waters L S, Storz G	
期刊/页码	Cell, 136（4）：615-628	
年度	2009	
DOI	10.1016/j.cell.2009.01.043	
被引次数	1168	
序号	45	
标题	**The Challenge of Finding a Cure for HIV Infection**	
作者	Richman D D, Margolis D M, Delaney M, et al	
期刊/页码	Science, 323（5919）：1304-1307	
年度	2009	
DOI	10.1126/science.1165706	
被引次数	695	

续表

序号	46
标题	Hepatitis B Virus Infection
作者	Dienstag J L
期刊/页码	New England Journal of Medicine, 359（14）：1486-1500
年度	2008
DOI	10.1056/NEJMra0801644
被引次数	781
序号	47
标题	Rates of Evolutionary Change in Viruses: Patterns and Determinants
作者	Duffy S, Shackelton L A, Holmes E C
期刊/页码	Nature Reviews Genetics, 9（4）：267-276
年度	2008
DOI	10.1038/nrg2323
被引次数	1018
序号	48
标题	How Ebola and Marburg Viruses Battle the Immune System
作者	Mohamadzadeh M, Chen L P, Schmaljohn A L
期刊/页码	Nature Reviews Immunology, 7（7）：556-567
年度	2007
DOI	10.1038/nri2098
被引次数	108
序号	49
标题	Origins of Major Human Infectious Diseases
作者	Wolfe N D, Dunavan C P, Diamond J
期刊/页码	Nature, 447（7142）：279-283
年度	2007
DOI	10.1038/nature05775
被引次数	964
序号	50
标题	Who Puts the Tubercle in Tuberculosis?
作者	Russell D G

期刊/页码	Nature Reviews Microbiology, 5（1）：39-47
年度	2007
DOI	10.1038/nrmicro1538
被引次数	464
序号	51
标题	**Bats：Important Reservoir Hosts of Emerging Viruses**
作者	Calisher C H, Childs J E, Field H E, et al
期刊/页码	Clinical Microbiology Reviews, 19（3）：531-545
年度	2006
DOI	10.1128/CMR.00017-06
被引次数	1026
序号	52
标题	**Global Patterns of Influenza a Virus in Wild Birds**
作者	Olsen B, Munster V J, Wallensten A, et al
期刊/页码	Science, 312（5772）：384-388
年度	2006
DOI	10.1126/science.1122438
被引次数	1430
序号	53
标题	**Pathogen Recognition and Innate Immunity**
作者	Akira S, Uematsu S, Takeuchi O
期刊/页码	Cell, 124（4）：783-801
年度	2006
DOI	10.1016/j.cell.2006.02.015
被引次数	8935
序号	54
标题	**Smallpox**
作者	Moore Z S, Seward J F, Lane J M
期刊/页码	Lancet, 367（9508）：425-435
年度	2006

续表

DOI	10.1016/S0140-6736（06）68143-9
被引次数	75
序号	55
标题	Systematic Review: A Century of Inhalational Anthrax Cases from 1900 to 2005
作者	Holty J E C, Bravata D M, Liu H, et al
期刊/页码	Annals of Internal Medicine, 144（4）: 270-280
年度	2006
DOI	10.7326/0003-4819-144-4-200602210-00009
被引次数	191
序号	56
标题	The Double Burden of Communicable and Non-Communicable Diseases in Developing Countries
作者	Boutayeb A
期刊/页码	Transactions of the Royal Society of Tropical Medicine and Hygiene, 100（3）: 191-199
年度	2006
DOI	10.1016/j.trstmh.2005.07.021
被引次数	369
序号	57
标题	The Emerging Diversity of Rickettsia
作者	Perlman S J, Hunter M S, Zchori-Fein E
期刊/页码	Proceedings of the Royal Society B-biological Sciences, 273（1598）: 2097-2106
年度	2006
DOI	10.1098/rspb.2006.3541
被引次数	312
序号	58
标题	CTX Phi and Vibrio Cholerae: Exploring a Newly Recognized Type of Phage-Host Cell Relationship
作者	McLeod S M, Kimsey H H, Davis B M, et al

期刊/页码	Molecular Microbiology, 57（2）: 347-356
年度	2005
DOI	10.1111/j.1365-2958.2005.04676.x
被引次数	68
序号	59
标题	Immunology of Chlamydia infection: Implications for a Chlamydia Trachomatis Vaccine
作者	Brunham R C, Rey-Ladino J
期刊/页码	Nature Reviews Immunology, 5（2）: 149-161
年度	2005
DOI	10.1038/nri1551
被引次数	478
序号	60
标题	Immunology of Hepatitis B Virus and Hepatitis C Virus Infection
作者	Rehermann B, Nascimbeni M
期刊/页码	Nature Reviews Immunology, 5（3）: 215-229
年度	2005
DOI	10.1038/nri1573
被引次数	1410
序号	61
标题	Influenza: Lessons from Past Pandemics, Warnings from Current Incidents
作者	Horimoto T, Kawaoka Y
期刊/页码	Nature Reviews Microbiology, 3（8）: 591-600
年度	2005
DOI	10.1038/nrmicro1208
被引次数	563
序号	62
标题	Some Lessons from Rickettsia Genomics
作者	Renesto P, Ogata H, Audic S, et al
期刊/页码	Fems Microbiology Reviews, 29（1）: 99-117

年度	2005	
DOI	10.1016/j.femsre.2004.09.002	
被引次数	63	
序号	63	
标题	The Natural History of Ebola Virus in Africa	
作者	Pourrut X, Kumulungui B, Wittmann T, et al	
期刊/页码	Microbes and Infection, 7（7-8）：1005-1014	
年度	2005	
DOI	10.1016/j.micinf.2005.04.006	
被引次数	217	
序号	64	
标题	Viruses in the Sea	
作者	Suttle C A	
期刊/页码	Nature, 437（7057）：356-361	
年度	2005	
DOI	10.1038/nature04160	
被引次数	1487	
序号	65	
标题	Bacterial Invasion: The Paradigms of Enteroinvasive Pathogens	
作者	Cossart P, Sansonetti P J	
期刊/页码	Science, 304（5668）：242-248	
年度	2004	
DOI	10.1126/science.1090124	
被引次数	803	
序号	66	
标题	Communicable Diseases in Complex Emergencies: Impact and Challenges	
作者	Connolly M A, Gayer M, Ryan M J, et al	
期刊/页码	Lancet, 364（9449）：1974-1983	
年度	2004	
DOI	10.1016/S0140-6736（04）17481-3	

续表

被引次数	275
序号	67
标题	**Comparative and Evolutionary Genomics of Yersinia Pestis**
作者	Zhou D S, Han Y P, Song Y, et al
期刊/页码	Microbes and Infection, 6（13）：1226-1234
年度	2004
DOI	10.1016/j.micinf.2004.08.002
被引次数	72
序号	68
标题	**Epstein-Barr Virus：40 Years On**
作者	Young L S, Rickinson A B
期刊/页码	Nature Reviews Cancer, 4（10）：757-768
年度	2004
DOI	10.1038/nrc1452
被引次数	1629
序号	69
标题	**Genomic Islands in Pathogenic and Environmental Microorganisms**
作者	Dobrindt U, Hochhut B, Hentschel U, et al
期刊/页码	Nature Reviews Microbiology, 2（5）：414-424
年度	2004
DOI	10.1038/nrmicro884
被引次数	808
序号	70
标题	**Influenza：Old and New Threats**
作者	Palese P
期刊/页码	Nature Medicine, 10（12）：S82-S87
年度	2004
DOI	10.1038/nm1141
被引次数	485
序号	71

续表

标题	**Intracellular Parasite Invasion Strategies**
作者	Sibley L D
期刊/页码	Science, 304（5668）: 248-253
年度	2004
DOI	10.1126/science.1094717
被引次数	357
序号	72
标题	**Hepatitis B Virus Infection—Natural History and Clinical Consequences**
作者	Ganem D, Prince A M
期刊/页码	New England Journal of Medicine, 350（11）: 1118-1129
年度	2004
DOI	10.1056/NEJMra031087
被引次数	2011
序号	73
标题	**Mycoplasma Pneumoniae and Its Role as a Human Pathogen**
作者	Waites K B, Talkington D F
期刊/页码	Clinical Microbiology Reviews, 17（4）: 697-728
年度	2004
DOI	10.1128/CMR.17.4.697-728.2004
被引次数	972
序号	74
标题	**Pathogenic Escherichia Coli**
作者	Kaper J B, Nataro J P, Mobley H L T
期刊/页码	Nature Reviews Microbiology, 2（2）: 123-140
年度	2004
DOI	10.1038/nrmicro818
被引次数	3335
序号	75
标题	**The Challenge of Emerging and Re-Emerging Infectious Diseases**
作者	Morens D M, Folkers G K, Fauci A S

期刊/页码	Nature, 430 (6996): 242-249
年度	2004
DOI	10.1038/nature02759
被引次数	1263
序号	76
标题	The Role of Sexually Transmitted Diseases in HIV Transmission
作者	Galvin S R, Cohen M S
期刊/页码	Nature Reviews Microbiology, 2 (1): 33-42
年度	2004
DOI	10.1038/nrmicro794
被引次数	561
序号	77
标题	The Roles of Anthrax Toxin in Pathogenesis
作者	Moayeri M, Leppla S H
期刊/页码	Current Opinion in Microbiology, 7 (1): 19-24
年度	2004
DOI	10.1016/j.mib.2003.12.001
被引次数	226
序号	78
标题	Are We Ready for Pandemic Influenza?
作者	Webby R J, Webster R G
期刊/页码	Science, 302 (5650): 1519-1522
年度	2003
DOI	10.1126/science.1090350
被引次数	525
序号	79
标题	Filamentous Phages Linked to Virulence of Vibrio Cholerae
作者	Davis B M, Waldor M K
期刊/页码	Current Opinion in Microbiology, 6 (1): 35-42
年度	2003

续表

DOI	10.1016/S1369-5274（02）00005-X	
被引次数	161	
序号	80	
标题	**Influenza**	
作者	Nicholson K G, Wood J M, Zambon M	
期刊/页码	Lancet, 362（9397）：1733-1745	
年度	2003	
DOI	10.1016/S0140-6736（03）14854-4	
被引次数	711	
序号	81	
标题	**Planning for Smallpox Outbreaks**	
作者	Ferguson N M, Keeling M J, Edmunds W J, et al	
期刊/页码	Nature, 425（6959）：681-685	
年度	2003	
DOI	10.1038/nature02007	
被引次数	266	
序号	82	
标题	**Tuberculosis**	
作者	Frieden T R, Sterling T R, Munsiff S S, et al	
期刊/页码	Lancet, 362（9387）：887-899	
年度	2003	
DOI	10.1016/S0140-6736（03）14333-4	
被引次数	774	
序号	83	
标题	**Viral Hepatitis B**	
作者	Lai C L, Ratziu V, Yuen M F, et al	
期刊/页码	Lancet, 362（9401）：2089-2094	
年度	2003	
DOI	10.1016/S0140-6736（03）15108-2	
被引次数	716	

续表

序号	84
标题	**Diversity Considerations in HIV-1 Vaccine Selection**
作者	Gaschen B, Taylor J, Yusim K, et al
期刊/页码	Science, 296（5577）：2354-2360
年度	2002
DOI	10.1126/science.1070441
被引次数	707
序号	85
标题	**Diagnosis and Management of Smallpox**
作者	Breman J G, Henderson D A
期刊/页码	New England Journal of Medicine, 346（17）：1300-1308
年度	2002
DOI	10.1056/NEJMra020025
被引次数	269
序号	86
标题	**Genome Sequence of the Human Malaria Parasite Plasmodium Falciparum**
作者	Gardner M J, Hall N, Fung E, et al
期刊/页码	Nature, 419（6906）：498-511
年度	2002
DOI	10.1038/nature01097
被引次数	3641
序号	87
标题	**Global Control of Hepatitis B Virus Infection**
作者	Kao J H, Chen D S
期刊/页码	Lancet Infectious Diseases, 2（7）：395-403
年度	2002
DOI	10.1016/S1473-3099（02）00315-8
被引次数	678
序号	88

续表

标题	Allergy, Parasites, and the Hygiene Hypothesis
作者	Yazdanbakhsh M, Kremsner P G, van Ree R
期刊/页码	Science, 296（5567）：490-494
年度	2002
DOI	10.1126/science.296.5567.490
被引次数	1133
序号	89
标题	Pathogen Population Genetics, Evolutionary Potential, and Durable Resistance
作者	McDonald B A, Linde C
期刊/页码	Annual Review of Phytopathology, 40：349-379
年度	2002
DOI	10.1146/annurev.phyto.40.120501.101443
被引次数	1536
序号	90
标题	Immunology of Tuberculosis
作者	Flynn J L, Chan J
期刊/页码	Annual Review of Immunology, 19：93-129
年度	2001
DOI	10.1146/annurev.immunol.19.1.93
被引次数	1746
序号	91
标题	Emerging Infectious Diseases of Wildlife—Threats to Biodiversity and Human Health
作者	Daszak P, Cunningham A A, Hyatt A D
期刊/页码	Science, 287（5452）：443-449
年度	2000
DOI	10.1126/science.287.5452.443
被引次数	2886
序号	92

备注：被引次数检索时间为2023年5月。

中文期刊文献

标题	全球新型冠状病毒变异株研究进展
作者	冯晔囡，宋洋，王世文，陈操，许文波
期刊	病毒学报
年度	2021
被引次数	31
序号	1
标题	新型冠状病毒变异株 VOC 202012/01 的全球早期传播与刺突蛋白进化特征分析
作者	冯晔囡，陈志肖，梦遥，赵翔，宋洋，王佶，许文波，陈操，王世文
期刊	病毒学报
年度	2021
被引次数	13
序号	2
标题	基于 SEIR 的新冠肺炎传播模型及拐点预测分析
作者	范如国，王奕博，罗明，张应青，朱超平
期刊	电子科技大学学报
年度	2020
被引次数	149
序号	3
标题	基于大数据回溯新冠肺炎的扩散趋势及中国对疫情的控制研究
作者	赵序茅，李欣海，聂常虹
期刊	中国科学院院刊
年度	2020
被引次数	98
序号	4
标题	新冠肺炎疫情大数据分析与区域防控政策建议
作者	周成虎，裴韬，杜云艳，陈洁，许珺，王姣娥，张国义，苏奋振，宋辞，易嘉伟，马廷，葛咏，张岸，姜莉莉
期刊	中国科学院院刊
年度	2020

续表

被引次数	145
序号	5
标题	新型冠状病毒（SARS-CoV-2）全球研究现状分析
作者	张龙浩，李柏宏，贾鹏，蒲剑，白蓓，李音，朱培嘉，李雷，曾国军，赵欣，董珊珊，刘梦菡，张楠
期刊	生物医学工程学杂志
年度	2020
被引次数	60
序号	6
标题	新型冠状病毒肺炎基本再生数的初步预测
作者	周涛，刘权辉，杨紫陌，廖敬仪，杨可心，白薇，吕欣，张伟
期刊	中国循证医学杂志
年度	2020
被引次数	143
序号	7
标题	2013—2018年我国流感流行特征分析
作者	马贵凤，祝洁，曹慧军，江滟
期刊	中国病原生物学杂志
年度	2019
被引次数	67
序号	8
标题	HPV疫苗在中国的应用现状
作者	张师前，王凯，张远丽
期刊	中国实用妇科与产科杂志
年度	2019
被引次数	64
序号	9
标题	中国部分省份手足口病传染率分析
作者	王燕芬，王旭峰，赵继军
期刊	中华疾病控制杂志
年度	2019

续表

被引次数	12
序号	10
标题	中国特色的艾滋病防治策略
作者	吴尊友
期刊	中华疾病控制杂志
年度	2019
被引次数	96
序号	11
标题	2006—2015年全国动物炭疽流行分析及防控
作者	周宇，张熙，李香，乔华，郭抗抗
期刊	中国兽医学报
年度	2018
被引次数	12
序号	12
标题	非洲猪瘟防控及疫苗研发：挑战与对策
作者	王涛，孙元，罗玉子，仇华吉
期刊	生物工程学报
年度	2018
被引次数	102
序号	13
标题	全球埃博拉病毒病应对及其对我国烈性传染病防控的启示
作者	黄翠，马海霞，梁慧刚，袁志明
期刊	军事医学
年度	2018
被引次数	16
序号	14
标题	我国的医院感染管理与防控现状调研及分析
作者	姚宏武，索继江，邢玉斌，曹晋桂，王志刚，蒋伟，范珊红，翟红岩，张群，罗爱武，刘运喜，马慧
期刊	中华医院感染学杂志
年度	2018

续表

被引次数	78
序号	15
标题	我国第二类疫苗接种现状及其影响因素研究进展
作者	张雪海，李娜，张双凤，夏时畅，张人杰
期刊	中国预防医学杂志
年度	2018
被引次数	41
序号	16
标题	在医学与政治之间——中国根除天花的国际认证
作者	苏静静，张大庆
期刊	自然科学史研究
年度	2018
被引次数	4
序号	17
标题	艾滋病流行现状及防治策略探讨
作者	唐琪，卢洪洲
期刊	复旦学报（医学版）
年度	2017
被引次数	61
序号	18
标题	全球人感染禽流感疫情及其流行病学特征概述
作者	姜慧，赖圣杰，秦颖，张志杰，冯录召，余宏杰
期刊	科学通报
年度	2017
被引次数	55
序号	19
标题	我国女性人乳头瘤病毒（HPV）感染的流行病学现状
作者	单玮，张涛，张铁军，赵根明
期刊	中华疾病控制杂志
年度	2017

续表

被引次数	241
序号	20
标题	我国实现艾滋病防治策略三个 90% 的进展与挑战
作者	吴尊友
期刊	中华疾病控制杂志
年度	2017
被引次数	136
序号	21
标题	抗乙型肝炎病毒药物的研究进展
作者	王宏亮，刘夏玲，曹爽
期刊	国际药学研究杂志
年度	2016
被引次数	28
序号	22
标题	全国重点寄生虫病的防控形势与挑战
作者	严俊，胡桃，雷正龙
期刊	中国寄生虫学与寄生虫病杂志
年度	2016
被引次数	95
序号	23
标题	中国病毒性肝炎流行状况 GIS 空间分析
作者	李扬，耿爱生，汪心海，尹德芬，李晓，焦华安，孙梦绮
期刊	中国卫生统计
年度	2016
被引次数	32
序号	24
标题	抗结核药物的研究进展
作者	殷春阳，冷东雷，何仲贵
期刊	沈阳药科大学学报
年度	2015

续表

被引次数	31
序号	25
标题	小儿肺炎支原体感染流行病学特征
作者	陈正荣，严永东
期刊	中国实用儿科杂志
年度	2015
被引次数	112
序号	26
标题	新发蜱传病原体——劳氏立克次体的研究现状
作者	闻静，焦丹，鞠文东，黄玉明，王悦，王建华，时晓杰，成洪艳，程成，孙毅
期刊	中国人兽共患病学报
年度	2015
被引次数	28
序号	27
标题	埃博拉病毒病：病原学、致病机制、治疗与疫苗研究进展
作者	程颖，刘军，李昱，刘翟，任翔，施一，高福，余宏杰
期刊	科学通报
年度	2014
被引次数	45
序号	28
标题	埃博拉病毒病：流行病学、生态学、诊断、治疗及控制
作者	李昱，任翔，刘翟，程颖，高福，余宏杰
期刊	科技导报
年度	2014
被引次数	38
序号	29
标题	埃博拉病毒疫苗研究进展
作者	杨利敏，李晶，高福，刘文军
期刊	生物工程学报
年度	2014

续表

被引次数	18
序号	30
标题	霍乱弧菌基因表达分析中内参基因的选择
作者	张翠彩，逄波，蒋秀高，阚飙
期刊	中国人兽共患病学报
年度	2014
被引次数	7
序号	31
标题	抗生素的使用与细菌耐药性
作者	孙涛
期刊	中国临床药理学杂志
年度	2014
被引次数	95
序号	32
标题	禽流感病毒研究概述
作者	谭伟，徐倩，谢芝勋
期刊	基因组学与应用生物学
年度	2014
被引次数	103
序号	33
标题	衣原体最新分类体系与分类鉴定方法研究进展
作者	李鹏，端青，宋立华
期刊	中国人兽共患病学报
年度	2014
被引次数	25
序号	34
标题	16S rRNA 基因序列分析法鉴定病原细菌
作者	朱飞舟，陈利玉，陈汉春
期刊	中南大学学报（医学版）
年度	2013

续表

被引次数	116
序号	35
标题	基于环境危险要素的中国霍乱分区预测
作者	徐敏,曹春香,王多春,阚飙,贾慧聪,许允飞,李小文
期刊	科学通报
年度	2013
被引次数	6
序号	36
标题	鼠疫耶尔森氏菌的进化研究:从系统发育学到系统发育基因组学
作者	崔玉军,宋亚军,杨瑞馥
期刊	中国科学:生命科学
年度	2013
被引次数	20
序号	37
标题	鼠疫自然疫源地学说的探讨
作者	张涛,李丽,赵建华
期刊	中国媒介生物学及控制杂志
年度	2013
被引次数	32
序号	38
标题	我国新发人畜共患寄生虫病的流行现状
作者	朱宏儒,刘璐,杨国静
期刊	中国血吸虫病防治杂志
年度	2013
被引次数	22
序号	39
标题	疫苗佐剂最新研究进展
作者	周洋,耿兴超,汪巨峰,李波
期刊	中国新药杂志
年度	2013

续表

被引次数	62
序号	40
标题	浙江省人感染 H7N9 禽流感流行特征与防控对策
作者	陈恩富，柴程良，孙继民，吕华坤，刘社兰，余昭，龚震宇，丛黎明
期刊	中国公共卫生
年度	2013
被引次数	156
序号	41
标题	2001—2011 年内蒙古炭疽流行病学特征分析
作者	李澄，闫绍宏，郭卫东，王文瑞
期刊	中国人兽共患病学报
年度	2012
被引次数	12
序号	42
标题	84 个炭疽暴发案例流行病学调查文献系统评价
作者	许汝福，沈渝菊，林辉，李亚斐，向颖，许斌，张耀，黄国荣
期刊	第三军医大学学报
年度	2011
被引次数	17
序号	43
标题	CRISPR-Cas 系统与细菌和噬菌体的共进化
作者	李铁民，杜波
期刊	遗传
年度	2011
被引次数	101
序号	44
标题	埃博拉出血热
作者	刘阳，马志永，史子学，王水明，王志亮，马玉堃
期刊	中国人兽共患病学报
年度	2011

续表

被引次数	24
序号	45
标题	肺炎支原体肺炎发病机制研究进展
作者	刘洋，李敏，徐佩茹
期刊	临床儿科杂志
年度	2011
被引次数	160
序号	46
标题	抗结核一线药物及结核分枝杆菌的耐药分子机制
作者	贾平平，余利岩，岑山
期刊	中国抗生素杂志
年度	2011
被引次数	48
序号	47
标题	鼠疫研究进展
作者	张涛，冯志勇，李丽
期刊	中国人兽共患病学报
年度	2011
被引次数	35
序号	48
标题	我国寄生虫病防治形势与今后防治科研重点
作者	周晓农
期刊	中国血吸虫病防治杂志
年度	2011
被引次数	102
序号	49
标题	中国鼠疫自然疫源地研究进展
作者	海荣
期刊	中国媒介生物学及控制杂志
年度	2011

续表

被引次数	31
序号	50
标题	北京市SARS流行的特征与时空传播规律
作者	曹志冬，曾大军，郑晓龙，王全意，王飞跃，王劲峰，王小莉
期刊	中国科学：地球科学
年度	2010
被引次数	35
序号	51
标题	非结核分枝杆菌病的流行趋势、诊断及治疗
作者	吴琪茵，黎友伦
期刊	中国人兽共患病学报
年度	2010
被引次数	35
序号	52
标题	抗流感病毒药物研究进展
作者	张强，赵庆杰，熊瑞生，李剑峰，沈敬山
期刊	药学学报
年度	2010
被引次数	54
序号	53
标题	人乳头瘤病毒在国人宫颈病变中感染及型别分布特征的Meta分析
作者	张东红，林美珊
期刊	中国全科医学
年度	2010
被引次数	116
序号	54
标题	鼠疫研究进展与展望
作者	周冬生，杨瑞馥
期刊	解放军医学杂志
年度	2010

续表

被引次数	32	
序号	55	
标题	云南省人和家畜立克次体病血清流行病学调查	
作者	常利涛，刀志宏，梁长威，李娟，李云德，赵景波，禹惠兰，张丽娟	
期刊	中国人兽共患病学报	
年度	2010	
被引次数	31	
序号	56	
标题	中国西部地区男男性行为人群艾滋病相关知识及行为调查分析	
作者	佘颖，钟晓妮，张燕，彭斌，梁浩，邹云锋，罗锦昆，彭鸿斌，黄爱龙	
期刊	重庆医科大学学报	
年度	2010	
被引次数	32	
序号	57	
标题	艾滋歧视与护理行为的相关性研究	
作者	严谨，韩扬扬，刘化侠	
期刊	中国现代医学杂志	
年度	2009	
被引次数	5	
序号	58	
标题	丙型肝炎病毒感染的流行病学	
作者	付涌水	
期刊	中国输血杂志	
年度	2009	
被引次数	34	
序号	59	
标题	霍乱的研究进展和预防控制	
作者	王树坤，吴强，杨汝松，姚颖波，刘红雁	
期刊	中国微生态学杂志	
年度	2009	

续表

被引次数	12
序号	60
标题	**加强乙型肝炎防治**
作者	庄辉
期刊	北京大学学报（医学版）
年度	2009
被引次数	53
序号	61
标题	**抗菌药物滥用与医院感染管理**
作者	崔兰贵，张磊，朱铁梁，吴志恒，赵榕慧，朱洁
期刊	中华医院感染学杂志
年度	2009
被引次数	84
序号	62
标题	**流感病毒感染介导的免疫病理损伤研究进展**
作者	吕进，王希良
期刊	生物化学与生物物理进展
年度	2009
被引次数	72
序号	63
标题	**人体寄生虫学学科发展的历史性思考**
作者	季旻珺，吴观陵
期刊	中国寄生虫学与寄生虫病杂志
年度	2009
被引次数	23
序号	64
标题	**细菌内毒素研究进展**
作者	郭萌，李冠民，黄清泉
期刊	中国实验动物学报
年度	2009

续表

被引次数	109
序号	65
标题	新世纪流感大流行的思考
作者	王革非，李康生
期刊	生物化学与生物物理进展
年度	2009
被引次数	50
序号	66
标题	支原体、衣原体感染与不孕症的关系及耐药性分析
作者	周淑群，韦柳华，周定球，莫善颖
期刊	中华医院感染学杂志
年度	2009
被引次数	47
序号	67
标题	SARS 流行病传染动力学研究
作者	李铮，陈曦，滕虎，修志龙，孙丽华，冯恩民
期刊	生物化学与生物物理进展
年度	2004
被引次数	17
序号	68

备注：被引次数检索时间为 2023 年 3 月。